Lost at School

Why Our Kids with Behavioral Challenges Are Falling Through the Cracks and How We Can Help Them

ROSS W. GREENE, Ph.D.

Scribner

New York   London   Toronto   Sydney

Many people have teachers they remember fondly as the ones who believed in them and helped them reach their fullest potential. This book is dedicated to Marshall Stearns, my sixth-grade teacher at North Miami Elementary School in 1968.

SCRIBNER
A Division of Simon & Schuster, Inc.
1230 Avenue of the Americas
New York, NY 10020

First Scribner trade paperback edition October 2009

SCRIBNER and design are registered trademarks of The Gale Group, Inc., used under license by Simon & Schuster, Inc., the publisher of this work.

For information about special discounts for bulk purchases, please contact Simon & Schuster Special Sales at 1-800-456-6798 or business@simonandschuster.com.

Designed by Kyoko Watanabe
Text set in Sabon

Manufactured in the United States of America

11 13 15 17 19 20 18 16 14 12

Library of Congress Control Number: 2008012479

ISBN 978-1-4165-7226-8
ISBN 978-1-4165-7227-5 (pbk)
ISBN 978-1-4165-8367-7 (ebook)

Excerpt from "Across the Great Divide" by Kate Wolf copyright Another Sundown Publishing Company, used with permission.

Praise for *Lost at School*

"No one in America has thought more deeply about the problems of disruptive children in school than Ross Greene. In his brilliant new book, he goes inside the minds of children and school personnel to explain why old-fashioned school discipline and zero-tolerance policies have failed. Then he offers original and tested new strategies for working with the most behaviorally challenging children. Every teacher and administrator who has ever felt that traditional discipline isn't working should read *Lost at School*."

—Dr. Michael Thompson, school consultant, coauthor of
Raising Cain, and author of *Best Friends, Worst Enemies*

"We cannot ignore difficult student behaviors any longer. Dr. Greene's book is a timely contribution to the literature on how schools must support *all* students, and his approach fits well with Response to Intervention (RTI)."

—Rachel Brown-Chidsey, Ph.D., NCSP, associate professor,
School Psychology Program, University of Southern Maine,
and coauthor of *Response to Intervention*

"A positive and practical approach for teachers who want to work redemptively with kids whose classroom behavior is an impediment to academic and social success."

—Carol Ann Tomlinson, Ed.D., Curry School of Education,
University of Virginia

"Accessible advice for parents and teachers concerned about children with behavior problems."

—*Booklist*

Contents

I hope that someday we will learn the terrible cost we all pay when we ignore or mismanage those people in society who most need our help.

THE HON. JUDGE SANDRA HAMILTON,
PROVINCIAL COURT OF ALBERTA, CANADA

The finest hour I have seen
Is the one that comes between
The edge of night and the break of day . . .
It's when the darkness rolls away.

KATE WOLF (SONGWRITER),
FROM "ACROSS THE GREAT DIVIDE"

Introduction

The wasted human potential is tragic. In so many schools, kids with social, emotional, and behavioral challenges are still poorly understood and treated in a way that is completely at odds with what is now known about how they came to be challenging in the first place. The frustration and desperation felt by teachers and parents is palpable. Many teachers continue to experience enormous stress related to classroom behavior problems and from dealing with parents, and do not receive the support they need to help their challenging students. Half of teachers leave the profession within their first four years, and kids with behavioral challenges and their parents are cited as one of the major reasons.[1] Parents know there's trouble at school, know they're being blamed, feel their kids are being misunderstood and mistreated, but feel powerless to make things better and are discouraged and put off by their interactions with school personnel.

School discipline is broken. Not surprisingly, tightening the vise grip hasn't worked. A task force of the American Psychological Association has recently concluded that zero-tolerance policies, which were intended to reduce violence and behavior problems in our schools, have instead achieved the opposite effect. A review of ten years of research found that these policies have not only failed to make schools safe or more effective in handling student behavior, but have actually increased behavior problems and dropout rates.[2] Yet public elementary and secondary schools in the United States continue to dole out a whopping 110,000 expulsions and 3 million suspensions each year, along with countless tens of millions of detentions.[3]

Behind the statistics, behind each expulsion, suspension, and detention, are human beings—kids, teachers, parents—doing the best they can with the tools they have. Dramatic changes are needed to help them. And my experience suggests that these changes won't be as painful and difficult as many fear. We cannot keep doing things the way we always have and continue losing kids on a scale that is truly astounding. This book is about doing things a different way.

I interact with hundreds of challenging kids every year. These kids would like nothing better than to be able to handle the social, emotional, and behavioral challenges being placed on them at school and in life, but they can't seem to pull it off. Many have been getting into trouble for so long that they've lost faith that any adult will ever know how to help them.

I work with hundreds of teachers every year, too. The vast majority care deeply about kids and devote massive amounts of time and energy to the kids they teach. But most readily acknowledge that understanding and helping challenging kids wasn't a major part of their education, and that they could use some serious help with some of these students and their parents. And most are so caught up in the daily demands of teaching and all the new initiatives imposed on them that they simply don't have time to reflect on how to better help the challenging kids in their classrooms.

I also work with hundreds of parents of challenging kids every year. Most are eager to work with school personnel in addressing their kids' challenges in an effective and compassionate way, but they aren't exactly sure how to make it happen.

Ten years ago I published a book called *The Explosive Child* that was primarily geared toward parents. Since then, the model I described in *The Explosive Child*—called Collaborative Problem Solving (CPS)—has been implemented not only in thousands of households but also in dozens of inpatient psychiatric units, residential facilities, systems of juvenile detention, and general and special education schools. It's become clear that a book delineating how the CPS model is applied in schools is sorely needed.

Now you know why I wrote this book and for whom I wrote it. So let's talk a little about the how.

Helping kids with social, emotional, and behavioral challenges is not a mechanical exercise. Kids aren't robots, adults aren't robots, and helping them work together isn't robotic. The work is hard, messy, uncomfortable, and requires teamwork, patience, and tenacity, especially as the work also involves questioning conventional wisdom and practices. This book contains lots of material and examples to help you better understand challenging kids, how to implement the CPS model, and how to work collaboratively toward the common goal of helping these kids more effectively.

But there's also a running story about some challenging kids, their teachers, their parents, and the leaders of their school . . . and their messy, uncomfortable, collective attempts to make things better. The running story helps accomplish several goals. First, it moves the book rapidly from ideas to pragmatic reality. Second, it helps bring to life the challenges, pressures, stressors, doubts, obstacles, and anxieties of each constituency. Third, it provides readers with the actual words to use under various conditions. So often people say, "I understand the CPS model, but I need to know what it *looks* and *sounds* like in action!" or "I need to get a feel for the *language* of Collaborative Problem Solving." And they ask, "Is it truly realistic to think that an entire school could do this?" Toward this end, the story is abundant with real-life examples and dialogue.

All of the characters are based on educators, parents, and kids I've known and worked with, the actual challenges they tried to overcome, and how they did it. Some characters are composites, and names and details have been changed to protect identities. I could have presented the characters in the best possible light, but then they wouldn't have been very authentic. So the principal in the story isn't *every* principal, she's just the principal of the school in this story. Same deal for the kids, parents, teachers, and other characters. They aren't stereotypes, nor are they intended to be representative . . . they're just the characters I chose to help me demonstrate the difficulties and complexities inherent in transforming the disciplinary culture in a classroom and school.

I'm also not very specific about the type of school being depicted. It's clearly a public school, and a lot of the action takes place in the sixth grade, but I've been intentionally vague about its precise grade representation and the ethnicity and socioeconomic status of its population. While these details sometimes matter at the fringes, they don't have a dramatic impact on outcomes when people are using the CPS model. Although there are many females exhibiting challenging behavior at school, for ease of exposition I refer to challenging kids in this book primarily in the male gender. While the book is about kids with *social, emotional,* and *behavioral* challenges, I use the terms *kids with behavioral challenges* and (though I try to be sensitive to people-first phraseology) *challenging kids* to encompass all three domains. Also, the work of other authors is referred to at various points throughout the text; these references are contained in a separate section at the end of this book.

This book is not about academics. There are plenty of initiatives in the field of education to make sure kids get what they need academically. This book is about the kids those initiatives inexplicably left behind.

This book does not bash or blame educators. Nor, for that matter, does it bash or blame challenging kids or their parents. It's about the need to make dramatic changes in a system that isn't working for teachers, parents, or challenging kids, and how to go about making those changes. Three massive shifts are required: (1) a dramatic improvement in understanding the factors that set the stage for challenging behavior in kids; (2) creating mechanisms for helping these kids that are predominantly proactive instead of reactive; and (3) creating processes so people can work on problems collaboratively.

Different people will take different things from this book. For some, the fact that challenging behavior can be traced back to lagging cognitive skills will be quite novel. For others, the limitations of consequences could be an eye-opener. For still others, the specific ingredients of Collaborative Problem Solving, and how these ingredients differ from (and are often more productive than) other ways of talking with and caring about challenging kids, will be enlightening. And for still others—perhaps those who have become a bit jaded or cynical—this book may offer a fresh perspective and new hope.

As always, to get the most out of what you're about to read, the primary prerequisites are an open mind and imagination of the possibilities.

Ross W. Greene

Boston, Massachusetts

CHAPTER 1

School of Hard Knocks

It was early October, and the students in Mrs. Lori Woods' sixth-grade class were hard at work on a social studies assignment. There was, however, one clear exception, a boy named Joey. Mrs. Woods had already had a few difficult moments with Joey, especially at times when he refused to work on class assignments. That Joey was clearly not working on his social studies project was an irritation; that he was now distracting two other kids pressed Mrs. Woods into action. She walked over to Joey's table.

"Joey, is there a problem?" Mrs. Woods whispered. "Because you're bothering the students around you."

Joey looked up at his teacher. "I don't know what to do."

"Joey, the instructions are on the board. How can you not know what to do?"

Two kids seated near Joey snickered.

"Because I don't!"

Now most of the other kids were watching.

"Back to work everyone," said Mrs. Woods. She turned her attention back to Joey. "Joey, let's talk about it at my desk so we don't disturb your classmates." She began walking toward the front of the room, but Joey didn't budge. Mrs. Woods turned back around.

"Joey, come up to my desk, please."

"No way," Joey said under his breath, but loudly enough to once again draw the attention of his classmates.

"Excuse me?"

Joey's face reddened. "I'm not coming up to your desk."

The entire class was now riveted, awaiting the teacher's response.

"Joey, if you don't come up to my desk now, I'll have to send you to the office."

"I'm not going there, either."

"Joey, *now!*"

"No way."

Mrs. Woods walked over to one of the students near the front door of the classroom. "Taylor, please go to the office and tell Mrs. Westbrook that we have a problem in our classroom and that we need Mr. Middleton to come immediately." Mrs. Woods hoped that the threatened arrival of the assistant principal might persuade Joey to rethink his stance.

Taylor dutifully jumped out of her seat and ran to the office. Mrs. Woods walked to the doorway of the classroom and turned to address the rest of her students. "I don't want to have to say this again: Get back to work."

"What's up?" asked Mr. Middleton when he arrived, a little out of breath. Mr. Middleton had been an assistant principal for twelve years (a science teacher for sixteen years before that), and was known among the faculty as a congenial, even-keeled man who was probably miscast as the school's primary disciplinarian.

"Joey was disrupting the class so I told him to come up to my desk and he refused. Then I told him that he had to go to the office and he refused. So there he sits." Mrs. Woods motioned in Joey's direction.

Mr. Middleton looked over his glasses into the classroom. "Let's see what I can do."

Mr. Middleton walked over to Joey, leaned down, and spoke softly. "Joey, I understand we have a problem. Why don't we talk about it in my office?"

Joey exploded. He jumped out of his seat, his head hitting Mr. Middleton in the jaw. *"I'm not going to the freaking office!"* he screamed and ran toward the door. The other kids gasped. Stunned by the blow to his jaw, Mr. Middleton grasped vainly at Joey. Joey pushed Mrs. Woods out of the way, screaming *"I hate your guts!"* As he passed Taylor's desk, he blurted, *"I'm going to kill you!"* Taylor recoiled as Joey ran out of the classroom. He ran down the hallway to the front of the school and out of the building with Mr. Middleton giving chase. As Mr. Middleton ran past the main office, he yelled to Mrs. Westbrook, the secretary, "Get Mrs. Galvin!" Mrs. Westbrook hurried into the principal's office and told Mrs. Galvin, the school principal, that Joey had just run out of the building with Mr. Middleton in his wake. Mrs. Galvin bolted out of her office to assist in the chase. Mr. Sizemore, one of the physical education instructors, heard the commotion from the copy room and sprinted after Joey as well.

Mr. Middleton and Mr. Sizemore found Joey hiding behind a car in the school parking lot and forcibly escorted him back into the school. The two men planted Joey in a chair in Mrs. Galvin's office. "Call his mother," puffed Mrs. Galvin to Mrs. Westbrook as she reentered the office.

With Mr. Sizemore and Mr. Middleton still holding his arms, Mrs. Galvin looked sternly at Joey. "Are you going to sit in that chair without them holding you?"

Joey strained against the grasp of the two men. "Get these creeps off of me."

"They will let go of you when you calm down and tell me you'll sit in that chair until your mother arrives."

Joey tried to break out of the hold of the two men, his face red, tears streaming down his cheeks. "Get them off of me!"

Mrs. Galvin was still catching her breath. "They will let go of you when you calm down. We will not have this kind of behavior in our school."

Joey continued to struggle against the two men. "Joey, just calm down," Mr. Middleton tried to soothe despite the pain in his jaw.

"Screw you," said Joey, struggling slightly less.

"Joey, we don't talk that way in this school, either," said Mrs. Galvin.

"Screw you, too," said Joey, glaring at the principal but struggling still less.

"Come on, Joey, just relax," said Mr. Middleton. "I don't want to hold you like this."

"So let go!" Joey seethed. "You already hurt my arm."

"We don't want to hurt you," said Mr. Middleton, "but we can't let you go running out of the school again. It's dangerous. Please just calm down so we can let go."

Joey's mother, Ms. Lowell, arrived ten minutes later. "What's going on here?" she demanded breathlessly.

"They hurt me," Joey glared at Mrs. Galvin.

Ms. Lowell looked at Joey's arms, then at Mrs. Galvin, seeking an explanation. Mrs. Galvin was a straight-talking administrator who prided herself on running a tight ship and making sure that the kids in her school got a good education.

"He threatened the life of one of his classmates," the principal said. "That's just unacceptable. He then ran out of the school and needed to be physically escorted back. That's why his arms are a little red."

Ms. Lowell tried not to raise her voice. "Joey, you threatened another kid?"

"I didn't mean it."

"Why did you run out of the school?" asked Ms. Lowell.

"I didn't know what to do on the social studies project," Joey mumbled.

Ms. Lowell was uncomprehending. "You didn't know what?"

"Apparently he was refusing to do his work," said Mr. Middleton. "Mrs. Woods asked him to come up to her desk and he refused to do that, too. Then she told him to go to the office and he refused again. Then I tried to talk to him and he ran out of the classroom."

"I didn't know what to do!" Joey insisted.

"I should add that he hit Mr. Middleton in the jaw and shoved Mrs. Woods during this episode," said Mrs. Galvin. "That's called assault, and it is just totally unacceptable in this building."

Joey slumped in his seat, again mumbling, "It was an accident."

"Joey, I can't believe you did that," said his mother. Joey's eyes welled up.

"On purpose or not, Joey will be spending the next five days at home," said Mrs. Galvin.

Ms. Lowell looked at the principal, eyes wide. "What do you mean?"

"I mean he's suspended from school for five days. We will not tolerate this sort of thing in our school. Joey's classmates have a right to a safe learning environment, and that right was violated today. I also need to talk with the superintendent about whether other action needs to be taken."

"Other action? Like what?"

"When a student assaults a teacher in this school system and threatens to kill people, our school discipline code says we need to notify the police. And Mr. Middleton and Mrs. Woods will have to decide whether they want to press charges."

"The *police?*" shrieked Joey's mother. "For an *accident?*"

"Based on what I've heard, I don't share Joey's view that it was accidental," said Mrs. Galvin. "For now, you need to take Joey home. We can discuss other developments once I have more information. Joey needs to understand that this type of behavior is unacceptable."

"He already knows this behavior is unacceptable," said Ms. Lowell.

This observation was met with silence.

Ms. Lowell had heard enough. "Let's go, Joey." She looked at Mr. Middleton. "I'm very sorry you were hurt." Joey followed his mother out of the office, his hands jammed deep in his jeans pockets, his head low.

The two administrators watched through the window as Joey and his mother got into the car and drove off.

What are we going to do about Joey?

More than ever, that's the big question. Because there sure are a lot of Joeys out there. Kids who can't seem to function in a classroom, have a hard time getting along with other kids, don't seem to respect authority, aren't responding to the school discipline program. Kids whose problems don't get better. Sometimes we read about them in the newspaper and see them on TV, especially if they hurt someone badly enough or are led out of the school in handcuffs. The stakes are high. When we don't help the Joeys, we lose them.

How are we going to help Mrs. Woods? Another big question. Mrs. Woods' classroom is full of kids with all kinds of academic, behavioral, emotional, and social challenges. She'd like nothing better than to be able to give all of them the help they need. She's put a lot of time and energy into helping her challenging students over the years, but often hasn't had much to show for her efforts. At a minimum, she needs some way of making sure the challenging kids in her class don't disrupt the learning of the other kids. But she also has high-stakes testing to worry about, lessons to plan, countless meetings to attend, and the latest school system initiatives to digest and implement, so she's pressed for time as it is. When we don't help Mrs. Woods, we lose her, too.

What about Ms. Lowell? It's a scary, lonely, callous, frustrating world out there for parents of challenging kids, even more so if the kid is challenging at school. Ms. Lowell has grown accustomed to feeling blamed for her son's difficulties, accustomed to the stares of people who identify her as the parent of *"that* kid." She's all too familiar with the different medicines used to treat challenging kids, along with the books and TV shows that characterize her as a passive, permissive, uncaring, unmotivated, uneducated parent. There are millions of Ms. Lowells out there, all wishing there was a better way, one that actually worked.

If we're going to start helping Joey and Mrs. Woods and Ms. Lowell, we need to start paying much closer attention to what we now know about how kids come to be challenging. Then we need to consider some important questions. Does the way we're disciplining kids in our schools address the actual factors that set the stage for kids' social, emotional, and behavioral challenges? If not, then what should we be doing instead?

What we've been thinking about challenging kids—that they're manipulative, attention-seeking, coercive, unmotivated, limit-testing, and that these traits have been caused by passive, permissive, inconsistent, noncontingent parenting—is way off base most of the time. As a result, the interventions that flow from these ways of thinking have been way off base as well. You see, if you believe that passive, permissive, inconsistent, noncontingent parenting has caused a kid to behave maladaptively, then you're going to put a great deal of effort into being rigid, firm, consistent, and contingent, typically through use of consequences (rewards and punishments). We live in a culture where many adults think of only one word, only one intervention, to deal with kids who don't meet adult expectations: *consequences*. Consequences can mean rewards (in schools, this might include special privileges or stickers, happy faces, and tickets or points that can be exchanged for tangible prizes) for appropriate behavior, or punishments (being deprived of privileges, being given extra assignments, time-outs, suspension, detention, expulsion) for undesirable behavior. Consequences are wonderful when they work. They are less wonderful when they don't work. And they often don't work for the kids to whom they are most frequently applied.[1]

That's because there are really only two goals imposed consequences help us achieve: (1) teaching kids basic lessons about right and wrong ways to behave, and (2) giving kids the incentive to behave the right way. But—and this is important—the vast majority of challenging kids *already know how we want them to behave.* They know they're supposed to do what they're told. They know they're not supposed to disrupt the learning of their classmates or run out of the school when they're upset or embarrassed. And they know they're not supposed to hit people, swear, or call out in class. So they don't need us to put lots of effort into teaching them how we want them to behave. And while this may be hard to believe, most challenging kids *already want to behave the right way.* They don't need us to continue giving them stickers, depriving them of recess, or suspending them from school; *they're already motivated.* They need something else from us.

The premise of this book is that kids with behavioral challenges *lack important thinking skills,* an idea supported by research in the neurosciences over the past thirty years on kids who are aggressive and have difficulty getting along with people and those diagnosed with ADHD, mood and anxiety disorders, oppositional defiant disorder, conduct disorder, and language-processing disorders. The thinking skills involved aren't in the traditional academic domains—reading, writing, and arithmetic—but rather in domains such as regulating one's emotions, considering the outcomes of one's actions before one acts, understanding how one's behavior is affecting other people, having the words to let people know something's bothering you, and responding to changes in plan in a flexible manner. In other words, these kids have a *developmental delay,* a learning disability of sorts. In the same way that kids who are delayed in reading are having difficulty mastering the skills required for becoming proficient in reading, challenging kids are having difficulty mastering the skills required for becoming proficient in handling life's social, emotional, and behavioral challenges.

How do we help kids who have traditional developmental delays? First, we assess the factors that are interfering with skill acquisition and then provide specialized instruction to teach them the skills they're lacking in increments they can handle. When you treat challenging kids as if they have a developmental delay and apply the same compassion and approach you would use with any other learning disability, they do a lot better. Continue treating them as if they're unmotivated, manipulative, attention-seeking, limit-testing . . . continue relying heavily on consequences to address their difficulties, well, they often don't do better. That's because consequences don't teach kids the thinking skills they lack or solve the problems that set the stage for their challenging behavior. Why have we been so zealously overapplying consequences to kids with behavioral challenges? Because we didn't realize they had a developmental delay.

If conventional school discipline isn't working for kids with social, emotional, and behavioral challenges, the only reason to keep using it would be because it *is* working for the kids who do not have these challenges. The reality is that well-behaved students aren't behaving themselves because of the school discipline program. They're behaving themselves because they have the skills to handle life's challenges in an adaptive fashion. Thus, rethinking how to go about addressing the needs of challenging kids can be approached without great trepidation: The school discipline program *isn't working for the kids who aren't doing well* and *isn't needed by the kids who are.*

Now back to our original questions: What are we going to do about Joey? And how are we going to help Mrs. Woods and Ms. Lowell?

Just as we would with any other developmental delay, we're going to help Mrs. Woods and Ms. Lowell better *understand* Joey's difficulties (in other words, help them identify the skills he's lacking) and pinpoint the *situations* in which he is most likely to have these difficulties (these are called *unsolved problems*). And we're going to help them learn how to work *with* Joey so the problems can be solved, the skills can be taught, and he won't be as challenging anymore.

No, it's not going to be easy, and it's definitely going to take time.

Helping kids with behavioral challenges is never easy and is always time-consuming. But intervening in ways that aren't working is always harder and more time-consuming than intervening in ways that are working. Of course, a lot hinges on your definition of "working." All too often, "working" refers only to the successful minimization of the impact of a challenging kid on his classmates. While this is a noble goal, it is often accomplished by sacrificing the challenging kid. What if it were possible to help him solve the problems that are setting the stage for his challenging behavior, simultaneously teach him the skills he's lacking, minimize the negative impact he has on his classmates, and prevent his inexorable slide toward alienation?

We're losing a lot of kids and a lot of teachers because we still view challenging kids the wrong way and handle them in ways that don't address their true difficulties. It's an exercise in frustration for everyone involved, and it's time to get off the treadmill.

CHAPTER 2

Kids Do Well If They Can

Kids with social, emotional, and behavioral challenges lack important thinking skills. Now there's an idea that can take some getting used to. Let's begin by considering your philosophy of kids: what kids are about, why they do what they do, what they're up to (if they're really up to anything).

Many adults have never given much thought to their philosophy of kids. But if you're trying to help kids with behavioral challenges, you're going to need one, because it's your philosophy of kids that's going to guide your beliefs and your actions in your interactions with them, especially when the going gets tough. The philosophy that serves as the foundation of this book is the title of this chapter: "kids do well if they can."

This philosophy may not sound earth-shattering, but when we consider the very popular alternative philosophy—"kids do well if they want to"—the significance becomes clear. These two disparate philosophies have dramatically different ramifications for our assumptions about kids and how to proceed when they do not meet our expectations.

When the "kids do well *if they want to*" philosophy is applied to a child who's not doing well, then we believe that the reason he's not doing well is because he *doesn't want to*. This very common assumption is usually wrong and causes adults to believe that their primary role in the life of a challenging kid (and the goal of intervention) is to *make the kid want to do well*. This is typically accomplished by motivating the kid, by giving him the incentive to do well, by rewarding him when he behaves in an adaptive fashion and punishing him when he behaves in a maladaptive fashion.

By contrast, the "kids do well if they can" philosophy carries the assumption that if a kid *could* do well he *would* do well. Doing well is always preferable to not doing well, but only if a kid has the skills to do well in the first place. If a kid isn't doing well, he must be lacking the skills. What's the most important role an adult can play in the life of such a kid? First, assume he's already motivated, already knows right from wrong, and has already been punished enough. Then, figure out what skills he's lacking so you have the clearest possible understanding of what's getting in his way. *Understanding why a kid is challenging is the first and most important part of helping him.*

This can be a radical philosophical shift for a lot of people. But don't abandon ship yet. There's much at stake, not only for kids with behavioral challenges but also for their classmates, teachers, and parents. This chapter is aimed at familiarizing you with the skills challenging kids lack and how to identify these lagging skills in the kids you're trying to help.

LAGGING SKILLS

If you identify the skills a kid is lacking, you'll understand *why* he's challenging. You'll also know which skills the kid needs to learn, and you'll be better equipped to anticipate the situations in which his challenging behavior is most likely to occur. If you don't know what skills a kid is lacking, you won't possess a true understanding of his challenges, it will be much harder to anticipate his worst moments, the skills won't get taught, his challenges will linger (or get worse), and he will become increasingly frustrated, hopeless, and alienated, just as most of us would if we had a problem no one seemed to be able to understand and were being treated in a way that made the problem worse.

When is challenging behavior most likely to occur? *When the demands being placed on a kid exceed his capacity to respond adaptively.* Of course, that's when all of us exhibit maladaptive behavior. The problem for kids with behavioral challenges (and those around them) is that they're responding much more maladaptively than the rest of us, and much more often. You see, there's a spectrum of things kids do when life's demands exceed their capacity to respond adaptively. Some cry, or sulk, or pout, or whine, or withdraw—that would be the milder end of the spectrum. As we move toward the more difficult end of the spectrum, we find screaming, swearing, spitting, hitting, kicking, destroying property, lying, and truancy. And as we move even further to the extreme end of the spectrum, we find behaviors that are injurious to oneself or others: self-induced vomiting, cutting, drinking or using drugs to excess, stabbing, and shooting. But all of these behaviors occur under the same conditions: when the demands being placed on a kid exceed that kid's capacity to respond adaptively. Why do some kids respond at the milder end of the spectrum while others are at the more severe end? Some kids have the *skills* to "hold it together" when pushed to their limits and some don't.

With this new perspective on challenging kids, much of what we say about them no longer makes sense. Take a look:

- *"He just wants attention."* We all want attention, so this explanation isn't very useful for helping us understand why a kid is struggling to do well. And if a kid is seeking attention in a maladaptive way, doesn't that suggest that he lacks the skills to seek attention in an adaptive way?
- *"He just wants his own way."* We all want our own way, so this explanation doesn't help us achieve an understanding of a kid's challenges. Adaptively getting one's own way requires skills often found lacking in challenging kids.
- *"He's manipulating us."* This is a very popular, and misguided, characterization of kids with behavioral challenges. Competent manipulation requires various skills—forethought, planning, impulse control, and organization, among others—typically found lacking in challenging kids. In other words, the kids who are most

often described as being manipulative are those least capable of pulling it off.

- *"He's not motivated."* This is another very popular characterization that can be traced back to the "kids do well if they want to" mentality, and it can lead us straight to interventions aimed at giving a kid the incentive to do well. But why would any kid *not* want to do well? Why would he choose *not* to do well if he has the skills to do well? Isn't doing well always preferable?

- *"He's making bad choices."* Are you certain he has the skills and repertoire to consistently make good choices?

- *"His parents are incompetent disciplinarians."* My experience is that parents of well-behaved kids get too much credit for the fact that their children are well-behaved, and that parents of challenging kids get far too much blame for the fact that their children are not well-behaved. Blaming parents doesn't help anyone at school deal effectively with the kid in the six hours a day, five days a week, nine months of the year that he's there.

- *"He has a bad attitude."* He probably didn't start out with one. "Bad attitudes" tend to be the by-product of countless years of being misunderstood and overpunished by adults who didn't recognize that a kid was lacking crucial thinking skills. But kids are resilient; they come around if we start doing the right thing.

- *"He has a mental illness."* While he may well meet diagnostic criteria for a psychiatric disorder and may even benefit from psychotropic medication, this description is a nonstarter. Fifty years ago, a psychiatrist named Thomas Szasz understood that "mentally ill" was a limiting (and potentially inaccurate and derisory) way to describe people with social, emotional, and behavioral challenges. He advocated for reconceptualizing these challenges as "problems in living," a more fitting and productive way of viewing things.

- *"His brother was the same way."* Ah, so it's the gene pool! Alas, we can't do anything about the gene pool, and it's likely that his brother was lacking some important thinking skills, too.

While many of these explanations enjoy tremendous popularity, most are simply clichés that lead caregivers down an intervention dead-end. Once you become comfortable with the idea that challenging kids lack important thinking skills, these explanations no longer make much sense. In fact, such explanations have a tendency to cause adults to view kids with behavioral challenges as "the enemy" and push them away.

The following list is much more useful. It's the list of many skills frequently found lagging in challenging kids:

- Difficulty handling transitions, shifting from one mind-set or task to another
- Difficulty doing things in a logical sequence or prescribed order
- Difficulty persisting on challenging or tedious tasks
- Poor sense of time
- Difficulty reflecting on multiple thoughts or ideas simultaneously
- Difficulty maintaining focus
- Difficulty considering the likely outcomes or consequences of actions (impulsive)
- Difficulty considering a range of solutions to a problem
- Difficulty expressing concerns, needs, or thoughts in words
- Difficulty understanding what is being said
- Difficulty managing emotional response to frustration so as to think rationally
- Chronic irritability and/or anxiety significantly impede capacity for problem-solving or heighten frustration
- Difficulty seeing the "grays"/concrete, literal, black-and-white thinking
- Difficulty deviating from rules, routine
- Difficulty handling unpredictability, ambiguity, uncertainty, novelty
- Difficulty shifting from original idea, plan, or solution
- Difficulty taking into account situational factors that would suggest the need to adjust a plan of action
- Inflexible, inaccurate interpretations/cognitive distortions or biases (e.g., "Everyone's out to get me," "Nobody likes me," "You always blame me," "It's not fair," "I'm stupid")
- Difficulty attending to and/or accurately interpreting social cues/ poor perception of social nuances

- Difficulty starting conversations, entering groups, connecting with people/lacks other basic social skills
- Difficulty seeking attention in appropriate ways
- Difficulty appreciating how one's behavior is affecting other people
- Difficulty empathizing with others, appreciating another person's perspective or point of view
- Difficulty appreciating how one is coming across or being perceived by others

You may have noticed that this list contains no diagnoses. That's because diagnoses don't give us any information about the cognitive skills a kid may be lacking. In other words, "bipolar disorder" provides no information about the specific skills a kid is lacking. Nor does "fetal alcohol syndrome" or "lead poisoned" or "brain injured" or "Asperger's disorder" or "ADHD" or "oppositional defiant disorder" or "antisocial" or "sociopath." All too often adults get caught up in the quest for the right diagnosis, assuming that a diagnosis will help them know what to do next. The reality is that diagnoses aren't especially useful for understanding kids with behavioral challenges or for helping adults know what to do next. Plus, kids don't generally exhibit challenging behavior in a vacuum. It usually takes two to tango: a kid who's lacking skills *and* an environment (teachers, parents, peers) that demands those skills. Durable, effective intervention must focus both on the kid (who has skills to learn and problems to solve) and on people in the kid's environment (who need to understand the true nature of the kid's difficulties and provide opportunities for the problems to be solved and the skills to be learned and practiced). Diagnoses don't reflect that reality, they simply pathologize the child.

While diagnoses do tend to make adults take a kid's difficulties more seriously, a kid doesn't need a diagnosis, or a special education designation, to have a problem. He just needs a *problem* to have a problem. Of course, if a school system requires a kid to have a diagnosis to access certain services, most mental health professionals are happy to oblige; it's just that we shouldn't operate on the assumption that a diagnosis provides a great deal of *useful* information. A kid shouldn't need a diagnosis to access help.

Let's focus on some of the lagging skills on the list for the purpose of making clear the connection between lagging skills and how they can contribute to challenging behavior.

IN FOCUS

Difficulty handling transitions, shifting from one mind-set or task to another

---

This lagging skill is often referred to as a *shifting cognitive set,* which is required any time a person moves from one task to another (for example, from gathering supplies and books from one's locker to getting down to work in class) or from one environment to another (from recess to quiet time). Each task or environment involves different norms and expectations and therefore a different mind-set: "In recess it's OK to run around and make noise and socialize" versus "During quiet time we sit at our desks and read quietly and don't talk to other kids." If a kid has difficulty with this skill, there's a good chance he'll be thinking and acting as if he's still in recess long after quiet time has started.

When you're telling a kid what to do, that also requires a shift in cognitive set, especially if what you're telling him to do isn't what he was doing in the first place (as a general rule, that's when kids usually get told what to do). Paradoxically, it's the kids who have trouble shifting set who wind up getting told what to do most often.

Difficulty shifting set contributes to many maladaptive behaviors in kids. When is the likelihood of maladaptive behavior greatly heightened in kids who lack this skill? When the environment demands that the kid shift cognitive set. It's just like any other learning disability. Kids who have difficulty reading are more likely to struggle when life demands that they read. Kids who have difficulty shifting cognitive set are more likely to struggle when life demands that they shift cognitive set. One of the important tasks of development is to learn how to shift gears efficiently when the environment demands it. It's a skill many challenging kids do not yet possess.

This doesn't mean that adults should stop telling kids what to do or completely eliminate demands for shifting cognitive set. But it does mean that if we want to help a kid whose challenging behaviors are set in motion by difficulty shifting cognitive set, the first step is to recognize that he's lacking that skill. Then we'd identify the specific situations (unsolved problems) in which that lagging skill is causing the most difficulty. Then we'd start working on solving those problems. How? That's covered in Chapters 4 and 5. For now, the most important thing is to understand that the kid isn't testing limits or being manipulative or controlling; rather, he's lacking an important skill.

IN FOCUS

Difficulty reflecting on multiple thoughts or ideas simultaneously (disorganized)

Difficulty considering a range of solutions to a problem

Difficulty considering the likely outcomes or consequences of one's actions (impulsive)

When you're faced with a problem or frustration, your primary task is to solve the problem that caused your frustration. To accomplish this task, these three skills will be absolutely essential. That's because problem-solving requires a great deal of organized, planful thinking.

Let's ponder that for a moment. To solve a problem you must first identify the problem you're trying to solve. Then you'll need to think of solutions to the problem. And then you'll need to anticipate the likely outcomes of those solutions so as to pick the best one. That's how people make decisions.

Many kids are so disorganized in their thinking—they have so much difficulty sorting through their thoughts—that they're unable to figure out what's frustrating them, in which case the process of problem-solving comes to an abrupt halt, the problem doesn't get solved, and their frustration heightens (often setting in motion one of the behaviors on the spectrum). Many are so disorganized that even if they can manage to figure out what problem they're trying to solve, they can't think of more than one solution to the problem. Many are so impulsive that even if they can think of more than one solution, they've already done the first thing that popped into their heads. The bad news? Our first solution is often (not always, but often) our worst. Good solutions usually come to mind after we've inhibited our less optimal initial impulses and considered our better options in a more organized fashion. Many kids—often the disorganized, impulsive ones—are notorious for putting their "worst foot forward." In other words, there are many kids who are responding to life's challenges in a maladaptive fashion because they aren't very skilled at organizing their thoughts, thinking of alternative solutions, or anticipating likely outcomes.

Approaching problems in an organized, planful manner, considering a variety of solutions, and reflecting on their likely outcomes are crucial developmental skills. Most two-year-olds don't yet possess these skills. Neither do a lot of challenging kids who—chronologically, at least—are a lot older.

Clearly, these kids need our help! But if the school discipline program emphasizes consequences, they're not going to get the help they need. Again, consequences only remind kids of what we don't want them to do, and give them the incentive to do something more adaptive instead. But they already know what we don't want them to do, and they're already motivated to do something more adaptive instead. They need something else from us.

By the way, a lot of kids who are disorganized and impulsive are diagnosed with ADHD. But whether a kid meets criteria for ADHD isn't the important part. Knowing that he is a disorganized, impulsive problem-solver gives you a much clearer understanding of his difficulties and provides more useful information about what kind of help he needs from you.

> **IN FOCUS**
> Difficulty expressing concerns, needs, or thoughts in words

Much of our daily lives involve language and communication skills, so it's no accident that kids who are lacking such skills have trouble handling the social, emotional, and behavioral demands that are placed upon them. For example, many kids have trouble finding the words to tell someone what's the matter or what they need. If you don't have the wherewithal to let people know that you "don't feel like talking," that "something's the matter," that you "need a minute to think," that you "don't know what to do," that you "need a break," or that you "don't like that," then you may express these things in ways that are far less ideal. The reminder "Use your words" won't help at all if a kid doesn't have the words. Some kids cry or become withdrawn when they don't have the skills to communicate effectively. Other kids make their thoughts or feelings or needs known with "Screw you," "I hate you," "Shut up," and other more colorful expressions (that's right, *disrespect* is just a sign that a kid is lacking important skills. . . . if the kid could communicate in a more respectful way, he would). And still others express themselves physically (shoving, hitting, throwing things, destroying property, running out of the classroom).

Regrettably, language-processing and communication-skills difficulties are frequently overlooked. Adults often don't think to assess these skills when they're trying to figure out why a challenging kid is challenging. And sometimes the testing instrumentation used when these skills are being assessed doesn't pick up on finer-grained lagging skills that may be involved; in such cases, the test results may not only fail to pinpoint the kid's difficulties, but also erroneously conclude that the kid has no language-processing or communication difficulties at all.

Can kids be taught to articulate their concerns, needs, and thoughts more effectively? Absolutely. But not until adults understand that it's the lack of these skills that is setting the stage for challenging behavior.

IN FOCUS

Difficulty managing emotional response to frustration so as to think rationally (separation of affect)

Chronic irritability and/or anxiety significantly impede capacity for problem-solving

---

Separation of affect refers to the ability to separate the *emotions* (affect) you're feeling in response to a problem or frustration from the *thinking* you must do to resolve the problem. While emotions can be quite useful for mobilizing or energizing people to solve problems, thinking is how problems get solved. Kids skilled at separating affect tend to respond to problems or frustrations with more *thought* than emotion, and that's good. But kids who lack skill in this domain tend to respond to problems or frustrations with more *emotion* and less (or no) thought, and that's not good at all. Learning how to put your emotions "on the shelf" so as to be able to think rationally is an essential developmental skill, and one many challenging kids have failed to develop.

At the milder end of the spectrum, kids who are having difficulty separating thought from emotion may become highly anxious over, for example, an upcoming test, a new social situation, not understanding an assignment, or being embarrassed in front of their classmates. They may cry over a bad grade, at not being picked first for a team, or when they feel socially excluded. At the more extreme end of the spectrum, their emotions may burst through in such a powerful way that they scream, swear, throw something, hit somebody, or worse. These kids may actually feel themselves "heating up," but often aren't able to stem the emotional tide until later, when the emotions have subsided and rational thought has returned. Naturally, the heating-up process will be greatly intensified if adults or peers respond in a way that adds fuel to the fire.

While separation of affect refers to momentary difficulties in managing emotions, other kids have more chronic difficulties regulating their emotions. All kids are a little sad, irritable, agitated, grumpy, cranky, grouchy, and fatigued, or a little anxious, worried, scared, and nervous some of the time. No one responds especially well to problems or frustrations when they're irritable or anxious, but some kids experience these emotions far more often and far more intensely. Kids who are frequently irritable or anxious often respond poorly to problems and frustrations. Because they haven't developed the skills they need for modulating their emotions and solving problems, they respond to problems and frustrations in a way that more closely resembles what we might see in a much younger child. When it comes to managing their emotions and solving problems, these kids *are* functioning at a much younger developmental level.

We've witnessed a disturbing trend in recent years: the almost automatic inclination to use medication to treat kids who have difficulty regulating their emotions. While medication can be useful, even indispensable, in some instances, jumping the gun on medicating kids whose difficulties are poorly understood is far too common. Pills don't teach skills, and there are many factors that could set the stage for a kid to be irritable or anxious that medication won't address. Some kids are irritable or anxious because of *chronic problems that have never been solved,* such as school failure, poor peer relations, being bullied, or having an unrecognized learning disability. Medication doesn't solve these problems.

Equally disturbing is the recent tendency to diagnose kids who have difficulty regulating their emotions as having bipolar disorder. In my experience, the vast majority of kids who have been called bipolar have been poorly assessed and inappropriately diagnosed.[1] These kids certainly don't meet criteria for adult bipolar disorder, and there are no universally accepted criteria for childhood bipolar disorder. Unfortunately, the recent popularity of the diagnosis accounts for a corresponding and disturbing increase in the use of a fairly new, relatively unproven class of medication in kids whose difficulties, in many cases, are very poorly understood. In a nutshell, that's one reason psychotropic medications are overprescribed: Not enough people are familiar with the cognitive factors that can set the stage for social, emotional, and behavioral challenges, and sometimes it's just easier to give a kid a pill than to figure out what's truly getting in his way.

Can irritable or anxious kids be helped to better regulate their emotions and respond to life's frustrations and anxieties more adaptively? Certainly. But not by putting a lot of effort into coming up with new and creative ways to punish them.

IN FOCUS

Difficulty seeing the "grays"/concrete, literal, black-and-white thinking

Difficulty deviating from rules, routine

Difficulty handling unpredictability, ambiguity, uncertainty, novelty

> Difficulty shifting from original idea or solution/difficulty
>   adapting to changes in plan
> Inflexible, inaccurate interpretations/cognitive distortions
>   or biases

Young kids tend to be fairly rigid, black-and-white, literal, inflexible thinkers. They're still making sense of the world and it's easier to put two and two together if they don't have to worry about exceptions to the rule or alternative ways of looking at things. As kids develop, they learn that, in fact, most things in life are "gray," that there are exceptions to the rule and alternative ways of interpreting things. Sometimes we have a substitute teacher, a field trip needs to be rescheduled because of the weather, someone is sitting in our usual seat in the cafeteria, recess has to be indoors instead of outdoors.

Unfortunately, for some kids, "gray" thinking doesn't develop as readily. Though some of these kids are diagnosed with disorders such as nonverbal learning disability or Asperger's disorder, it's more useful to think of them as *black-and-white thinkers living in a gray world*. Predictably, these kids are most likely to exhibit challenging behavior when the world places demands on them for gray thinking.

Many such kids are quite comfortable with factual information because it's black-and-white but grow uncomfortable when life demands problem-solving because it's gray.

TEACHER: *Class, what's the highest mountain in North America?*
    Andrew?
ANDREW *(black-and-white thinker): Mount McKinley!*
TEACHER: *Excellent, Andrew. Now, I'd like you and Susie to do*
    a presentation on Mount McKinley for the rest of the class.
    You guys can do it anyway you like, but you have to talk
    about it and agree on a plan. OK?
ANDREW: *OK.*
(2 minutes later)
ANDREW: *Mrs. Huggins, Susie won't do it right!*
TEACHER: *What do you mean, Andrew?*

ANDREW: *When you do a presentation on mountains, first you have to show everyone a picture of the mountain you're talking about. Susie says it doesn't matter when you show the picture. She's wrong!*

It sounds like Andrew has some pretty clear ideas about how to do a presentation on Mount McKinley, and is having difficulty moving off his original idea. Spoiled brat? No. Control freak? Wouldn't be the best choice of words. Black-and-white thinker living in a gray world? Classic case.

These kids love details (black-and-white) but aren't so adept at handling ambiguity (gray) and often miss the "big picture" (gray). They love predictability (it's black-and-white) but don't do so well when things are unpredictable (gray). They love certainty (black-and-white) and routines (black-and-white) but don't handle uncertainty (gray) or changes in plan (gray) very well.

TEACHER: *Class, we're not going out for recess today at ten-fifteen because we have an assembly.*

ANDREW: *What do you mean we're not going out for recess at ten-fifteen? We always go out for recess at ten-fifteen! I'm going out at ten-fifteen!*

Tough way to go through life. No one would choose to be that way.

These black-and-white kids tend to interpret the world in some pretty rigid ways, too. These are the kids who are prone to make black-and-white statements such as "I'm stupid," or "You always blame me," or "Nobody likes me," or "You're mean," or "It's not fair," or "Things will never work out for me," or "People are out to get me." These rigid ways of thinking—sometimes called cognitive biases or cognitive distortions—can cause these kids to respond to even the most benign circumstances in powerful (and challenging) ways. Can you imagine interpreting common social stimuli—a friend's smirk, peers whispering, a slap on the back—as evidence that people were out to get you? That would set the stage for some pretty maladaptive responses.

The Andrews of the world often present significant challenges to their teachers and classmates as they struggle to apply concrete rules and interpretations to a world where few such rules apply. Some sulk or become anxious when events don't conform to their original configuration, or when they've interpreted an event in a distorted fashion. Some scream. Some swear. Or throw things. Of course, those are the things they *do*. All that tells you is where they are on the spectrum of challenging behaviors. Now you know *why* and *when* they're doing them. That's where the action's at.

Can black-and-white thinkers be helped to think more flexibly? To move from an original way of thinking and adapt to circumstances or perspectives they may not have taken into account? Most definitely . . . so long as adults recognize that it's hard to teach kids to be more flexible by being inflexible themselves.

IN FOCUS

Difficulty appreciating how one's behavior is affecting other people; often surprised by others' responses to his/her behavior

Difficulty empathizing with others, appreciating another person's perspective or point of view

---

Many kids with behavioral challenges have difficulty understanding another's perspective and appreciating how their behavior is affecting others. These are crucial skills, for they help us gauge whether we've caused someone pain or pleasure, whether our behavior is being well- or poorly received. Whether a joke was funny. Whether a pat on the back was too hard. Whether a comment was embarrassing or humiliating or hurtful. This information helps us decide whether to repeat the behavior or change course.

Kids who lack these skills are prone to behave in ways that fail to take the needs of others into account and to repeat behaviors that are causing emotional or physical discomfort. These are not endearing traits, and kids who lack these skills are frequently punished in one way or another. Here's the hitch: Punishment may not be a terribly effective way to teach kids how to take another's perspective or to appreciate how their behavior is affecting others. Many adults are incredibly vigilant in ensuring that kids suffer immediate, adult-imposed consequences for maladaptive behavior, yet helping kids appreciate how their behavior is affecting others is a much more reliable mechanism for ensuring that kids do the right thing without adult assistance.

Appreciating how our behavior is affecting others, taking others' needs and concerns into account, and modifying our behavior in response to the feedback we receive are vital developmental skills that many challenging kids have yet to master. Can these skills be taught? Yes, usually. Of course, it does take a while, and we'll need some new methods.

So now you know, if you didn't already, that the skills required for adaptive social, emotional, and behavioral functioning don't come naturally to all kids. We adults tend to think that all kids are created equal in these capacities, but this simply isn't true. You also know that challenging behavior occurs when life demands skills that a child lacks, and that there's a whole spectrum of challenging behaviors that can occur—some relatively mild, others much more severe—under these circumstances.

By the way, there's a big difference between interpreting the lagging skills described above as "excuses" rather than as "explanations." When lagging skills are invoked as excuses, the door slams shut on the process of thinking about how to teach the kid the skills he lacks. Conversely, when lagging skills are invoked as *explanations* for a kid's behavior, the door to helping swings wide open. As you shall see.

UNSOLVED PROBLEMS

I've described some of the lagging skills that can set the stage for challenging behavior, but there's a crucial piece of information missing. Those lagging skills are especially problematic in specific situations. We need to identify the specific conditions or situations (sometimes called triggers or antecedents) in which challenging behavior occurs. I prefer to call these situations *unsolved problems*. How do we know these problems are *unsolved*? Because they're still precipitating challenging behavior. If you don't identify the problems that are precipitating a kid's challenging behavior, it will be hard to know what you're working on, the problems will remain unsolved, and the kid's challenging behavior will persist. But if you identify the kid's unsolved problems, you can work with him to solve them, and his challenging behavior will subside.

For example, if a kid is having some of his greatest difficulties during circle time, then circle time is an unsolved problem precipitating challenging behavior. If a kid is having difficulty getting along with other kids during recess, then getting along with other kids during recess is an unsolved problem precipitating challenging behavior. And if a kid is refusing to work when paired with a particular classmate, then working with that particular classmate is an unsolved problem precipitating challenging behavior. A lot of adults nominate the word "no" as a trigger. But it's not specific enough. It's what the adult is saying "no" to—going to the bathroom (yet again), sharpening a pencil (yet again), excessive talking or teasing—that helps adults know the specific problem they need to solve (so they don't have to keep saying "no" so often).

Difficulties getting along with other kids on the school bus, behaving appropriately in the cafeteria or in the hallways, transitioning from one activity to another, interacting with a certain teacher or peer, getting started and maintaining effort on specific academic tasks, completing classwork or homework, working with other students cooperatively—these are all problems that commonly precipitate challenging behavior. What's the next goal? Work with the students in a way that moves these problems from the "unsolved" category to the "solved" category.

NEW LENSES
AND A NEW TOOL

There are many lenses through which challenging behavior in kids can be viewed. Some people view challenging behavior through the prism of diagnoses. Now you know why that's not my focus. Some people see passive, permissive, inconsistent, noncontingent parenting when they're observing a child's challenging behavior. Now you should be clear as to why that won't be our emphasis, either. Here's the mantra that encapsulates the view of this book:

Behind every challenging behavior
is an unsolved problem and a lagging skill.

Whether a kid is sulking, pouting, whining, withdrawing, refusing to talk, crying, spitting, screaming, swearing, running out of the classroom, kicking, hitting, destroying property, or worse, you won't know what to do about the challenging behavior until you understand why it's occurring (lagging skills) and pinpoint the situations in which it occurs (unsolved problems). Lagging skills are the *why* of challenging behavior. Unsolved problems tell us *with whom, over what, where,* and *when* the behavior is occurring.

Of course, you're going to need a mechanism for assessing and keeping track of the lagging skills and unsolved problems that are setting the stage for challenging behavior in a given kid, so this is a good time to introduce you to the Assessment of Lagging Skills and Unsolved Problems (ALSUP) shown on page 287. The ALSUP includes a list of the lagging skills you learned about earlier in this chapter, along with a section for identifying unsolved problems. You'll want to bring copies of the ALSUP to meetings in which a child's challenges are being discussed. Along with the child's other adult caregivers (the team), achieve a consensus on the skills the kid seems to be lacking. Next, achieve a consensus on the unsolved problems (in the Unsolved Problems section) that seem to be precipitating the kid's challenging behavior. This information leaves you at the doorstep of what to do next. (Though I don't think "quantifying" and "understanding" are synonyms, many schools find "quantifying" necessary, therefore the ALSUP is also available in Likert-scale format at lostatschool.org.

Why is it important to take the time to achieve a consensus on lagging skills and unsolved problems? Because if caregivers have disparate notions about what's getting in a kid's way, and those differences remain unresolved, then there will be no coherent treatment plan and, quite probably, little or no progress because all the adults will be working on something different and doing it in different ways. The time devoted to hashing out and coming to a consensus about a kid's lagging skills and unsolved problems is usually very well spent (if a kid is still exhibiting challenging behavior, it's a pretty surefire bet no one's figured these things out yet).

NEW TIMING

Once you have a decent handle on a kid's lagging skills and unsolved problems, you've taken a major step in the right direction because the kid's challenging episodes are now highly predictable, which is good news if you're a teacher and have a class full of twenty-five other students. It's also good news if you're a parent who wants to play an active role in making sure things go better for your child at school. See, the process of teaching skills and solving problems is a lot easier if it's done *proactively*. If you're a teacher, you don't have to wait until the kid disrupts the class before you try to solve the problem that causes the disruption; you can do it in advance because the problem and the disruption are predictable. And if you're a parent—let's face it, you're not there when your child is disrupting the class—you can collaborate with your child's teachers and play a role in solving the problems and teaching the skills as well. A lot of adults find it hard to believe that a kid's challenging behaviors are highly predictable, believing instead that such behaviors are unpredictable and occur out of the blue. But that's not true, not if you know what skills the child is lacking and what his triggers are.

Most challenging kids will have many lagging skills and many unsolved problems, and this can feel overwhelming. But you can't fix everything at once, so you shouldn't try. Better to prioritize two or three unsolved problems to work on first. If you solve these and other problems *collaboratively*, you'll simultaneously teach the kid many of the skills he's lacking.

A FEW LIVE ONES

At this point, it might be helpful to meet a few kids and give you an opportunity to contemplate the lagging skills and unsolved problems that are contributing to their challenging behavior.

Cody

Cody is a six-year-old first grader whose biggest problem is physical aggression toward his classmates. His teacher observes that Cody often hits other kids when they disagree with him, when he feels left out, or when he perceives that kids are laughing at him. When Cody hits, he is deprived of recess or removed from an activity. These punishments cause him to scream, cry, and threaten, prompting visits to the principal's office. His teacher has tried talking with Cody about the hitting, but these conversations aren't terribly productive. "He won't talk," says Cody's teacher. "When I try talking with him, he either denies that there's a problem, or shrugs, or walks away." Lately, she's noticed that Cody has burst out crying in some situations in which he might previously have lashed out physically, but the hitting continues to be a major area of concern. Her most pressing concerns are "How do I talk to Cody about the hitting when he refuses to discuss it?" and "What do I do to keep the other kids safe?"

Academically, Cody is an average student with no apparent learning disabilities. He impresses with his excellent knowledge of the constellations and of reptiles. Socially, he can be quite friendly and engaging, but kids tend to stay away from him for fear of being hit.

In an effort to better understand the *why* of Cody's hitting, his teacher completed the ALSUP and endorsed many items. She prioritized the following lagging skills:

- Difficulty considering a range of solutions to a problem
- Difficulty managing emotional response to frustration so as to think rationally (separation of affect)

- Difficulty shifting from original idea or solution and adapting to changes in plan or new rules

Cody's teacher also identified the unsolved problems (*who, what, where,* and *when*) that were prompting his hitting:

- Disagreements with classmates
- Feeling left out
- Feeling that he is being laughed at

Kelvin

Kelvin is a ten-year-old fourth grader who was retained in the first grade because of "immaturity" and academic difficulties. Cognitive testing in his second year of first grade documented below-average verbal skills, well-below-average nonverbal skills, and well-below-average processing speed. Recent testing has shown that Kelvin is still well below grade level in all academic skill areas.

Because of his academic and behavioral challenges, Kelvin has, for the past three years, been placed in a self-contained special education classroom that includes one teacher, an aide, and six other students. The classroom operates on a point and level system, whereby each student receives privileges for adhering to behavioral expectations (such as staying on task, completing assignments, and using appropriate language) and loses privileges when these expectations are not met. Kelvin continues to have trouble maintaining a high level, and the loss of points or his level often precipitates major challenging episodes, including screaming, swearing, and destruction of property. On some occasions Kelvin has had to be physically restrained. Otherwise, Kelvin is usually in a pretty good mood.

Kelvin's teachers report that most of his difficulties occur when they are trying to help him with difficult academic tasks ("He just won't let us help him," says his teacher) and in transitioning from one activity to another. "He always wants the current activity to continue," she says. "If he's playing a board game during choice time with one of his classmates, he wants it to go on forever. We can't let him play board games the whole day."

Kelvin also has difficulty handling uncertainty and ambiguity. For example, if he asks, "Can we play Uno today during choice time?" and his teacher responds, "We might be able to do that today," the word "might" frustrates him and he will demand a more definitive answer. Phrases such as "in a while" and "we have to stop the game soon" are confusing for him as well.

Kelvin's teachers are concerned about his screaming, swearing, destruction of property, difficulty ending one activity and moving on to another, difficulty staying on task, and difficulty using appropriate language. To achieve a better understanding of his difficulties and to target specific skills and unsolved problems for intervention, they completed the ALSUP. They found the ALSUP to be a useful discussion tool for helping them shift away from motivational explanations for Kelvin's difficulties, and identified the following lagging skills:

- Difficulty handling transitions and shifting from one mind-set or task to another (shifting cognitive set)
- Difficulty considering the likely outcomes or consequences of actions (impulsive)
- Difficulty handling unpredictability, ambiguity, uncertainty, novelty; and difficulty seeing the "grays"/concrete, literal, black-and-white thinking

They also identified the following unsolved problems:

- Losing points or his level
- Moving from choice time to an academic activity
- Receiving help for his academic challenges

Elena

Elena is a thirteen-year-old seventh grader who is several years below grade level in almost all academic areas and is completing very little work, but it is her behavior that concerns her teachers the most. Elena has to be reminded numerous times to get started on academic assignments and, after several reminders, responds defiantly with comments like "Shut up," "This is stupid," and "I hate this . . . why do I need to do this?" When she's partnered with a classmate she especially dislikes, she'll refuse to do any work. If she doesn't understand an assignment, she won't ask for help and won't attempt the assignment. Several times a month, Elena comes into class, puts her head on her desk, and goes to sleep. She's received numerous detentions for refusing to remove her iPod headphones and for skipping class.

Her teachers have a variety of hypotheses for why she's having so much difficulty at school. "Her behaviors are an attempt to get us to give her the attention she doesn't get at home," says one of her teachers. Another teacher isn't so sure. "I think she acts the way she does to push us away because she's so certain we're going to reject her." Interestingly, some of Elena's teachers never see her defiant side. "She's fine for me," says one. "You just can't get into power struggles with her." Yet another teacher feels strongly that Elena's academic difficulties are the root cause of her behavior problems: "If we could just get her caught up academically—if she'd let us—then all this stuff that's related to her poor self-esteem would improve." Some of Elena's teachers have become very discouraged about the prospects of helping her. Says one, "I've tried talking with her about her difficulties and about what she needs to do to turn things around. But you put all that time into helping her, and the next day she's back behaving the same way she did the day before. I'm starting to think she's a lost cause."

The four teachers in Elena's learning community met to discuss her ongoing difficulties and completed the ALSUP in an attempt to better understand the factors setting the stage for her challenging behavior. They homed in on several key lagging skills that they felt were coming into play:

- Difficulty adapting to changes in routine
- Difficulty shifting from an original idea or solution
- Difficulty considering the consequences of her actions and inhibiting her impulses
- Difficulty appreciating how her behavior is affecting other people

They identified the following high-priority unsolved problems:

- Being partnered with a classmate she doesn't like
- Being reminded to get started on academic assignments

- Being pushed to complete academic assignments
- Being prompted to adhere to elements of the school discipline code

Rodney

When describing Rodney, a sixteen-year-old tenth grader, the first thing his teachers mention is his charisma and popularity. They also describe him as a capable, albeit somewhat distracted and inconsistent, student. Then they get to the challenging parts. With some teachers, Rodney can be hostile and disrespectful, especially when they set limits on his use of profane language. Rodney argues that profanity is commonplace among his friends and family, and that at school these words "just slip out," but his teachers feel he derives some satisfaction from the reactions of his classmates. The many dozens of detentions and occasional suspension he has received over the years for using profanity have not had any effect.

His teachers also feel that when Rodney senses weakness or vulnerability in a classmate or teacher, he "goes in for the kill." One of his classmates commonly erupts when Rodney whispers things, out of earshot of the teacher, that he knows will upset her. One teacher tells the story of a shy, timid kid who was formerly in Rodney's science class. Rodney verbally tormented the student so relentlessly that he eventually transferred out of the class in order to escape him.

Rodney's teachers report that trying to talk with him about these issues is an exercise in futility. Reports one teacher, "He won't talk. He always changes the topic. And if you press him on something, he just gets up and leaves the room."

When Rodney's teachers completed an ALSUP, they endorsed virtually every item, including the following:

- Difficulty expressing needs, thoughts, or concerns in words
- Difficulty empathizing with others and appreciating another person's perspective or point of view
- Difficulty maintaining focus for goal-directed problem-solving

As regards unsolved problems, they prioritized the following:

- Being corrected or reprimanded for using profanity

- Being corrected or reprimanded for his mistreatment of classmates
- Whenever you don't watch him like a hawk

ILLOGICAL CONSEQUENCES

Before moving on, let's consider in greater detail why common interventions are not terribly effective. Kids learn how we want them to behave because we tell them. In the case of challenging kids, it's not that they don't know how we want them to behave, it's that they're lacking the skills to execute what they know. You may want to catch yourself the next time you're on the verge of asking a kid "How many times do I have to tell you . . . ?" Instead, figure out why he's having such difficulty consistently acting on what he knows—in other words, identify the skills he's lacking—and pinpoint the specific situations (unsolved problems) in which those lacking skills are causing the most trouble.

But that's not what usually happens. Instead, the kid gets those powerful, inescapable, *natural* consequences: praise, approval, being scolded, being disliked, not being invited to things, and so forth. Challenging kids experience lots of natural consequences, though they're likely to experience the punishing variety far more often than their less challenging counterparts. Natural consequences are effective at reducing the challenging behavior of some kids, but not the kids this book is about. That's because natural consequences don't solve the problems or teach the lagging skills that are precipitating their challenging behavior.

So the challenging behavior persists, or worsens. In response, adults usually add even more consequences, those of the imposed, "logical," "unnatural," or "artificial" variety. These include punishments such as staying in from recess, time-out from reinforcement, detention, suspension, and expulsion; rewards such as special privileges; and record-keeping devices such as stickers, points, levels, and the like. A word of caution on referring to such consequences as "logical": If a kid hasn't responded to *natural* consequences, then simply adding imposed consequences may not be very logical at all! Imposed consequences don't solve the problems or teach the lagging skills that are precipitating challenging behavior, either.

These kids clearly need something else from us. They need adults who know that lagging skills give rise to challenging behavior and that such behavior occurs under specific conditions. They need adults who can identify those lagging skills and unsolved problems and know how to solve those problems (collaboratively) so that the solutions are durable, the skills are taught, and the likelihood of challenging behavior is significantly reduced.

And yet, the debate is a common one: Is it that the kid *can't* do well or *won't* do well? If he can't do well, then lagging skills are the logical explanation. If he won't do well, then poor motivation would seem to make sense. Things are seldom so simple, but here's a graphic that might help you think this through; it shows the different combinations of motivation and skills and their logical outcomes:

Motivation

		YES	NO
	YES	*Adaptive*	*Maladaptive*
Skills			
	NO	*Maladaptive*	*Maladaptive*

If a child has the requisite skills and is motivated (Yes/Yes), we should expect to see adaptive behavior. If a child does not possess the requisite skills and is not motivated (No/No), we are unlikely to see adaptive behavior. And if a child does not possess the requisite skills and is motivated (No/Yes), adaptive behavior is also unlikely. Which brings us to the fourth possibility: Yes Skills/No Motivation. Many adults believe they see this combination most often; that's why motivational strategies are so popular. However, I'm not sure I've ever seen it. When people make use of the ALSUP, they find that kids who they thought were unmotivated were, in fact, lacking lots of skills. In other words, when adults change their understanding of challenging behavior, things finally begin moving in the right direction.

We've covered a lot of ground in this chapter, so a summary of the key points might be helpful:

- Viewing challenging behavior as the result of lagging skills (kids do well *if they can*) rather than as poor motivation (kids do well *if they want to*) has significant ramifications for how adults interact with kids with behavioral challenges and try to help them.
- A wide range of lagging skills can set the stage for challenging behavior.
- Challenging behavior usually occurs in predictable situations called unsolved problems.
- Adults have a strong tendency to automatically apply consequences to challenging behavior. Whether of the natural or artificial variety, consequences do not teach lagging cognitive skills or help kids solve problems.
- The first step in helping a challenging kid is to identify the skills he's lacking and the problems that are precipitating his challenging moments, and this is best accomplished by having relevant adults use the ALSUP as a tool for achieving a consensus.

Q & A

Question: If lagging cognitive skills and unsolved problems set the stage for social, emotional, and behavioral challenges in kids, what is the fate of the functional behavior assessment (FBA) routinely performed in schools to better understand challenging behavior?
Answer: For the unfamiliar, an FBA (sometimes called a functional analysis) is a procedure through which the function (causes, purposes, goals) of a kid's challenging behavior is identified. Though FBAs are common in schools, the information gathered through and inferences drawn from a functional analysis vary depending on the orientation, training, and experience of the evaluator conducting the procedure.

But a core assumption guiding most FBAs is that maladaptive behavior is "working" for a kid by allowing him to "get" something desirable (e.g., attention, peer approval) or "escape" or "avoid" something undesirable (e.g., a difficult task). The belief that challenging behaviors are somehow "working" for a kid leads many adults to the conclusion that those behaviors are purposeful (what could be referred to as the *intentionality attributional bias*). This popular conclusion can set the stage for misguided statements such as "It must be working for him or he wouldn't be doing it," and invariably sets the stage for interventions aimed at punishing kids' challenging behaviors so the behaviors don't "work" anymore, and rewarding adaptive replacement behaviors to encourage ones that "work" better. This is the foundation of most school discipline programs.

But this definition of "function" reflects what I call the "first pass" of a functional assessment. There's an indispensable "second pass"—a deeper level of analysis—that, regrettably, often goes neglected. And that is: *What lagging skills help us understand why the kid is getting, avoiding, and escaping in such a maladaptive fashion?* The second pass begins with some very important questions: If the kid had the skills to go about getting, escaping, and avoiding in an adaptive fashion, then why is he going about getting, escaping, and avoiding in such a maladaptive fashion? Doesn't the fact that he's going about getting, escaping, and avoiding in a maladaptive fashion suggest that he doesn't have the skills to go about getting, escaping, and avoiding in an adaptive fashion? These questions spring from the core mentality of the CPS model (kids do well if they can) and from the belief that doing well is always preferable to not doing well (but only if a kid has the skills to do well in the first place). *The essential function of challenging behavior is to communicate to adults that a kid doesn't possess the skills to handle certain demands in certain situations.* This definition sets the stage for interventions aimed at solving the problems that are giving rise to challenging behavior and teaching the kid the skills he's lacking.

So, back to the original question: What is the fate of the FBA? I can't think of a reason to stop doing them. But if you want an FBA to help you get to the *core* of challenging behavior—lagging skills and unsolved problems—you'll want to focus on the second pass rather than the first. By the way, you don't need to do a full-blown FBA to complete the ALSUP and achieve a consensus on a kid's lagging skills and unsolved problems.

Question: I'm not quite clear about what you mean by "unsolved problems." Can you explain further?

Answer: Challenging kids aren't challenging every minute. They're challenging sometimes, under certain conditions, usually when the environment is demanding skills they aren't able to muster or presenting problems they aren't able to solve. As you've read, lagging skills are the *why* of challenging behavior. Unsolved problems are the *who, what, where,* and *when* of challenging behavior and help adults pinpoint the specific circumstances or conditions under which a kid's challenging behavior is most likely to occur.

So if a kid is having difficulty in his interactions with a particular classmate (a "who") or teacher (another "who"), and those interactions are setting the stage for challenging behavior, then getting along with that particular classmate or teacher is an unsolved problem. If a kid is having difficulties with a particular assignment (a "what"), and those difficulties are setting the stage for challenging behavior, then difficulty with that assignment is an unsolved problem. Difficulties on the school bus, in the cafeteria, or in the hallway (all "where" and "when") are also unsolved problems. If the kid could resolve these problems in an adaptive manner, he would.

I use the terms "unsolved problems," "triggers," "circumstances," "antecedents," and "situations" interchangeably, but they all refer to the same thing. I like "unsolved problems" best, though, because it unambiguously tells us that there's a problem the child is having difficulty solving on his own.

Question: What research supports the idea that challenging behavior is a form of developmental delay?
Answer: Much of the research is, for better or worse (mostly worse), tied to specific diagnoses, but the link between lagging skills and challenging behavior is unequivocal. For example, the association between ADHD and lagging executive skills (e.g., difficulty shifting cognitive set, doing things in a logical sequence, having a sense of time, maintaining focus, controlling one's impulses) is well-established. Equally well-established is the fact that kids with ADHD are at increased risk for other diagnoses (and much more serious challenging behavior), such as oppositional defiant disorder (ODD: temper outbursts, arguing with adults, and defiance) and conduct disorder (CD: bullying, threaten-

ing, intimidating, fighting, physical aggression, stealing, destroying property, lying, truancy).[2]

There are also convincing data documenting increased rates of ODD and CD in kids with mood disorders (i.e., those who have difficulty with skills related to the regulating of one's emotions, including managing one's emotional response to frustration so as to think rationally [separation of affect]),[3] and in kids who are socially impaired (including skills such as accurately interpreting social cues, seeking attention in appropriate ways, appreciating how one's behavior is affecting others, empathizing, and appreciating how one is being perceived by others).[4] The research literature has increasingly shown that kids with language processing delays (including skills such as considering a range of solutions to a problem; expressing concerns, needs, or thoughts in words; and understanding what is being said) are at significantly greater risk for ODD and CD as well.[5] And there is a persuasive and growing literature documenting the very challenging behaviors that can accompany autism spectrum disorders and nonverbal learning disability (and the black-and-white, concrete, literal thinking that typifies these disorders).[6]

We've learned a lot about children's brains in the last thirty years. We now know how challenging kids come to be challenging. It's time for our actions to reflect our knowledge.

Question: You mentioned that kids with behavioral challenges aren't usually challenging every second of every waking hour. Some kids are challenging at home and not at school, others at school and not at home, and others in both places. If it's true that the kid is lacking skills, then why would he be exhibiting challenging behavior in one place and not another? Isn't the discrepancy in behavior between home and school proof that he's *choosing* to behave one way in one place and another way in the other? Isn't that a sign that the kid is doing well when he wants to?

Answer: Actually, it's proof that challenging behavior is specific to certain conditions: those where skills are being required that the child does not yet sufficiently possess or where he continues to confront problems that he hasn't been able to solve.

Especially in cases where a kid is more challenging at home than school, it's common for people to explain the disparity as the result of poor parenting. Now you know better. The school environment may have advantages that reduce the likelihood of challenging behavior in some kids. School environments tend to be more structured and predictable than home environments, and this can reduce the likelihood of challenging behavior in some (but by no means all) challenging kids. Often medicines that are helpful for reducing challenging behavior at school have worn off by the time the kid arrives home. And some kids can manage to stay tightly wrapped during the school day and then completely unravel—some would say decompensate—once they're at home again. Of course, most of us look a lot better when we're outside the home than when we're inside it!

Even when the reverse is true—if a kid's challenges are greater at school than at home—it's common for the finger to be pointed at parents ("The parents just let him do whatever he wants at home. No wonder he doesn't act up with them."). The more plausible and productive explanation is that the school is placing demands on the kid—for focused learning, self-starting, organizing, sustained effort, and getting along with others—that may not be nearly as intense at home. Best for adults to stop pointing and start identifying the kid's lagging skills and unsolved problems.

The Story Continues . . .

Joey and his mother rode home in silence, Joey staring out the window from the backseat, Ms. Lowell feeling alone, frustrated, and at a loss. Joey attempted a quiet, "I'm sorry."

His mother was trying hard not to scream or cry. "Don't talk to me, Joey. I don't want to hear anything right now."

What's the point of screaming and crying? she thought. Joey had been on the receiving end of many of her lectures and punishments over the years, but his problems remained.

It angered her that the people at school acted as though Joey's problems were all her fault. But they weren't any better at dealing with Joey than she was. Worse, in fact. They just expected her to retrieve him when they decided they'd had enough.

She briefly considered calling her ex-husband, Joey's father. The guy who had left it up to her to raise Joey. Actually, his lack of involvement, while an irritant, was better than the alternative. They had never agreed on how to deal with Joey anyway. Still, it sure would be nice to have *someone* to help out.

Joey's mom conjured up the list of mental health professionals who'd worked with her and Joey over the years, seven at last count. The ones who told her to be more consistent, set firmer limits, use more consequences, and hold him accountable. The ones who prescribed medication that usually didn't make things much better and often made things worse. Eventually, Joey just refused to keep going to therapy and taking medicine, and his mother didn't see the point in forcing the issue anymore. None worth calling now.

Finally, they were home. When they entered the house, Joey went to his room and Ms. Lowell to her own. She sat down on her bed and started to cry.

Joey could hear his mother crying. He walked quietly to her room and knocked on the door. She quickly wiped away her tears as he opened it.

"Mom, I didn't mean to hurt Mr. Middleton."

"I know."

"I'm sorry I screwed everything up again."

"Me too."

"I don't know what to do."

"Me either."

"I'm sorry you're crying."

"I'll live."

"Maybe I should go live with Dad."

"Why, you think your father has any great ideas for how to keep you from going nuts at school?"

"I don't know."

"Do *you* have any great ideas for how to keep you from going nuts at school?"

"No."

"Well, me either, Joey. So there it is. No one knows what to do. You've got us all baffled, pal."

Joey didn't say anything else. He closed the door, went back to his room, and buried his head in his pillow.

Mrs. Woods sat glumly at her desk at the end of the school day. She tried grading a few papers. She tried reading a memo from the superintendent. But something was gnawing at her. Joey.

She'd seen her share of challenging kids over the years, but she was still in disbelief about how quickly things had escalated in her classroom only a few hours earlier. She recalled what she'd heard about Joey from last year's teachers: "Joey is like Jekyll and Hyde. One minute he's minding his own business, the next minute he's exploding, usually over practically nothing. I think he's still upset over his parents' divorce. I hear his mother has a pretty nasty temper, too!"

I guess I saw Hyde today, she thought. She sighed as she recognized a familiar knot growing in her stomach. How many of those had she experienced over the past five or six years?

Her team teacher, Mrs. Franco—known for running a tight ship and for her strong irreverent streak—stuck her head in the door. "You OK?"

"I don't really know."

Mrs. Franco walked into the room. "Tough day. What happened?"

"Which part? The blowing up, the telling Taylor he was going to kill her, or Mr. Middleton getting his jaw hurt?"

Mrs. Franco winced sympathetically.

Mrs. Woods picked up the superintendent's memo from her desk. "Have you seen this? Here we are, trying to keep our heads above water with all these kids who need our attention, and we're constantly being reminded that every kid needs to get over the same bar before the school year's out. Like it's a bunch of robots we're teaching. Like I'm some sort of magician."

"You've had a tough day," said Mrs. Franco. "But look at the bright side."

"What bright side?"

"It's Friday. And Joey won't be in your class for the next five days."

* * *

Mrs. Woods' husband could always tell when she'd had a bad day at school. Normally, when he arrived home from work, she'd be listening to classical music and looking over her students' work. On bad days the house was silent. He found her in the backyard watering annuals that had just suffered through the first frost.

"Looks like those flowers are done for," he said.

"What makes you say that?" she snapped.

"Just that the frost seems to have got to 'em," he said.

Mrs. Woods felt her eyes stinging. "They'll be fine."

"Tough day at school?"

"You could say that."

"Want to talk about it?"

"I want to water my dead flowers a little longer."

"Want me to make dinner tonight?"

"That would be nice."

Mr. and Mrs. Woods had raised a son and daughter together, both well-behaved, both good students, both now in college. His wife's increasing unhappiness and frustration at work were at odds with Mr. Woods' vision of what should now be their "easy years." As he began preparing dinner, he reminded himself not to give his wife advice about how to run her classroom. Mrs. Woods always grew impatient when she tried to explain to her husband that she couldn't run her classroom like he ran his hardware store.

Mrs. Woods came in from the backyard. "Am I losing my mind, or did I just spend twenty minutes watering dead flowers?"

"You're definitely losing your mind. So what happened at school today?"

"I had an ugly scene in my classroom. One of my kids lost it, Mr. Middleton got hit in the jaw, another of my kids got threatened, the kid who lost it ran out of the school and got suspended for five days . . ."

"Geez," said Mr. Woods. "Middleton got hit in the jaw? Why'd the kid go nuts?"

"I asked him to come up to my desk because he wasn't doing his work."

"Middleton OK?"

"I don't know. I didn't see him after school."

Mr. Woods' eyes narrowed as he looked at his wife. "You OK?"

"Well, I didn't get hit in the jaw, but the whole thing was pretty upsetting."

"The kid went nuts because you asked him to come up to your desk? What's the matter with him?"

"I don't know. I mean . . . that's probably the most upsetting part. I don't know what's the matter with him. I couldn't believe what was happening in my classroom."

"So the kid got what he had coming to him," said Mr. Woods. "I guess he's going to learn that you don't go nuts in Betty Galvin's school."

"Betty Galvin isn't going to have the kid in her classroom when he comes back from being suspended."

"Maybe"—Mr. Woods could feel himself slipping perilously into advice-giving mode—"Maybe it's time for you to start thinking about . . ."

"This is exactly why I don't like to tell you what happens in my classroom! If you start with that hardware store speech again I will leave!"

Mr. Woods recovered. "OK, OK, no hardware store speech. But I hate to see you upset like this. It's just not worth it."

"It *is* worth it! I *like* teaching!" said Mrs. Woods. "Well, I *used* to like teaching. But I'm not the type to run away from a problem."

"That's why you were out there watering dead flowers."

"Very funny."

"See, that's my point. You keep telling me about how the kids keep getting more and more difficult. You keep telling me you don't like to run away from problems, you want to help them. Maybe trying to help these kids is like watering dead flowers. Maybe there's no helping them."

Mrs. Woods thought for a moment. "I don't believe that," she said softly.

"All I know is if our kids ever acted that way . . ."

"Garrett and Lisa were easy," said Mrs. Woods. "I don't have trouble with the easy kids in my class. They're easy. I have trouble with the *tough* kids. I don't know what to do with the tough kids!"

"Well, I don't know what to tell you," said Mr. Woods, turning his attention back to making dinner. "If you're bound and determined to help the tough kids, then I guess you'll have to find some way to figure it out."

On Tuesday, Joey's mother received a phone call at work.

"Hi, is this Mrs. Turner?" asked an unfamiliar voice.

"No, this is not Mrs. Turner," she responded impatiently.

"Um, is Mrs. Turner there?"

"There is no Mrs. Turner here," she said with curt satisfaction.

She heard the caller fumbling with papers. "Oops, uh . . . sorry. Oh, I see here, Turner's your husband's name . . ."

"He's not my husband anymore," she said tersely, while feeling slight pity for the confused-sounding man on the other end of the phone. "Who is this anyways?"

"Oh, um . . . I'm sorry. Yes, now I see . . . Ms. *Lowell,* yes?"

"You got it. What can I do for you?"

"My name is Carl Bridgman. I'm the new psychologist at Joey's school. Is this a good time?"

Oh, great, Joey's mother thought. Another shrink. She tried to suppress her well-established frustration with the mental health profession. "No," she lied, "this is not a good time."

"Sorry about the confusion. I'm kind of new to the school system, and I just received Joey's file this morning. I understand there was a problem at school last week."

"You could say that."

"I'd really like to understand what happened in that classroom," said Dr. Bridgman.

"You're not the only one," said Joey's mother.

"It sounds like this is a bad time for you, but I'm thinking it might be a good idea for me to meet you and Joey, you know, so I can start to get a handle on things."

"Mr. Bridgman . . . that's what you said your name was?" asked Joey's mother.

"Well, it's Doctor Bridgman, but whatever."

"Doctor Bridgman," said Joey's mother, "if you can get a handle on what's going on with my son, you'll be the first to accomplish the feat."

"Hmm . . . I take it others have tried."

"You'd be number eight."

"Sounds like Joey's been struggling for quite a while."

"I thought you said you had his file in front of you."

"Well, I must confess, I haven't looked at it very closely," said Dr. Bridgman. "But since it sounds like no one's gotten a handle on Joey's problems yet, I'm not sure whether the information would be terribly useful anyway."

Joey's mother found herself warming slightly to the psychologist.

"Joey's been difficult since he was a toddler, things got worse once he started school, and things are still bad now. And to tell you the honest truth"—she could feel herself starting to get emotional—"to tell you the honest truth, I don't know what I'm going to do."

"Look, I can't make any promises," said Dr. Bridgman. "I know how hard it can be to deal with schools, especially if you have a challenging kid. All I can tell you is that I'll listen to you and try to understand what's going on with Joey and do my best to make things better. But I can't do any of those things unless you'll come in with Joey and meet with me."

What do I have to lose? thought Ms. Lowell. "Joey probably won't talk to you," she said.

"I guess I can't fault him for that," said Dr. Bridgman. "But maybe you'll talk to me."

"You don't have to worry about that."

Ms. Lowell was already apprehensive as she knocked on the door to Dr. Bridgman's office several days later, with a reluctant Joey by her side. Her anxiety spiked when he opened the door. Dr. Bridgman was a large man, his clothes didn't quite fit, his shirt was partially untucked, his tie hung loosely around his neck, and his thick-rimmed glasses slid down his nose. His office was extraordinarily unkempt.

"Hi, Carl Bridgman," he said, shaking her hand. Then he turned his attention to Joey. "You're Joey, yes?"

Joey nodded.

"Come in, let's talk a little." Dr. Bridgman guided Joey and his mother into his office and removed stacks of files from two chairs so his guests could sit. "This office is already a mess, and I've only been here a month," he said to no one in particular.

"Where exactly did you come from?" asked Ms. Lowell, scanning the office.

"Oh, I've worked in a few different states over the years," Dr. Bridgman replied. "But my office has always been a complete mess no matter what state I've been in."

Joey chuckled.

"And you say you're a psychologist?" asked Ms. Lowell.

"School psychologist," said Dr. Bridgman. "At least that's what my degree says I am."

"What do you say you are?" asked Ms. Lowell.

"At the moment, I'm the guy who'd like to help things go better at school for you and Joey," Dr. Bridgman responded. "It would be nice if what happened the other day didn't happen again."

"That would be nice," said Ms. Lowell, still skeptical.

"Joey," said Dr. Bridgman, "can you tell me what happened the other day?"

Joey was silent.

"Joey, he can't help us if you don't talk," said Ms. Lowell.

"I don't want to do this," mumbled Joey, looking at his mother.

"I don't blame you," said Dr. Bridgman. "The thing is, if I don't hear your ideas about what happened, then I'll have to rely on everyone else's ideas, and I'm not sure you want me relying on what everyone else is saying about what happened."

Joey considered his options.

"Joey, please," said Ms. Lowell.

Dr. Bridgman looked carefully at Joey. "You've talked to a lot of doctors, Joey. And I'm betting you don't think they've done you much good. I mean, all those doctors, and you're still suspended for five days. So I can't say that I blame you for not wanting to talk to a perfect stranger."

Joey was still silent.

Dr. Bridgman continued. "Now, I don't know what all those other doctors did. I'm sorry they didn't help you very much. I don't know if I'll be able to help you or not. But I know I can't help unless I hear what you have to say."

Joey surprised his mother and started talking. "All the teachers hate me. They like embarrassing me . . . and getting me in trouble."

"The teachers like embarrassing you," said Dr. Bridgman. "And you're probably not too keen on being embarrassed . . . or getting into trouble."

"I don't care about getting into trouble. I'm used to it."

"So what happened the other day that made you run out of the school?" asked Dr. Bridgman.

"Um . . . I was sitting at my desk and I didn't know what to do on the social studies project. And Mrs. Woods got a little mad at me because I didn't know what to do. So she told me to come up to her desk, and I didn't want all the kids looking at me. So I told her I didn't want to go up to her desk. So she had Mr. Middleton come in the class and he wanted me to go to the office, and then *everyone* was looking at me. So I jumped out of my seat. I guess that's when Mr. Middleton got hurt . . . but I didn't mean for him to get hurt. That's when I ran out of the classroom . . . and then they found me and grabbed my arms and Mrs. Galvin," Joey's facial expression and tone signaled his dislike of the school principal, "suspended me."

Dr. Bridgman was listening intently. "Sounds pretty scary. Were you scared, Joey?"

"Um, no . . . not really."

"What were you?"

"Um, I don't know . . . *embarrassed*?"

Ms. Lowell interrupted. "Mrs. Galvin said she was going to see about pressing charges. Do you know anything about that?"

"No, I don't," Dr. Bridgman replied. "Hard to imagine that would fix anything."

Ms. Lowell was surprised by Dr. Bridgman's candor. She couldn't recall having ever heard school staff question the wisdom of the school's leaders.

"Am I going to get arrested?" asked Joey.

"I hope not," said Dr. Bridgman. "But we do need to get a handle on what's going on so we can make sure things don't get out of control again."

"How do we do that?" asked Joey's mother.

"Well, I know everyone's focused right now on what Joey did," said Dr. Bridgman. "You know, jumping out of his chair so Mr. Middleton got hurt, telling Taylor he was going to kill her, running out of the school. But I usually find it's a lot more helpful to focus on the problem that set the stage for Joey to do that stuff in the first place. If we can find a way to solve it, that should keep it from causing trouble again."

CHAPTER 3

Lesson Plans

You now know that *kids do well if they can*; that if a kid *could* do well he *would* do well. And that behind every challenging behavior is either an unsolved problem or a lagging skill. You're also familiar with the lagging skills that usually set the stage for social, emotional, and behavioral challenges, along with two tools—the *ALSUP* and the *situational analysis*—to help you pinpoint the specific lagging skills and unsolved problems that may be involved. And you know that once a kid's lagging skills and unsolved problems are pinpointed, his challenging behavior becomes *highly predictable,* which means that his difficulties can be addressed *proactively.* You're ready to consider your options. But let's first think about what your expectations are, because *unmet* expectations let you know you have a skill to teach or a problem to solve.

If you're an educator, you presumably have the expectation that the kids in your classroom (or school or school system or caseload) will learn what they need to learn in a given school year. Maybe you expect that they'll learn not only the requisite academic material, but also maybe even develop a love of learning, a curiosity about the world around them, and the ability to think about, analyze, and solve problems. Certainly you expect your students to conduct themselves in ways that are safe, respectful, and don't disrupt the learning of their classmates. And you want to pursue these expectations in ways that are fair, respectful, humane, and effective.

If you're a parent, you want pretty much the same things. You want your child to learn the requisite academic material and maybe even develop a love of learning, a curiosity about the world, and the ability to think about, analyze, and solve problems. You want your child and his classmates to conduct themselves in ways that are safe, respectful, and don't disrupt anyone's learning. And you want your child to be treated fairly, respectfully, humanely, and effectively by school staff.

Looks like everyone's on the same page. When these expectations are being met, kids, teachers, and parents tend to be pretty satisfied. But if these expectations are *not* being met, you need a plan.

There are basically three options for handling unmet expectations. I call these options plans, as in Plan A, Plan B, and Plan C.

Plan A is when adults *impose their will* in response to an unmet expectation. Plan A is far and away the most popular way adults handle problems or unmet expectations with kids, and not only in schools. Often, Plan A implies the preferred option, but not in this book. More on Plan A soon—but not much more, since it won't be our primary focus.

Plan C involves *dropping an expectation completely,* at least temporarily. At first glance, Plan C may sound like "giving in," but, as you'll read below, that's not the case. More on Plan C soon—but not much more, since it won't be our primary focus, either.

Plan B refers to *Collaborative Problem Solving,* in which the child and adult are engaged in a process of *resolving a problem or unmet expectation in a realistic and mutually satisfactory manner.* As you'll soon discover, this is the Plan with the greatest potential for durably solving the problems and teaching the lagging skills giving rise to kids' social, emotional, and behavioral challenges in a way that is fair, respectful, humane, and effective. As you may have guessed, Plan B is what the rest of this book is about.

Let's take a closer look at each option.

PLAN A

If a kid isn't meeting a given expectation, one way to approach the problem is by imposing your will. Let's say a kid is badgering one of his classmates and causing the classmate to become agitated, and the teacher has already asked the kid to stop badgering. The teacher would be using Plan A if she said, "Rodney, go stand in the hallway now! Come back when you're ready to treat people kindly."

Or if a kid says, "I'm not doing this assignment unless I can work with my friend," and the teacher has already made it clear that he expects the kid to partner with a different student, then a potential Plan A response would be "Elena, you're not working with Hector. Let me know if a detention is necessary to help you understand that."

Or if a kid is distracting his classmates because he doesn't understand an assignment and the teacher says, "Joey, let's talk about it at my desk so we don't disturb your classmates," and Joey refuses to comply, then a potential Plan A response would be, "Joey, if you don't come up to my desk now, I'll have to send you to the office."

At first glance, these probably sound like perfectly ordinary, reasonable responses. However, there are a few problems with responding in this manner to kids who aren't meeting expectations. The first is that *Plan A greatly heightens the likelihood of challenging behavior in challenging kids.* When we "rewind the tape" on most of the challenging episodes that occur in schools (and homes), we discover that the vast majority of these episodes are precipitated by an adult responding to an unmet expectation using Plan A. The second problem is that *Plan A doesn't help us figure out why the kid isn't meeting our expectations in the first place.* Third, *Plan A doesn't teach lagging skills or durably resolve problems giving rise to challenging behavior.* In view of these shortcomings, it's not clear that Plan A qualifies as fair, respectful, humane, or effective treatment.

Are you thinking that you do a lot of Plan A? If so, you're not alone. Most adults use Plan A when kids aren't meeting expectations. Are you wondering if it's still Plan A if you impose your will nicely? Yes, that's still Plan A (it's called Gentle A, but it's Plan A all the same). Are you thinking that Plan A usually "works" with "ordinary" kids? If so, you're right. But, once again, it depends on your definition of "works." If, by "works," you mean that the kid ultimately complied when you imposed your will, then yes, Plan A usually works with ordinary kids. But even ordinary kids have skills that need to be taught and problems that need to be solved, and Plan A doesn't teach skills or solve problems.

PLAN C

Plan C involves dropping a given expectation completely, at least temporarily. When you're using Plan C, you're not solving any problems or teaching any lacking thinking skills. But Plan C can help adults remove low-priority expectations, thereby helping a kid to be more "available" to work on higher-priority problems or skills and reducing the likelihood of challenging behavior.

If Liam is sharpening his pencil for the seventh time in the past hour, and it's the teacher's expectation that Liam remain in his seat because all that pencil sharpening is distracting other kids or making it hard for Liam to complete his work, and the teacher has already made it clear to Liam that his pencil sharpening is excessive and disruptive, but the teacher chooses to say nothing about the pencil sharpening because she has bigger fish to fry with Liam, then what the teacher chose to do is Plan C.

If a particular kid says "I'm not doing my homework," and his teacher has already decided that homework isn't a high priority right now given other more pressing issues with this kid, then letting the kid know he needn't do the homework is Plan C.

You probably still need convincing that Plan C is not the same thing as "giving in." The definition of "giving in" is when you start with Plan A and end up using Plan C because the kid made your life miserable.

But when you start with Plan C, your reasoning is: "I understand why this kid is challenging, and I know I can't fix everything at once. I also know what unsolved problems we're working on right now, and this is not one of them. I'm going to drop this expectation, at least for now, so the kid is more available to work on our high-priority problems."

Does this mean you're supposed to drop all your expectations so a kid won't exhibit challenging behavior? No. But, again you may find it productive to let go of some lower-priority expectations so you and the kid aren't overwhelmed by the large number of problems that need to be solved. Moreover, sometimes Plan C makes sense as a matter of timing. In other words, you may feel that it would be better to discuss a given problem at a more opportune moment, which sometimes means Plan C now and Plan B shortly thereafter.

PLAN B

Plan B involves Collaborative Problem Solving. Plan B helps adults clarify and understand a child's concerns about or perspective on a particular unsolved problem, be it excessive badgering of other kids, refusing to work, pencil sharpening, incomplete homework, or class disruptions. Plan B also helps the kid understand the adult's concerns about the problem. And Plan B helps adults and kids work together toward mutually satisfactory solutions so that both parties' concerns are addressed, the problem gets solved, and, as will become clear as we move forward, lagging skills get taught.

Is the kid going to need help for the rest of his life? Actually, the reason you're helping him now is so he won't need your help for the rest of his life.

This next part is important. There are two ways to use Plan B: *Emergency B* and *Proactive B*. When I first describe Plan B, it's common for adults to come to the erroneous conclusion that the best time to use Plan B is at the precise moment when a kid is beginning to show signs of challenging behavior. That's Emergency Plan B, and the timing is actually not the best because the kid may already be upset or heated up and because, if you're a teacher, you've got a lot of other things going on in your classroom at that moment. Few of us do our clearest thinking, resolve difficult problems, and learn new skills when we're already upset, so crisis *management* is not your best long-term strategy. You'll go much further with crisis *prevention*. As I mentioned earlier, because challenging behavior tends to be highly predictable, you don't have to wait until a kid is in the midst of a challenging episode to try to solve the problem that caused the episode. The goal is to get the problem solved or the skill taught *proactively*—before it comes up again. That's Proactive Plan B.

When Mrs. Woods threatened to send Joey to the assistant principal because he wouldn't come up to her desk, that was Plan A. Could she have used Emergency Plan B instead? Yes, and Emergency Plan B would have worked out a lot better for Mrs. Woods, Mr. Middleton, Joey, and the other kids in the class. But if Mrs. Woods had previously observed that Joey became confused on assignments and was easily embarrassed in front of his classmates, then Proactive Plan B would have been even better. Will anarchy ensue in Mrs. Woods' classroom if she doesn't use Plan A? No, it won't.

By the way, there's another reason to be using Plan B instead of Plan A: If you want to help a kid, you're going to need a helping relationship to accomplish the mission. Time and time again, research (and practical experience) has shown that the most reliable factor leading people to change—by far—is the relationship they have with the person helping them change. And while you may have thought that helping is the sole domain of professional helpers—medical doctors, mental health professionals, clergy, and the like—educators often find themselves in a position to help kids who are in distress.

Why would kids need the help of a teacher on nonacademic problems? Because, either in their own eyes or the eyes of others, they are involved in problem situations they are not handling well. What is the goal of the helping relationship? To help kids not only better manage a given problem, but to apply the learning to sorting out other problems and to preventing problems from occurring in the first place. Helping provides kids with tools to become more effective self-helpers and more responsible "agents of change" in their own lives.

As noted by Dr. Gerard Egan, author of *The Skilled Helper: A Problem-Management and Opportunity-Development Approach to Helping,* helping is messy. Helping is a working alliance, a two-way collaborative process, and a two-person team effort. Helping is not something that teachers do to kids; rather, it is a process that teachers and kids work through together.

In trying to forge a helping relationship with a challenging kid, it can be useful to think about the qualities you'd seek in someone you were hoping could help you. Are you seeking someone who cares? Whom you feel you can trust? Who takes the time to listen to you? Who asks the right questions and truly tries to understand your concerns? Who has the wisdom and know-how to help in ways that are effective and durable? Who involves you in the process? Is this the type of relationship you're forging with the challenging kid you're trying to help?

Plan B is a relationship-building process. Plan A pushes kids away.

Q & A

Question: Doesn't helping kids with behavioral challenges take a lot of time?
Answer: Yes, helping, especially the kind that involves teaching skills and solving problems durably, takes time. But perpetually dealing with kids' challenges in ways that aren't working takes much more time. And don't forget, Proactive Plan B is taking place at opportune moments, not under emergent conditions.

Question: Like when? Don't forget, I have twenty-five kids in my class, I'm the only one in there, and I have a bunch of kids who are on special education programs and need my attention.
Answer: Most teachers find that Proactive Plan B can be done during the times they're devoting individual attention to other student problems (for instance, academic challenges), such as before school, after school, during recess, or during lunch; whenever they can spare five or ten minutes. I've also found that most principals and assistant principals are happy to arrange coverage so that a classroom teacher has the time to do Plan B with a kid. You'll probably want to devote your initial Plan B efforts to helping the kids whose challenges are most severe and who are disrupting the classroom process the most. Then move on to the rest of the kids who need Plan B. You're devoting a lot of time to the kids with behavioral challenges already. While

Plan B takes a little extra time and planning up front, my experience is that it dramatically reduces the amount of time you're spending on challenging behavior overall.

Question: You said that this model doesn't require that adults suspend all of their expectations. Care to say more about that?

Answer: It would be impossible to teach, parent, or help kids without having expectations. The CPS model does not involve dropping all expectations. But since you can't fix everything at once, it makes sense to eliminate *some* low-priority expectations (in other words, use Plan C) and focus on the higher-priority expectations and problems that remain. Just because you're eliminating a given expectation now doesn't mean you won't come back to it once some higher-priority expectations have been met.

You will want to consider whether your expectations for each kid are truly realistic, and grade level and chronological age typically are not great indicators of a kid's developmental readiness for a particular expectation. We often place expectations on kids that we know they can't meet, and then punish them when they handle our expectations as poorly as we suspected they would. An unrealistic expectation is a challenging behavior waiting to happen.

Question: You also said that simply communicating an expectation to a kid is not the same as using Plan A. Can you explain that again?

Answer: This is an important point to clarify. You're not using any Plan when you're communicating or reminding a kid of an expectation, and you don't need a Plan if a given expectation is being met. The three Plans represent your options for dealing with *unmet* expectations. That said, there's definitely such a thing as "style points" in how adults go about communicating or reminding a kid of their expectations. In other words, it's possible to communicate expectations in a way that will send some of the more volatile kids right over the edge.

Question: So when Mrs. Woods let Joey know that she wanted him to get back to work and stop disturbing his classmates, that wasn't Plan A?

Answer: No, that was Mrs. Woods reminding Joey of her expectations. She moved into Plan A in imposing her will when her expectation remained unmet. But the most important point is that Joey's difficulty getting started on assignments was a predictable problem, and one that would have been possible to clarify and address proactively.

Question: Isn't this model really just a sophisticated form of battle picking?
Answer: Plan B isn't a choice between battling and not battling. It's about getting concerns identified and addressed, solving problems, teaching skills, reducing challenging behavior, and forming a helping relationship. Prior to learning about Plan B, many adults thought they had only two options: impose their will or drop their expectations. If those are your only options, then picking your battles is precisely what you're doing.

Question: Does the CPS model mean there's no such thing as setting limits anymore?
Answer: "Setting limits" means adults have concerns they want to ensure are addressed. With Plan A, adults are making sure that their concerns are addressed (through imposition of adult will) but are disregarding kids' concerns. As you've read, there are significant drawbacks to this approach to setting limits because, as noted above, Plan A teaches no skills, solves no problems durably, and, in certain kids, increases the likelihood of challenging behavior. Even in "ordinary" kids, Plan A is just an application of "might makes right." Isn't "might makes right" the wrong turn that society took a long time ago? If there's another way to help kids meet adult expectations without teaching them that might makes right, shouldn't we be interested? With Plan B, adults are making sure that their concerns are addressed—the adults are setting limits—but are equally committed to ensuring that kids' concerns are also addressed. So long as the concerns of one party go unaddressed, the problem is not durably solved. But you're setting limits whether you're using Plan A or Plan B.

Question: Yes, but how will the kid be held accountable for his actions?
Answer: It depends on what you mean by "accountable." For some

folks, holding a kid accountable for his actions simply means making sure he pays the price for his challenging behavior. In the CPS model, holding a kid accountable means that the kid is participating in a process in which he's identifying and articulating his own concerns or perspectives, taking yours into account, and working toward a realistic and mutually satisfactory solution. One could make the case that Plan B is actually more effective at holding a kid accountable than Plan A, since the kid is participating in and actually thinking about a plan to reduce his challenging behavior (and taking your concerns into account) rather than merely being on the receiving end of endless adult ingenuity.

Question: Is it safe to assume that you're not too enthusiastic about zero-tolerance policies?

Answer: As noted in the Introduction, I believe zero-tolerance policies are a great example of a very fascinating and counterproductive human tendency to add more Plan A when it's clear Plan A isn't getting the job done.

Question: Is the CPS model a good fit with Response to Intervention (RTI)?

Answer: There is significant congruence between the goals, structure, and practices of RTI and the CPS model. For the unfamiliar, RTI represents an effort to move away from IQ-achievement discrepancies in identifying learning disabilities and permit schools to put in place intervention procedures for addressing a student's learning needs as soon as they are identified by a classroom teacher and confirmed with supporting data. Recent federal legislation—No Child Left Behind and the most recent reauthorization of the Individuals with Disabilities Act—mandates that RTI methods be applied to practices for instructional and behavioral intervention in classrooms.

In their 2005 book, *Response to Intervention: Principles and Strategies for Effective Practice,* school psychologists Rachel Brown-Chidsey and Mark Steege note that the impetus for RTI comes, at least partially, from the recognition that the needs of many students receiving services in special education could be met in general education classrooms. As such, the first and most important school personnel to implement intervention are classroom teachers. The CPS model is an excellent fit with RTI in this regard.

RTI also represents an attempt to introduce scientific, data-based methods into school classrooms to guide the selection, use, and evaluation of academic and behavioral interventions. Though it is a relatively new model, in many respects CPS is a good fit along these lines as well. The basic elements of the CPS model are well described in books, chapters, articles, and research papers. The research supporting the positive outcomes achieved by CPS[1] is understandable and fully described, has been conducted in a range of settings—families, schools, inpatient psychiatric units, and juvenile detention facilities—and is published (or in press) in peer-reviewed journals. These studies have been conducted using both experimental (randomized) and quasi-experimental designs. The effectiveness of CPS is being independently studied in multiple settings in North America and Europe. Among the most ambitious are a five-year National Institutes of Mental Health–funded study at the Virginia Tech Child Study Center and a three-year study in the seven public schools in Sanford, Maine, funded by the Maine Juvenile Justice Advisory Group.

The Story Continues . . .

It had been one week since Joey's suspension, and on the Friday before his return Mrs. Galvin called his reentry meeting to order. "As you know, we're meeting to discuss Joey's reentry into school on Monday." Mrs. Woods, Ms. Lowell, and Mr. Middleton nodded. But there was a conspicuous absentee: Dr. Bridgman. Mrs. Galvin, who had a penchant for starting and ending meetings on time, found this irritating. Joey's mother, whose trepidation about the meeting was tempered only by the hope that Dr. Bridgman would do a lot of the talking, was troubled, too.

Mrs. Galvin looked at her watch and made little effort to hide her annoyance. "I don't know where Dr. Bridgman is. Hopefully, he'll be here soon. The school psychologist writes the reentry plan, but it looks like we're starting without him."

"How is Joey doing?" Mr. Middleton asked Joey's mother.

"About as well as can be expected, under the circumstances," she sighed. "Mr. Middleton, I hope he didn't hurt you badly."

Mr. Middleton rubbed his jaw. "I must say, I can still feel it."

"We think we will need a different plan in place for Joey to return to the classroom," said Mrs. Galvin. "As you might imagine, Taylor's parents want some reassurance that Joey is not going to threaten to kill their daughter again."

"Look, I wasn't there," said Joey's mom. "I didn't see what happened. I've heard your version of what happened and I've heard Joey's. I'm very sorry Mr. Middleton got hurt and that Joey pushed Mrs. Woods. I can understand Taylor's parents being worried about their daughter's safety. But based on what Joey's told me, he doesn't deserve all the blame for this."

"We're not trying to blame anyone, Ms. Lowell," said Mrs. Galvin. "It's just that according to our school discipline code, there are certain procedures that we need to adhere to when things like this happen."

Ms. Lowell found herself unable to resist the opportunity for blunt honesty. "To tell you the truth, I've never noticed that the school discipline code has ever helped Joey."

Mrs. Galvin was unfazed. "Well, be that as it may, we do have rules that all our students need to follow. We can't send the message that Joey's behavior was acceptable. He's going to have to learn that he needs to follow the same rules as everyone else or he'll continue to suffer the consequences."

"Joey's been suffering the consequences since preschool!" Ms. Lowell exclaimed. "He *knows* the rules. He feels bad about what happened. But consequences aren't fixing the problem. From what Joey tells me, all of this started because he didn't understand a social studies assignment."

"From what I understand, Mrs. Woods wanted Joey to come up to her desk because he was disrupting her class," said Mrs. Galvin. "He refused to come up to her desk. Mrs. Woods has twenty-six other students in her class, and she simply can't have Joey interfering with the work of the other kids."

"Don't you think the way the problem *was* handled interfered with the work of the other kids? Mrs. Woods, nothing against you, but Joey said you embarrassed him in front of the class and that's why he wouldn't go up to your desk to talk to you."

Mrs. Galvin jumped in before Mrs. Woods. "Embarrassed or not, Joey needs to be held accountable for his actions. We can't have Joey becoming aggressive and running out of the school just because he's embarrassed or doesn't understand an assignment."

Mrs. Woods wasn't eager to appear unappreciative of her principal's support, but felt the need to speak for herself. "Well, now I . . . I've been thinking a lot about what happened. I think maybe there could have been a better way for me to handle things . . . you know, in hindsight. I just didn't expect Joey to react that way."

"Now, don't go beating yourself up, Mrs. Woods," said Mrs. Galvin. "Joey's behavior was completely inappropriate. Ms. Lowell, we're going to need your support to make sure this never happens again. That's why we're having this meeting."

"Look, no offense, but I've been coming to these meetings and trying to be supportive for a long time, and all I ever hear about is what *I* need to do with Joey," said Joey's mother. "What else do you want me to do? I'm not here when he blows up! I just come get him after he's been suspended."

"Maybe you can tell us what you think would work," said Mrs. Galvin.

"I don't *know* what will work!" said Ms. Lowell. "Look, Joey's no angel at home, either. He has his moments, believe me. And he's had more than his share of punishment. It just doesn't seem to affect him like it affects his brother. He's different that way. So I don't know what will work. I just know what you've been doing isn't working. If it was working we wouldn't be sitting here right now."

"I hate to ask personal questions, but is Joey still angry about your divorce?" asked Mrs. Galvin. "Is that what this is really about?"

Ms. Lowell responded tersely, uncertain if she'd be able to contain herself. "Joey had trouble with his anger before the divorce. His anger is no better or worse now than it was before the divorce."

"Is he looking for attention? Is it because he doesn't see his father as much anymore?" pressed Mrs. Galvin.

"He sees his father plenty," said Ms. Lowell. "And he did not do what he did the other day for attention! Hurting Mr. Middleton is not the kind of attention he's looking for! Being suspended from school isn't, either!"

"So what do you think it is? Why does he get so angry?" asked Mr. Middleton.

"I wish I knew," said Ms. Lowell.

Suddenly the door to the meeting room flew open and Dr. Bridgman barged in. "Sorry I'm late," he said as he sat down, a little out of breath. "I had another meeting run long."

"We were just discussing what might be causing Joey to feel so angry," said Mrs. Galvin, looking up from her watch. "We were wondering if it's related to his parents' divorce."

Dr. Bridgman was trying to find Joey's file in his briefcase. "Oh, I don't think that's it at all."

Mrs. Galvin appeared surprised by this statement. "Well, what do you think is causing him to be so angry?"

"I don't know that I'd call him angry," said Dr. Bridgman. "I did have a chance to meet with Joey and his mom a few days ago, so I was able to gather some information about the factors that set the stage for Joey to get upset." He looked at Mrs. Woods. "But it would be very helpful if I could spend a little while talking with you as well, just to get a sense for what Joey looks like in the classroom."

"That would be fine," said Mrs. Woods.

"What kind of hypotheses do you have?" asked Mrs. Galvin, trying to hide her skepticism.

"Well, only some very tentative ones so far," said Dr. Bridgman. "But I've heard that Joey is easily embarrassed in front of his classmates. Do you see that, too, Mrs. Woods?"

"Well, I . . . I guess so. I mean, that's what I'm hearing," said Mrs. Woods.

"And does he often appear confused about what to do on assignments?" asked Dr. Bridgman.

Mrs. Woods nodded. "Yes, that happens quite often."

"This is all very interesting," said Mrs. Galvin, "but how exactly is this information going to help us make sure that Joey doesn't blow up again?"

"This information will help us understand *why* and *when* Joey blows up," said Dr. Bridgman.

"Well, regardless of *why* and *when* he blows up, hopefully Joey has learned his lesson about what happens when he acts that way," said the principal. "Maybe he'll think twice before he does it again."

"Actually, why and when Joey acts that way is really important," said Dr. Bridgman. "See, I don't think he wanted to act that way. I think he doesn't have the skills to keep himself from acting that way . . . especially when he's frustrated or embarrassed."

Ms. Lowell couldn't tell if the ensuing silence was related to Dr. Bridgman's contradiction of the principal or whether everyone was simply giving his words some thought.

Mr. Middleton broke the silence. "You're saying that Joey didn't mean to blow up?"

"That's right," said Dr. Bridgman.

"Then why'd he do it?" asked Mr. Middleton.

"My bet is that he couldn't think of anything better to do," said Dr. Bridgman.

More silence, this time broken by Mrs. Galvin. "We don't have much time left. I'm wondering if maybe we should get on with our reentry plan."

"Hard to come up with a plan unless we know what we're trying to accomplish," said Dr. Bridgman.

"We are trying to accomplish Joey's coming back to school and not blowing up again," said Mrs. Galvin. "I think it's really quite simple."

Dr. Bridgman shifted in his chair. "I don't think it's going to be so simple. Helping Joey not blow up again is going to take a lot of work. If we don't put the work in, I predict he'll just blow up again."

Mr. Middleton rubbed his sore jaw. "Seems to me we've been working hard on Joey for a while now. We don't have anything against hard work. But it sure would be nice to have something to show for it. What kind of work are you talking about, Dr. Bridgman?"

"Well, from what I can gather, the work that's been done up until now has been for the purpose of giving Joey the incentive to do the right thing, mostly by punishing him when he does the wrong thing," said Dr. Bridgman. "But if Joey doesn't have the *skills* to do the right thing, well, all the incentives in the world won't teach him the skills he lacks."

"What skills?" asked Mr. Middleton.

"In Joey's case, I'm not sure yet," said Dr. Bridgman. "That's why I want to meet with Mrs. Woods and"—he looked at Mrs. Woods—"I'm sorry, I forgot the name of the teacher you're teamed with."

"Mrs. Franco," helped Mrs. Woods.

"Yes, Mrs. Franco . . . I'd like to meet with you both to get a better sense of the skills Joey's lacking and the situations in which Joey is likely to run into trouble. Then we'll have a much better sense of the work that needs to be done."

"So we're not having Joey sign a contract agreeing not to run out of the school or threaten his classmates again?" asked Mrs. Galvin.

"Joey can't agree to that right now," said Dr. Bridgman. "It's wishful thinking."

"So what's our reentry plan?" asked Mrs. Galvin.

"Well, once we have a handle on the skills Joey is lacking, we'll understand why he responds to certain problems so poorly. And then we can start solving the problems and teaching the skills. After that, Joey should be in pretty good shape . . . and we won't have to worry so much about him running out of school and threatening his classmates."

Mrs. Galvin was undeterred. "And then we'll have a reentry plan?"

"Oh, then we'll have something much better than a reentry plan," Dr. Bridgman reassured. "Then we'll have a *staying in school* plan."

Mrs. Woods usually looked forward to lunch with her colleagues. On most days, it was a chance to decompress and gather her thoughts, however briefly. She sat down next to Mrs. Franco and across from a seventh-grade teacher, Jerry Armstrong. Mr. Armstrong taught Joey's brother, and was known for his definite views about the way schools should be run and discipline administered.

"Big meeting today?" asked Mr. Armstrong.

"Well, it certainly was an interesting meeting," said Mrs. Woods, sitting down to eat.

"Joey's mother behave herself?" asked Mr. Armstrong.

Mrs. Woods began unpacking her lunch. "She did fine."

"Poor kid . . . can you imagine going home to *that* every day?" asked Mr. Armstrong. "And we're supposed to pick up the pieces when the kid comes to school. Unbelievable."

Mrs. Woods wasn't in the mood to go toe-to-toe with Mr. Armstrong. The man had his point of view and she'd never seen anyone make a dent in it. Still, she was feeling some empathy for Joey's mother, so, against her better judgment, she continued the dialogue. "What is it you think Joey's going home to every day?"

"From what I've heard, that lady's got a nasty temper," said Mr. Armstrong. "Looks like the apple didn't fall far from the tree."

"Oh, I don't know," said Mrs. Woods. "She's in a tough spot. Divorced, full-time job, two kids, one difficult. I'm not sure I'd handle all that with an even temper."

"Well, a lot of us didn't have it so easy ourselves," said Mr. Armstrong. Here we go again, thought Mrs. Woods. "You can't make excuses for these people," Mr. Armstrong continued. "Bleeding hearts and pity parties don't cut it where I come from."

Mrs. Woods was now regretting heading down this path. "No, I suppose not."

"He wouldn't have pulled that garbage with me," said Mr. Armstrong. "I'll tell you what I would've done with him."

Mrs. Franco laughed. "We know what you would've done with him."

"I don't think it's funny," said Mr. Armstrong. "If they're going to throw these kids at us and expect us to fix everything their families have screwed up, we shouldn't have our hands tied when they go nuts on us. You think a five-day suspension's going to fix what's broken about that kid?"

"No, actually, I don't," said Mrs. Woods.

"Well, me either," said Mr. Armstrong. "That's one messed-up boy. That kid shouldn't even be in this school. He should be done for the year."

"And how would that make anything any better when he shows up again next year?" asked Mrs. Franco.

"Look, in the real world—not this school, obviously, but the *real* world—there's a price to be paid for acting that way," said Mr. Armstrong. "In the *real* world they put kids like Joey away."

"Away where?" asked Mrs. Franco.

"Wherever they put messed-up kids so they don't screw up the learning of the other kids," said Mr. Armstrong, packing up his belongings. "We're not running a mental institution here."

Mrs. Woods was delighted to see Mr. Armstrong preparing to leave. "Jerry, I just want to enjoy my lunch, if that's OK. I appreciate your concern."

"No problem," said Mr. Armstrong, moving toward the door. "Let's not think about it until he kills somebody."

Mrs. Franco watched Mr. Armstrong leave the lounge. "Talk about broken records," she said under her breath. "So how *was* the meeting?"

"Interesting," said Mrs. Woods. "Betty Galvin and the new school psychologist got into it a little."

"Really! Over what?"

"Well, first of all, the psychologist, Dr. Bridgman—I don't know if you've met him yet—was late to the meeting," said Mrs. Woods.

"Whoo boy!" said Mrs. Franco, fully appreciating the seriousness of this offense. "He'll learn."

"Didn't seem to faze him," said Mrs. Woods. "But he gave us his theory about why Joey blew up, and I don't think Betty was buying it at all."

"What's his theory?" said Mrs. Franco.

"Well, I don't know that I could do justice to what he was saying, but it made sense to me at the time," said Mrs. Woods. "He's coming by this afternoon after school to talk about Joey. He'd like you to sit in, since you have Joey for some classes, too. Can you do it?"

"Sure," said Mrs. Franco. "I could use a new theory."

Dr. Bridgman arrived fifteen minutes late for his meeting with Mrs. Woods and Mrs. Franco, who were seated at a table in Mrs. Woods' classroom. "Sorry I'm late," he puffed. "This still a good time?"

The two teachers looked up from their conversation. "Um, sure," said Mrs. Woods.

Mrs. Franco stuck out her hand. "I'm Denise Franco. You must be Dr. Bridgman."

"Carl's fine," said Dr. Bridgman.

"OK, Carl, I understand you have some new theories about our friend Joey."

"I didn't think I could do justice to what you said in the meeting," Mrs. Woods said.

Dr. Bridgman pulled some papers out of his briefcase. "Oh, well, I'm not sure the theories are so new. But the basic idea is that challenging kids haven't developed a lot of the skills they need to solve problems, handle their emotions, shift gears, interact with other kids, those sorts of things."

"What did our principal think of your theory?" Mrs. Franco prodded.

"I'm not sure," said Dr. Bridgman. "I guess I'm accustomed to this being a little new for people."

"It's certainly new for me," said Mrs. Woods. "But I'm happy to be made a believer if you can help us out with Joey. And after that we've got a bunch of other kids you can work on."

"Well, our first task is to get a good handle on the thinking skills that Joey seems to be lacking," said Dr. Bridgman. "We also want to get a better idea of the circumstances or problems that cause him the most trouble."

"That's easy," said Mrs. Franco. "Any time things don't go the way he thought they would."

Dr. Bridgman handed both teachers a copy of the ALSUP. "Can you be a little more specific?"

"Let me think," said Mrs. Woods. "He doesn't like schedule changes. He doesn't like when his bus is late." She looked at Mrs. Franco. "Can you think of any others?"

"He doesn't like when he has a new math partner," said Mrs. Franco. "And sometimes he gets very confused about what to do on assignments that other kids don't have any trouble understanding. Does that help?"

"A lot," said Dr. Bridgman, thinking about some of the lagging skills that might explain these behaviors. "Like I said in the meeting, if we know the problems that cause Joey the most trouble, we can start working on those problems so they don't cause him so much trouble anymore."

"You're saying I should have seen it coming," said Mrs. Woods.

Mrs. Franco patted Mrs. Woods on the hand. "You have to be careful what you say to my friend here," Mrs. Franco cautioned Dr. Bridgman. "She's very hard on herself."

"Well, with all those kids in the class, it's not so easy to always see things coming," said Dr. Bridgman. "But I am saying that Joey's difficulties are pretty predictable if we're paying attention to the information he's giving us."

"So what's this?" asked Mrs. Franco, examining her copy of the ALSUP.

"That's a list of the skills challenging kids frequently lack," said Dr. Bridgman. "I'm betting some of the items on that list explain why Joey's been having so much trouble for so long."

Mrs. Franco scanned the list. "So we're supposed to figure out which ones apply to Joey?"

"Exactly. And then we'll decide which ones are the most important."

"So I'm a little lost," said Mrs. Franco. "Let's say we know something's giving Joey trouble. How are we supposed to prepare for it? I mean, I already make sure he has the same math partner every day so he doesn't get all agitated. But what about everything else?"

"I hope you won't think I'm being evasive," said Dr. Bridgman, "but first we really need to figure out the full range of skills Joey's lacking and the problems that cause him the most trouble."

"Oops, sorry," said Mrs. Franco. "Keep going."

"So which items seem to apply to our friend Joey?"

Mrs. Franco recited the first item. "Difficulty handling transitions, shifting from one mind-set or task to another . . ."

"That's him," Mrs. Woods confirmed. "Ooh, here's a big one: difficulty managing emotional response to frustration so as to think rationally."

"Yep," said Dr. Bridgman, checking off the items on the ALSUP. "Others?"

Mrs. Woods was carefully studying the ALSUP. "Here are three that describe him to a tee. Difficulty deviating from rules, routine, original plan; difficulty handling unpredictability, ambiguity, uncertainty, novelty; and difficulty shifting from original idea or solution. Then there's difficulty adapting to changes in plan or new rules . . . that's him, oh, and this one . . . difficulty taking into account situational factors that would suggest the need to adjust a plan of action."

Mrs. Franco added her own choices. "I'm wondering about these two: difficulty expressing concerns, needs, or thoughts in words, and difficulty understanding what was said . . ." She looked at Mrs. Woods. "Don't you think those apply, too?"

Mrs. Woods nodded. "I do."

Dr. Bridgman seemed pleased. "This is very helpful. Any others?"

The two teachers finished scanning the list and looked at each other. "I'd say that about covers it," said Mrs. Franco.

"Some of this seems so obvious," said Mrs. Woods. "How could I have missed it?"

"Join the club, honey," said Mrs. Franco. "But at least we're figuring it out now."

"I don't think it's so obvious," said Dr. Bridgman. "I used to miss this stuff on these kids, too, until I knew what to start looking for. By the way, I can add one that I heard when I met with Joey and his mom. Inflexible, inaccurate interpretations/cognitive distortions or biases."

Mrs. Franco looked puzzled. "Explain."

"He thinks teachers hate him, and like getting him into trouble, and like embarrassing him," said Dr. Bridgman.

"How do you know that?" asked Mrs. Franco.

"He told me," said Dr. Bridgman.

Mrs. Woods looked hurt. "I can't believe he thinks those things."

Dr. Bridgman tried to be reassuring. "Oh, those interpretations may not have anything to do with your interactions with him. My bet is that those ways of thinking have built up over the years. They're the best Joey can do to explain why he gets into trouble so much."

"But it's so terrible that he thinks those things about me," said Mrs. Woods.

"Yes, we'll have to convince him that those things aren't true," said Dr. Bridgman.

"How do we do that?" asked Mrs. Woods.

Dr. Bridgman looked at his watch. "I think that's probably another meeting. We have a few more things to accomplish in this meeting, and I want to be sensitive to the time."

"Oh, don't worry about the time," said Mrs. Franco. "It's having my time wasted that bothers me."

"Well, we now have a sense of the skills Joey may be lacking," said Dr. Bridgman. "I'd like to hear a little about the situations that cause him the greatest difficulty . . . the problems that trigger his worst moments."

"He just doesn't seem to understand what to do on assignments sometimes," said Mrs. Woods. "I mean, that seems to be what set him off a week ago. The entire class is working on a social studies assignment, and Joey's sitting there doing nothing. So I go over and ask him why he's not working, and he says he doesn't understand the assignment. How can he not understand the assignment?"

"We'll have to figure that out," said Dr. Bridgman.

Mrs. Franco held up her ALSUP. "I don't see that on here."

"Well, that's a trigger, so it's something you write in at the bottom where it says Unsolved Problems."

"Ah, yes, got it."

"And I guess being embarrassed is a trigger," said Mrs. Woods. "That seems to have been a factor, too."

"Yes, indeed," said Dr. Bridgman.

The teachers considered the question. "I'm going to have to think about triggers a little more," said Mrs. Woods. "I'm not coming up with anything else at the moment."

"Me, either," said Mrs. Franco.

"Well, you mentioned some other unsolved problems already—the bus being late, schedule changes," said Dr. Bridgman. "Let's go with what we've got. We have one more task. We need to decide what we want to start working on first."

"We have to pick?" asked Mrs. Franco.

"They all seem so important," said Mrs. Woods.

"Yes, it certainly sounds that way," said Dr. Bridgman. "But we can't work on everything at once. We'd get overwhelmed and so would Joey. So we need to prioritize to keep things manageable."

"Um, I know this is a bit off topic, Carl," said Mrs. Franco, glancing over at Mrs. Woods, "but how much do you think Joey's mom has to do with his difficulties?"

Dr. Bridgman looked a bit puzzled. "I'm not sure what you mean."

Mrs. Franco lowered her voice. "There are some people in this school who think Joey's difficulties have to do with his parents being divorced and his mother being a bit wacko."

"Interesting," said Dr. Bridgman. "His mother didn't strike me as being especially wacko. But to tell you the truth, I don't think Joey is lacking skills or getting confused on assignments or reacting badly to being embarrassed because his mother's wacko or his parents are divorced."

Mrs. Franco seemed satisfied. "So what are we working on?"

"I . . . I don't know that I can pick," said Mrs. Woods.

"OK," said Dr. Bridgman. "Let's make it easy. When people are new at this, the easiest place to start is with triggers. So let's start with two of the ones that we have: maybe being confused on some assignments and being embarrassed in front of his classmates. We could try to resolve those first."

"Yes, but how?" asked Mrs. Franco.

"Plan B," said Dr. Bridgman.

The teachers looked at each other.

Dr. Bridgman elaborated. "Collaborative Problem Solving—Plan B— will help us get a better idea of what's getting in the way for Joey on those two problems and help us come up with solutions so they can be resolved."

"You want us to come up with solutions?" asked Mrs. Woods.

"No, that's not Plan B," said Dr. Bridgman. "Joey needs to be part of the solution."

"Joey's going to help us come up with solutions?" asked Mrs. Woods.

"Exactly," said Dr. Bridgman.

"What makes you think he'll talk to us?" asked Mrs. Franco.

"Oh, once Joey recognizes that we're trying to understand what's going on with him and that we're trying to involve him in the solution, I bet he'll talk," said Dr. Bridgman.

"Does it concern you at all that we've never done this Plan B?" asked Mrs. Woods.

"Doesn't concern me at all," said Dr. Bridgman. "Most folks have never done Plan B."

The two teachers looked at each other again. Mrs. Woods turned to Dr. Bridgman. "I suppose I should do Plan B with Joey first. It is my classroom he ran out of."

———————

Here's what Joey's ALSUP looked like when it was completed. For a clean copy, see page 287.

Analysis of Lagging Skills and Unsolved Problems (ALSUP)

Child's Name _Joey Turner_____ Date _9-29-09_____

LAGGING SKILLS

_✓_ Difficulty handling transitions, shifting from one mind-set or task to another

____ Difficulty doing things in a logical sequence or prescribed order

____ Difficulty persisting on challenging or tedious tasks

____ Poor sense of time

____ Difficulty reflecting on multiple thoughts or ideas simultaneously

____ Difficulty maintaining focus

____ Difficulty considering the likely outcomes or consequences of actions (impulsive)

____ Difficulty considering a range of solutions to a problem

_✓_ Difficulty expressing concerns, needs, or thoughts in words

_✓_ Difficulty understanding what is being said

_✓_ Difficulty managing emotional response to frustration so as to think rationally

____ Chronic irritability and/or anxiety significantly impede capacity for problem-solving or heighten frustration

____ Difficulty seeing the "grays"/concrete, literal, black-and-white thinking

_✓_ Difficulty deviating from rules, routine

_✓_ Difficulty handling unpredictability, ambiguity, uncertainty, novelty

_✓_ Difficulty shifting from original idea or solution

_✓_ Difficulty taking into account situational factors that would suggest the need to adjust a plan of action

_✓_ Inflexible, inaccurate interpretations/cognitive distortions or biases (e.g., "Everyone's out to get me," "Nobody likes me," "You always blame me," "It's not fair," "I'm stupid")

____ Difficulty attending to or accurately interpreting social cues/poor perception of social nuances

____ Difficulty starting conversations, entering groups, connecting with people/lacking other basic social skills

____ Difficulty seeking attention in appropriate ways

____ Difficulty appreciating how his/her behavior is affecting other people

____ Difficulty empathizing with others, appreciating another person's perspective or point of view

____ Difficulty appreciating how s/he is coming across or being perceived by others

UNSOLVED PROBLEMS

HOME

____ Waking up/getting out of bed in the morning

____ Completing morning routine/getting ready for school

____ Sensory hypersensitivities

____ Starting or completing homework or a particular academic task

____ Food quantities/choices/preferences/timing

____ Time spent in front of a screen (TV, video games, computer)

____ Going to/getting ready for bed at night

____ Boredom

____ Sibling interactions

____ Cleaning room/completing household chores

____ Taking medicine
____ Riding in car/wearing seat belt

SCHOOL
____ Shifting from one specific task to another (specify)
_✓_ Getting started on/completing class assignment (specify) *Being confused*
_✓_ Interactions with a particular classmate/teacher (specify) *Having a new math partner*
____ Behavior in hallway/at recess/in cafeteria/on school bus/waiting in line (specify)
____ Talking at appropriate times
____ Specific academic tasks/demands, e.g., writing assignments (specify)
_✓_ Handling disappointment/losing at a game/not coming in first/not being first in line (specify) *The bus being late*

OTHER (list)
Being embarrassed
Schedule changes

CHAPTER 4

Let's Get It Started

If you're feeling like you don't know much about how to do Plan B yet, don't despair; you're about to find out. So far, what you know about Plan B is that it's one of three ways adults handle problems with kids, and that it's quite different from the usual ways. You also know that, depending on your timing, there are two forms of Plan B. Proactive B is used well before a challenging behavior occurs yet again, and is made possible by the fact that challenging episodes tend to be highly predictable. Emergency B is used in the midst of a challenging episode. Because Proactive B is far preferable, it will be our primary focus. A description of Emergency B comes later in the chapter.

Plan B allows adults to achieve five goals essential to helping kids with behavioral challenges.

- *Goal #1: Pursue unmet expectations and ensure that your concerns about a given kid's challenges are addressed.*

If a kid is doing something you wish he wasn't—for example, interfering with the learning of his classmates, calling out without raising his hand, treating other kids in an unkind manner, or making classmates feel unsafe—or not doing something you wish he was, such as not working on a given assignment, failing to complete homework, or not working cooperatively with the kids in his group, you have unmet expectations to pursue and concerns to be addressed.

- *Goal #2: Solve the problems precipitating a child's challenging episodes in a collaborative, mutually satisfactory, and durable fashion.*

Most kids with behavioral challenges have five or six unsolved problems that are routinely precipitating their challenging episodes. The goal is to resolve them one by one so that, after a period of time, they aren't causing challenging episodes anymore. But the collaborative and mutually satisfactory elements are crucial. As you've already read, solutions that don't stand the test of time usually fall flat because they fail to identify and resolve the concerns of both parties.

- *Goal #3: Teach the kid the skills he's lacking.*

The more adults use Plan B to solve problems, the more practice and help kids receive with a lot of the skills they're lacking. Plan B helps kids think about, identify, and articulate the concerns that are precipitating challenging behavior; take into account situational factors and others' perspectives; move off of their original solution; generate alternative solutions; consider whether those solutions are realistic and mutually satisfactory; and talk about problems without going over the edge—all things kids with behavioral challenges may not be very good at. Plan B doesn't teach these skills in one repetition, it takes multiple reps (as it does with any new skill).

- *Goal #4: Reduce challenging behavior.*

When adults better understand challenging behavior, solve problems durably and collaboratively, and simultaneously teach lagging thinking skills, challenging behavior is reduced. The work is often slow and messy. There's no way around that. CPS is not a quick fix. Of course, you don't fix a reading disability in a week, either. In fact, find a challenging kid people are trying to fix quickly and you'll see a

challenging kid it's taking a very long time to fix. There's no cookie
cutter, either. The approach must be tailored to the needs of each individual child to whom it is being applied.

- *Goal #5: Create a helping relationship.*

Why be adversarial, why be the enemy, when you and the kid can
be on the same team? In creating a process that helps you and the kid
collaborate on solutions that will address each others' concerns, Plan
B facilitates a helping relationship. The kid comes to feel that you
actually care about his concerns, that you feel his concerns are legitimate. He realizes that you're going to listen to him, try to understand
him, and make sure that his concerns are addressed. He knows you're
not mad, that he's not in trouble, that you're not going to tell him what
to do. He begins to trust you, to rely on you . . . as a helper.

Let's start with the basics of Plan B and go into more detail as we
move along. There are three steps for doing Plan B, and they are the
same whether you're doing Proactive B or Emergency B: (1) Empathy,
(2) Define the problem, (3) Invitation.

Each step brings crucial ingredients to the durable and collaborative resolution of problems. These ingredients are what distinguish
Plan B from other types of conversations or discussions and make
"talking with a kid" much more productive. Many people find it difficult to apply these ingredients, so you're in for some hard work.
Then again, if you're trying to help a challenging kid, you're already
working hard. Let's make sure you have something to show for your
hard work.

EMPATHY

The goal of the Empathy step is to achieve the best possible *understanding* of a kid's *concern* or *perspective* related to a given problem. Like
adults, kids have legitimate concerns: approval, hunger, fatigue, fear,
a desire to do certain things, a tendency to avoid things they're not
good at, a desire not to be embarrassed or humiliated, and so forth.

However, most kids are accustomed to having their concerns super-seded by the concerns of adults. If a kid's concerns about a problem remain unidentified and unaddressed, then the kid will have little investment in working with you and the problem will remain unsolved. You don't lose any authority by gathering information about and understanding a kid's concerns; you gain a problem-solving teammate.

Adults often feel they already know what a kid's concern or per-spective is, so they don't see the point in spending time figuring it out. Or they skip or rush through the Empathy step because they're nar-rowly focused on their own concerns. Or they are so consumed by a kid's challenging behavior that they lose sight of the fact that there are valid concerns precipitating that challenging behavior.

How do you get the information-gathering process rolling? If you're doing Proactive B, Empathy involves making a neutral obser-vation about a challenge or problem the kid is having, followed by an initial inquiry. In its most basic form, here's what that might sound like:

Example #1:
> ADULT *(Empathy step, kicking off Proactive B): I've noticed that you've been getting pretty mad at some of the other kids lately. What's up?*

Example #2:
> ADULT *(Empathy step, kicking off Proactive B): I've noticed that you haven't been getting much homework done lately. What's up?*

The *neutral* aspect of the neutral observation is important, because it requires that adults resist the temptation to jump to biased conclusions about the kid's concerns. Here are some examples of biased observations on the getting-mad problem:

> *"I guess you don't care about hurting other kids."*
> *"You know, you can't always have things your own way."*

Some biased examples on the homework problem:

"You must not be very interested in getting good grades."
"The homework must be too hard for you."

Right or wrong, these observations are definitely not neutral and certainly not the best way to get the kid to talk about the problem. In fact, such judgments often have the effect, especially in challenging kids, of ending the discussion before it has even started.

If you're lucky, after you ask "What's up?" the kid will say something. In most cases, what he says is going to require further clarification. If you're unlucky, he'll say "I don't know" or nothing at all, and such responses often cause great panic in adults who had the misimpression that Plan B was going to be smooth sailing. But "I don't know" may be a true statement. It's possible the kid has never thought about your question before, that he just needs some time to think about it, that he's going to need your help figuring it out, that he's not very comfortable talking about his concerns, that he doesn't quite trust you yet, or that he doesn't have the communication skills to say what he's thinking. More on these issues later. For the time being, - we're going to assume that the kid actually did say something:

ADULT *(Empathy step, kicking off Proactive B): I've noticed that you've been getting pretty mad at some of the other kids lately. What's up?*
CHILD: *They won't let me play with them.*
ADULT: *Ah, they won't let you play with them and that makes you mad.*

ADULT *(Empathy step, kicking off Proactive B): I've noticed that you haven't been getting much homework done lately.*
OLDER KID: *I've been getting some homework done.*
ADULT *(clarifying the concern): Yes, some, that's true. But a lot less than usual, yes?*
OLDER KID: *Yeah.*
ADULT: *So, what's up? How come you're getting less done than usual?*
OLDER KID: *Most of the homework lately is our geography projects, and I don't know what to do. I don't know how to look that stuff up. Plus—don't take this wrong—it's not that*

interesting. I got stuck with Uzbekistan, or whatever it's called.

ADULT: *That's true, we have been spending a lot of time on our geography projects. And it sounds like you're not too interested in the country you were assigned.*

The Empathy step is now rolling. But you're probably not done yet. You don't move on to the next step until you feel that you have the clearest possible understanding of the kid's concern or perspective on the unsolved problem you're discussing, something I've referred to as an "aha!" moment. Achieving this understanding means you're probably going to need to "drill" a little. Notice the word isn't *grill*, it's *drill*, as in drilling for information. Here's what drilling might look like (using a different example):

ADULT: *I've noticed you've been having some trouble with swearing lately. What's up?*

KID: *Um . . . sometimes the words just pop out.*

ADULT: *Ah, that can happen sometimes. How come the words just pop out?*

KID: *You guys get more freaked out about swearing than my parents do. They don't think it's that big of a deal.*

ADULT: *Ah, so there's a lot of swearing at home?*

KID: *No, not really a lot, but my parents just don't care about it like you all do.*

ADULT: *So, I don't understand how that causes you to swear at school.*

KID: *It's not like I'm swearing all the time! Just some of the time.*

ADULT: *I'm wondering if we can figure out when those sometimes are.*

KID: *I don't know when I swear.*

ADULT: *Can you think of a time lately when you swore?*

KID: *I swore while I was taking the math test in Mrs. Thompson's class.*

ADULT: *What do you think it was about the math test that caused you to swear?*

KID: *Like I said, it just popped out.*

ADULT: *Yes, but I'm thinking there may have been something about the math test that caused it to just pop out. Can you remember?*

KID: *There was a problem I couldn't figure out.*

ADULT: *Ah, so that's why you swore.*

KID: *Yeah, maybe.*

ADULT: *Can you think of other times when a swear word might pop out?*

KID: *Um . . . well, sometimes when I'm messing around with my friends and I didn't know an adult was listening.*

ADULT: *I can see how that could happen. Any other times?*

KID: *Um . . .*

ADULT: *Take your time. There's no rush.*

When you're drilling, you're trying to gather more specific information about something that's still pretty general ("the words just pop out"), often by probing about the who, what, where, when, and sometimes why, of the problem. You can also seek greater clarity by saying things like, "I don't quite understand," "Can you tell me more about that?" "I'm confused," or "How so?" or by asking for the kid's thoughts on why the behavior or problem occurs in one situation and not another. All along, you're asking yourself, "Does this make sense to me yet? Do I feel like I fully understand his concerns on this problem?" If not, keep drilling.

Sometimes kids put a *solution* on the table rather than a *concern.* Your job is ensure that the kid's concern ends up on the table. Here's how you might get that ball rolling:

ADULT: *I've noticed you've been having some trouble with swearing lately. What's up?*

KID: *I've decided to work really hard on that so I don't swear anymore.*

ADULT: *Oh . . . uh, I'm delighted to hear that. Though I was still hoping we might be able to figure out why you're swearing so much, and maybe also figure out when it's happening.*

KID: *Um . . . sometimes the words just pop out. . . .*

Feeling heard and understood tends to be calming. But Empathy alone isn't sufficient for keeping some kids, especially the highly reactive ones, calm enough to hang in there with Plan B. They might need some reassurance as well. Reassurance about what? First and foremost, reassurance that you're not using Plan A. You see, these kids have had a lot more Plan A in their lives than Plan B, so they're probably still betting on the Plan A horse. This being the case, early on they may get heated up in response to Plan B because they're not yet accustomed to your trying to collaborate with them to solve problems. They're going to need some reassurance on that count. But since they don't know what Plan A is, you can't say, "I'm not using Plan A." Instead, you could say something like, "I'm not saying no," or "I'm not saying you must," or "I'm not saying you can't." Of course, you're not saying "yes," or "you don't have to" or "you can," either. Other examples of reassurance are "I'm not mad," "You're not in trouble," "I'm not going to tell you what to do," and "I'm just trying to understand."

When adults struggle with the Empathy step, it's usually because they aren't sure exactly what words to use (luckily, there are tons of examples throughout this book). Some adults fear that the Empathy step is a prelude to capitulating to the kid's wishes. Don't worry, you're not about to capitulate. You're about to *collaborate*.

DEFINE THE PROBLEM

In the second step of Plan B the adult brings his or her concern about a problem or unmet expectation into consideration. This is called the Define the Problem step because a problem is defined simply as *two concerns that have yet to be reconciled*: the kid's and yours. Out of the three options (Plans A, B, and C) for responding to problems or unmet expectations, Plan B is the only option in which there are two concerns being entered into consideration. By the way, there's an easy way to recognize which Plan you're using. If the only concern on the table is the Adult's concern, you're using Plan A. If the only concern on the table is the Child's, you're using Plan C. Only Plan B ensures that Both concerns are on the table.

Like kids, adults are prone to putting *solutions* on the table instead of concerns. Plan B is dead in the water if there are two solutions on the table, a circumstance we'll call *dueling solutions,* also known as a "power struggle." When an adult puts a solution on the table during the Define the Problem step, that's usually a pretty clear sign that the process has shifted from Plan B to Plan A. Examples: "You need to use your words so you don't hit kids when you're mad at them" or "You have to do the writing or you'll never get better at it." In a power struggle, two parties are engaged in the battle to determine whose solution is going to win and whose solution is going to lose. Power struggles are a win/lose proposition. But with Plan B, there's no such thing as a power struggle, because you and the kid are engaged in a completely different activity: trying to find solutions that will address both parties' concerns. That's a win/win proposition. *The child needs to become convinced that you're just as invested in making sure his concern gets addressed as you are in making sure yours gets addressed.* Again, so long as the concerns of one party or the other are unaddressed, the problem is not durably solved.

But getting your concern on the table can take some practice. While many adults are certain that they have a concern about a given problem or unmet expectation, they often struggle with how to identify and articulate it. Many adults have an informal (and sometimes quite exhaustive) list of things they think kids "should" or "shouldn't" do, but have never given any thought to *why* kids "should" or "shouldn't" do those things. Some concerns are easier for a kid to comprehend and to take into account than others. In general, the fact that a kid's behavior violates the rules or isn't meeting your expectations wouldn't be explicit enough. Better to let the kid know that his behavior is interfering with his or someone else's learning, or that it's affecting other people adversely by hurting or offending them, making them feel unsafe, or hurting their feelings, or that it's making it difficult for him to be part of the community of which he is a valued member. These are concerns that kids can identify with and take into account.

Here are some examples of how it might sound (note that these are continuations of some of the Proactive Plan B dialogues above):

ADULT *(Empathy step, kicking off Proactive B): I've noticed that you've been getting pretty mad at some of the other kids lately. What's up?*

CHILD: *They won't let me play with them.*

ADULT *(clarifying the concern): Ah, they won't let you play with them and that makes you mad.*

CHILD: *Yep.*

ADULT *(reassurance, then Defining the Problem): I'm not saying you shouldn't get mad when they won't let you play with them. The thing is, we want everyone to feel safe in our classroom and to let one another know how we're feeling with our words. When you hit other kids, I think they get hurt and don't feel very safe . . . and they may not even know why you're mad.*

ADULT *(Empathy step, kicking off Proactive B): I've noticed that you haven't been getting much homework done lately.*

OLDER KID: *I've been getting some homework done.*

ADULT *(clarifying the concern): Yes, some, that's true. But less than usual, yes?*

OLDER KID: *Yeah.*

ADULT *(still clarifying): So, what's up? How come you're getting less done than usual?*

OLDER KID: *Most of the homework lately is our geography projects, and I don't know what to do. I don't know how to look that stuff up. Plus, don't take this wrong, it's not that interesting. I got stuck with Uzbekistan, or whatever it's called.*

ADULT *(still clarifying): That's true, we have been spending a lot of time on our geography projects. And it sounds like you're not too interested in the country you were assigned.*

OLDER KID: *Yeah, I mean, I don't really care about Uzbekistan. It's a boring country.*

ADULT *(clarifying further): So we have two things going on: You're not sure what to do to get your project going, and you're not too happy with the country you were assigned.*

OLDER KID: *Yep.*

ADULT *(clarifying further still): So help me understand. Are you*

having trouble getting going because you don't like your
country, or would you have difficulty getting going no
matter what your country is?

OLDER KID: *Well, the country I got assigned isn't helping. But*
you usually let us work with partners on stuff like this, and
now I'm on my own. And I don't know where to start, or
how to look it up.

ADULT *(Defining the Problem): I think I understand. The thing*
is, I wanted to have a few projects you did on your own . . .
you know, without someone helping you . . . otherwise it'll
always be really hard for you.

The first two steps of Plan B are reserved exclusively for concerns.
You don't even consider solutions until the third step. It doesn't make
much sense to brainstorm solutions until you know what concerns
you're trying to address.

INVITATION

Now that you have two concerns on the table, and not a moment
before, you and the kid are ready to brainstorm potential solutions
that will address those concerns. This step involves restating the two
concerns that have now been identified so as to summarize the problem to be solved (usually starting with the words *"I wonder if there's*
a way . . ."). This step is called the Invitation because the adult is lit-
erally *inviting* the kid to solve the problem collaboratively. The Invitation lets the kid know that solving the problem is something you're
doing *with* him—in other words, *together*—rather than *to* him. Here
are examples of Invitations corresponding to the dialogues above.
Note that the adult is recapping the two concerns so as to ensure that
the kid understands the problem to be resolved:

INVITATION: *I wonder if there's a way for you to let me know*
you're mad that the other kids won't let you play with them
without you hitting them. Do you have any ideas?

INVITATION: *I wonder if there's a way for us to help you get*

started on your project and look things up, but do it
independently so I can be sure you know how to do it on
your own. Do you have any ideas for how we could do that?

The fact that you're giving the kid the first crack at generating a solution ("Do you have any ideas?") doesn't mean the kid is the only one on the hook for generating solutions. You're both on the hook. After all, you're on the same team. But giving the kid the first opportunity to think of solutions is good strategy, especially for kids who are accustomed to having an adult's will imposed upon them, for it lets the kid know beyond a shadow of a doubt that you're interested in his ideas.

Many adults, in their eagerness to solve the problem, forget the Invitation. Just as they are on the precipice of actually collaborating with a kid and working toward a solution that addresses both concerns, they impose their will. What a shame. You see, while there is some chance that a kid won't be able to think of any solutions, there's actually an excellent probability the kid *can* think of good solutions—ones that will take your combined concerns into account—and has been waiting (often not so patiently) for you to give him the chance. So, as it relates to solving problems with kids, the important theme is:

Don't be a genius.

You'd think that most adults would breathe a sigh of relief at the news that they're no longer on the hook for coming up with instantaneous, ingenious solutions to all problems involving kids. In truth, it takes some getting used to. Many adults are absolutely certain they know exactly how a problem should be solved. It's no crime to have some ideas or proposals for how to solve a problem, but when you use Plan B you do so with the understanding that the solution is not predetermined. Solving a difficult problem *durably* requires a willingness to let the process of exploring solutions unfold without the adult's solution being prematurely invoked. If you already know how the problem is going to be solved before the conversation takes place, then you're not using Plan B, you're using Plan A. Plan B isn't merely a clever variant of Plan A.

So, the definition of an ingenious solution is: *Any solution that the two parties agree is* **realistic** *and* **mutually satisfactory.**

If a solution under consideration isn't realistic and mutually satisfactory, then the problem isn't solved yet and the problem-solving team (you and the child) still needs to explore other potential solutions.

The *mutually satisfactory* part should be of great comfort to adults who fear that, in using Plan B, their concerns will not be addressed. If a solution is mutually satisfactory, then by definition your concern *has* been addressed. So, to reiterate an earlier point, if you were thinking that Plan A is the only mechanism by which adults can "set limits," think again. You're setting limits when you're using Plan B, too.

The *realistic* part is important, too. Plan B isn't an exercise in wishful thinking. If you can't reliably follow through on the solution that's being considered, then don't agree to it just to end the conversation. Likewise, if you don't think the kid can follow through on the solution that's being agreed to, then you should express gentle skepticism on this count ("It would be wonderful if you could do that solution! I'm just not so sure you really can because I know that's been a struggle for you in the past. Let's try to come up with a solution we can both do.") and try to help him think of solutions that are more plausible.

Some kids' first stab at a solution is to simply repeat what they wanted in the first place (for example, "I don't want to talk about it. I'm not doing the project on my own."). This is often a sign that the kid is having a hard time moving beyond his original solution or is not especially proficient at generating solutions that are mutually satisfactory. In these cases, simply remind him that the goal is to come up with a solution that works for *both* of you, perhaps by saying, "Well, that's one idea. And I know that solution would probably work for you, because then you wouldn't have to look things up on your own, but it probably wouldn't work for me because I really want you to get some practice at doing that so it's not so hard for you anymore. Let's see if we can come up with an idea that will work for both of us." In other words, there's no such thing as a bad solution. Proposals for solutions are weighed solely on the basis of whether they are realistic and mutually satisfactory.

There's another reason the kid might be having difficulty moving off his original solution: He's been well trained. Kids who get a lot of Plan A thrown at them become good at throwing Plan A back. They may not have had much experience solving problems in any other way.

Just in case you're wondering what the general game plan is, over time—after multiple repetitions—Plan B should significantly reduce challenging behavior. Problems are being solved one at a time. The kid is learning that his concerns are being heard and addressed, so there's really nothing to get upset about. The kid is learning skills crucial to handling life's social, emotional, and behavioral challenges. It's all good.

Let's see how the three steps would look all together, once again assuming that things are going fairly smoothly. Forgive the redundancy . . . some learners benefit from multiple repetitions:

ADULT *(Empathy step, kicking off Proactive B): I've noticed that you've been getting pretty mad at some of the other kids lately. What's up?*

CHILD: *They won't let me play with them.*

ADULT *(clarifying the concern): Ah, they won't let you play with them and that makes you mad.*

CHILD: *Yep.*

ADULT *(reassurance, then Defining the Problem, then Inviting): I'm not saying you shouldn't get mad when they won't let you play with them. The thing is, we want everyone to feel safe in our classroom and to let one another know how we're feeling with our words. When you hit other kids, I think they get hurt and don't feel very safe . . . and they may not even know why you're mad. I wonder if there's a way for you to let me know you're mad that the other kids won't let you play with them without you hitting them. Do you have any ideas?*

CHILD: *You could tell them to let me play with them.*

ADULT: *Well, there's an idea. And I think we could work on that as a class. The thing is, I'm not always right there when they're not letting you join in, so I'm thinking there would still be times when you might get mad. So we would still*

*need to find a way for you to let me know you're mad at the
other kids without you hitting them. Yes?*

CHILD: *Yes.*

ADULT: *So, what do you think? Do you have any ideas?*

CHILD: *I could come tell you.*

ADULT: *Yes, you could. Do you think you could remember to do
that?*

CHILD: *Yes . . . well, maybe not always.*

ADULT: *What could we do so you don't forget?*

CHILD: *You could remind me before we go to recess or choice
time—that's when they're doing stuff I want to join in on.*

ADULT: *We could try that. And if our solution doesn't get the
job done, we'll get back together and talk about it some
more, yes?*

CHILD: *Yes.*

ADULT *(Empathy, kicking off Proactive B): I've noticed that you
haven't been getting much homework done lately.*

OLDER KID: *I've been getting some homework done.*

ADULT *(clarifying the concern): Yes, some, that's true. But less
than usual, yes?*

OLDER KID: *Yeah.*

ADULT: *So, what's up? How come you're getting less done than
usual?*

OLDER KID: *Most of the homework lately is our geography
projects . . . and I don't know what to do. I don't know how
to look that stuff up. Plus, don't take this wrong, it's not
that interesting. I got stuck with Uzbekistan, or whatever it's
called.*

ADULT *(still clarifying): That's true, we have been spending a lot
of time on our geography projects. And it sounds like you're
not too interested in the country you were assigned.*

OLDER KID: *Yeah, I mean, I don't really care about Uzbekistan
. . . it's a boring country.*

ADULT *(clarifying further): So we have two things going on:
You're not sure what to do to get your project going, and
you're not too happy with the country you were assigned.*

OLDER KID: *Yep.*

ADULT *(clarifying further still): So help me understand. Are you having trouble getting going because you don't like your country, or would you have difficulty getting going no matter what your country is?*

OLDER KID: *Well, the country I got assigned isn't helping. But you usually let us work with partners on stuff like this, and now I'm on my own. And I don't know where to start . . . or how to look it up.*

ADULT *(Defining the Problem): I think I understand. The thing is, I wanted to have a few projects you did on your own, otherwise it'll always be really hard for you.*

OLDER KID: *Uh-huh.*

ADULT *(Inviting): So I'm wondering if there's a way for us to help you get started on your project and look things up, but do it independently so I can be sure you know how to do it on your own. Do you have any ideas for how we could do that?*

OLDER KID: *You could help me.*

ADULT: *I could help you. But I don't want to do the whole thing for you . . . then you wouldn't be learning how to do it independently.*

OLDER KID: *Yeah, but you could, like, help me make an outline or something, just to get me going. Just so I know what topics I'm supposed to be looking up, so I know where to start.*

ADULT: *We could work on an outline together. You've done this before, so I'm betting you have more ideas than you think you do.*

OLDER KID: *Yeah, but I'm always partnered with Kenneth or Philip, and they know what they're doing.*

ADULT: *So should we work on an outline together?*

OLDER KID: *OK. But what about Uzbekistan?*

ADULT: *I take it you'd like to switch countries.*

OLDER KID: *Can I?*

ADULT: *Well, I don't have an incredible need for you to do Uzbekistan. And you haven't done any work on Uzbekistan*

yet, so it's not like you'll have wasted your time. But I
would like you to do a country in that region because I'm
trying to make sure we have good coverage of the entire
world. Is there another country in that region you'd like
to do?

OLDER KID: *I'll look.*

ADULT: *Just let me know which one you choose so I can make*
sure no one else is doing the same country. And if our
solution about the homework doesn't work, we'll talk
again and make sure we come up with something that does
work.

OLDER KID: *OK.*

If you're thinking that these issues don't have a high degree of difficulty, you're right, although many a major incident has begun with a seemingly minor issue, and hitting other kids isn't so minor. The two kids certainly did a good job of identifying and articulating their concerns, and they sure were good at coming up with solutions (actually, you'll be amazed at the number of kids who take the Plan B ball and run with it when given the chance, and we have the rest of the book to consider those who can't).

If you're also thinking that Plan B can take some time, you'd be right. On average, maybe about five to ten minutes (longer, at least initially, on complicated problems that have gone unresolved for a long time). But the conversations are usually taking place anyway. When you're using Plan B, the conversations are much more productive. You're not telling a kid he's making bad choices (if he *could* make better choices, he *would*). You're not reminding him of more desirable alternative behaviors (if he *could* exhibit these preferred alternative behaviors, he *would*). You're not imposing *your* solutions (that's Plan A). Plan B helps you get the information you need to establish what's getting in the kid's way and helps you solve the problem durably and collaboratively.

Sometimes adults feel they've somehow failed if they don't make their way through all three steps of Plan B on the first try. Don't sweat it. Very difficult problems—actually, even what seem like very simple problems—typically require more than one conversation. If, in your first attempt at Plan B on a chronic, time-consuming problem, you're able to identify the kid's concern, that's a success. Get back to the next two steps tomorrow.

You may have noticed that problems tend to be a little more complicated once you start talking about them, but if we don't talk about them we'll never discover that. You may also have noticed that Plan B always ends with an agreement to talk again if the solution doesn't go as well as hoped. Often the first solution doesn't solve the problem durably. That's not your signal to abandon the Plan B ship, only a sign that the solution you both thought would accomplish the mission probably wasn't as realistic or mutually satisfactory as it may have first seemed (a fairly common circumstance in the course of human affairs!). In life, most good solutions are improvements on prior solutions that didn't quite get the job done.

Now that we've made our way through basic, relatively straightforward Proactive Plan B, let's briefly turn our attention to Emergency B. The main difference between Proactive B and Emergency B is *timing* and the wording of the Empathy step. As regards the former, Emergency B occurs both in the heat of the moment and in front of all the other kids in the class. Doing Emergency B in front of the entire group isn't an unrealistic option, but it depends on your comfort level. Comfortable or not, Emergency B isn't the ideal way to solve problems durably, collaboratively, and reasonably. Nonetheless, you may have need for Emergency B every now and again.

When you're doing Emergency B, the Empathy step involves repeating the kid's concern back to him, sticking closely to his exact words. Some people call this "reflective listening." Here's what this would sound like, using the same characters that were helping us out earlier:

CHILD *(yelling at his classmates): You guys are making me mad!*
ADULT *(Empathy step, kicking off Emergency B): Looks like someone is getting very mad! What's up?*
KID: *I'm not doing this homework project!*

ADULT *(Empathy step, kicking off Emergency B): You're not doing this homework project! What's up?*

If you're a classroom teacher, you're probably wondering whether Emergency B is a viable option if, for example, the child in the first example had already hit one of his classmates. Yes, it is (*"Looks like we have a problem here, what's up?"* or *"Kelvin, you're very upset, what's up?"*). Not to beat a dead horse, but it's important to remember that problems that "suddenly" erupt are typically predictable in the first place, and that Proactive B would have been easier and more productive than Emergency B. Of course, Plan A (*"Stop hitting, now!"* or *"Kelvin, out in the hall, now!"*) is also an option at the moment a problem arises in the classroom, but Plan A does carry the risk of making the situation much worse.

On problems that "suddenly" come to the fore that do not involve safety (*"I'm not doing this assignment!"*), Plan C could also be a viable option (*"Richie, can you hang tight for a few minutes so I can make sure everyone else is set?"*), so long as it's understood that the issue will need to be addressed with the kid at the earliest opportune moment using Proactive Plan B.

Q & A

Question: Speaking of Plan C, are there some challenging kids who are so volatile and unstable that academics need to be deemphasized until things are calmer?

Answer: Absolutely. Some kids simply aren't "available" for academic learning until headway has been made on the challenges that may be impeding learning. In such instances, academics may have to take a backseat until progress occurs on these challenges. Plunging forward with academics when a kid is bogged down with other challenges is usually an exercise in futility.

Question: In the above examples, there was more going on in the Empathy step than just empathy.

Answer: This is an important point to clarify. While challenging kids are certainly deserving of our empathy, the primary goal of the Empathy step is to *gather information* and *achieve the clearest possible understanding of his concern or perspective*. In other words, there is a difference between an empathic statement ("That must feel terrible for you") and a clarifying or information-gathering statement ("I'm a little confused about what you're saying. . . . Can you tell me a little more about that?"). Both are wonderful, but the latter helps you achieve the primary goal.

Question: I don't think I do Plan A that often . . . but I've noticed that I do have a tendency to side step or bypass kids' concerns a lot. Is that the same thing?
Answer: Glad you brought that up. Adults do have a strong tendency to bypass, disregard, or dismiss kids' concerns. Here are some examples of what you may be referring to:

KID: *I don't know how to do this.*
ADULT: *Sounds like someone just needs to try harder.*

KID: *She's bothering me.*
ADULT: *Just ignore her.*

KID: *This is too much for me to do.*
ADULT: *Oh, come on, you can do it!*

KID: *Mr. Trumbull won't listen to me.*
ADULT: *You know, you're going to run into people like him in life, so it's good experience for you to be dealing with it now.*

KID: *This isn't fair!*
ADULT: *Life's not fair.*

These adult responses can have the same effect as Plan A. It's frustrating to have one's concerns dismissed (whether one is a kid or adult), but those who have the skills to handle this frustration tend to respond more adaptively than those who don't have the skills. And, of course, if a kid's concerns aren't identified and taken into account, the problem won't get solved and will simply reappear in short order.

Question: Shouldn't I still be using consequences for challenging behavior—even if I don't think they're working—so the other kids know I'm taking the challenging behavior seriously?
Answer: It's your choice, but the other kids don't need you to use consequences to know you're taking the problem seriously. They need to see that you've got a handle on the challenging kid's lagging skills and unsolved problems and that, slowly but surely, his challenging behaviors are decreasing. You don't improve your credibility by continuing to intervene in a way that isn't working or is making things worse. Remember, consequences are useful for two things: (1) teaching basic lessons about right and wrong, and (2) giving kids the incentive to do well. You'll want to use consequences if you think one or both of these things are coming into play. But, as mentioned earlier, kids with behavioral challenges already know the basic lessons about right and wrong and, because *kids do well if they can,* they already have the incentive to do well.

Question: Should I reward a kid for successfully participating in Plan B?
Answer: I generally recommend against it. The effects of Plan B—finally having one's concerns identified, making headway on getting a problem solved, learning new skills, resolving difficulties without conflict or challenging behavior—these are far more rewarding (and far more important for you and the kid to focus on) than any extrinsic reward you might offer.

Question: So Plan B doesn't undermine a teacher's authority with the other kids in the class?
Answer: Quite the contrary. The other kids are watching us closely. If you intervene in a way that accomplishes the goals delineated at the beginning of this chapter, you'll have done nothing to undermine your authority with the other kids. In fact, don't be surprised if they start asking if you'd begin addressing their problems in the same way.

Question: It's a Plan A world. If we're doing Plan B with a kid, aren't we setting him up for failure?

Answer: First off, don't be so sure it's a Plan A world. In fact, it's worth pondering which skill is most important for life in the "real world": the blind adherence to authority trained with Plan A, or working things out with people in a realistic and mutually satisfactory manner trained with Plan B. I humbly (but predictably) suggest that it's the latter. Second, the reason you're doing Plan B is to teach the kid the skills he lacks so he can handle problems he'll face in the real world, just as you would with any other developmental delay.

Question: For how long do the adults need to do Plan B with a kid?

Answer: Certainly until the high-priority lagging skills have been instilled, the most important unsolved problems are resolved, and the kid's challenging behavior has been dramatically reduced. But as you'll read in Chapter 7, there are many good reasons to keep using Plan B, not just with a specific challenging kid but with everyone in the class.

Question: Is it really fair to expect teachers, who are not trained as mental health professionals, to use Collaborative Problem Solving?

Answer: I don't know what's fair. I do know that teachers already have a lot on their plates. I know that an astounding number of challenging kids are needlessly slipping through the cracks and losing their futures. And I know that a mental health degree is not a prerequisite for using Collaborative Problem Solving. Teachers have always taught nonacademic skills to their students, skills related to handling life's social, emotional, and behavioral challenges. It's just that some kids and some challenges require that teachers have a different mind-set and skill-set. What are the key qualifications for helping kids with behavioral challenges? An open mind, a willingness to reflect on one's current practices and try on new lenses, the courage to experiment with new practices, and the patience and resolve to become comfortable with using the ALSUP and Plan B. If it makes you feel any better, most mental health professionals don't have training in Collaborative Problem Solving, either.

Question: It seems like you think teachers should be all things to all kids.

Answer: Not so, but this is a group of kids you could really help.

Question: Are you telling me I have to adjust what I'm doing for every kid I teach?

Answer: Not every kid—just the ones who are having trouble meeting your expectations.

The Story Continues . . .

"Is he here yet?" Mrs. Franco stuck her head inside Mrs. Woods' classroom after school on Friday afternoon.

Mrs. Woods looked up from writing comments on a student's paper. "No, not yet. Seems to be a pattern."

"Gotta feel for the man, though," said Mrs. Franco. "Apparently he's covering three schools. That's a lot of kids." Mrs. Franco spotted Dr. Bridgman walking briskly toward her. "Wait, here he is now."

"Good afternoon, ladies," said Dr. Bridgman. "Sorry I'm late. This still a good time?"

The two teachers nodded.

"Good, because I was thinking that it might be a good idea for Ms. Lowell to bring Joey in early Monday morning to meet with me and Mrs. Woods, and I want to make sure we're ready."

"Ready for what?" asked Mrs. Woods.

"Well, like we discussed, it would be good to talk with Joey about what to do the next time he gets confused about an assignment," said Dr. Bridgman. "You know, so it doesn't turn into a mess."

"That would be good," said Mrs. Woods. "So, what's he supposed to do?"

"We don't know—we haven't done Plan B with him yet," said Dr. Bridgman.

"Ah, yes, you mentioned this Plan B thing the other day," said Mrs. Woods. "I'm looking forward to watching you do it."

"Oh, um, we'll need you to do more than just watch," said Dr. Bridgman. "See, it's you and Joey who have to agree on a solution."

"Darn, you get to have all the fun," smiled Mrs. Franco.

Dr. Bridgman explained Plans A, B, and C, along with the three steps—Empathy, Define the Problem, and the Invitation—of doing Plan B. He also distinguished between Emergency B and Proactive B, and described the advantages of the latter. When he finished, he asked, "So should we give it a quick run-through? Because eventually it won't be me solving these problems with him, it should be you both."

Mrs. Franco looked at Mrs. Woods and laughed. "He's trying to turn us into psychologists."

"Oh, you don't have to be a psychologist to do Plan B," insisted Dr. Bridgman. "You probably do Plan B all the time with your husbands."

Mrs. Franco laughed again. "I don't work things out with my husband. I just tell him what to do."

"So let's think about what Plan B might look like with Joey on Monday," continued Dr. Bridgman. "The first step is Empathy . . . that's where we're trying to get Joey's concern on the table, trying to understand. If we're doing Proactive B, we're making an observation. Probably something like, 'We've noticed that you sometimes aren't sure what to do on some of your assignments.' But we don't know *why* Joey's not sure what to do. So we have to ask him. By saying something like, 'What's up?'"

"So what's he going to say?" asked Mrs. Woods.

"Beats me," said Dr. Bridgman.

"Well, if *you* don't know what's up, then how are *we* supposed to know what's up?" asked Mrs. Franco.

"We need to see what Joey says," said Dr. Bridgman.

"What if he doesn't know?" asked Mrs. Woods.

"We'll put our heads together and figure it out," said Dr. Bridgman. "Based on our conversation yesterday, we do have some theories."

"We do?" asked Mrs. Woods.

"Yes, I'm betting this has something to do with some of the skills he's lacking—you know, the ones we talked about the other day—although I'm open to any information Joey might give us about this problem. But our goal with the Empathy step is to achieve the clearest possible understanding of what's going on with Joey as it relates to his confusion over assignments. Then comes the Define the Problem step. That's where you get your concern on the table."

"My concern," Mrs. Woods looked uncertain.

"Yes, what's your concern about him blowing up and running out of your classroom?"

"Well, he just can't do that," said Mrs. Woods. "It's just not OK."

"Yes, but what's your *concern*?" asked Dr. Bridgman.

Mrs. Woods looked a bit perplexed. "You mean . . . like . . . that he'll get suspended again?"

"That's what's going to *happen* to him if he blows up again," said Dr. Bridgman. "But I don't know if that's your primary concern."

"You mean that it's not safe?" said Mrs. Woods, looking to Mrs. Franco for help. Mrs. Franco shrugged.

"Sure, that's a concern," encouraged Dr. Bridgman. "It's not safe, and we don't want anyone getting hurt, and it's scary for you and the other kids."

"So those are my concerns," said Mrs. Woods tentatively.

"I think so," said Dr. Bridgman.

"OK, so now we've told him my concerns," said Mrs. Woods.

Dr. Bridgman nodded. "Good. Next we invite him to solve the problem with us, and we'll give him the first crack at a solution. So you'll hear me saying something like, 'I wonder if there's a way for us to help you when you get confused about an assignment so you don't get so upset about it?'"

"What if he doesn't have any ideas?" asked Mrs. Franco. "He says 'I don't know' a lot."

"We'll help him come up with a solution," said Dr. Bridgman.

"So what's the solution?" asked Mrs. Woods.

"We don't know that yet, either," said Dr. Bridgman. "Something realistic and mutually satisfactory."

"We don't know the solution?" asked Mrs. Franco. "You're expecting Joey to tell us?" She cast a skeptical glance at Mrs. Woods.

"Well, if we already know the solution then we're not involving Joey in crafting the solution," said Dr. Bridgman. "Of course, if he doesn't have any ideas, we can offer some possibilities."

The two teachers were silent.

"How does that sound?" asked Dr. Bridgman.

"I'm glad you're doing this," said Mrs. Woods. "I mean, I'm just not accustomed to doing things this way."

"It does take some getting used to," said Dr. Bridgman. "But you probably don't teach reading the same way you did ten years ago, either. Plan A hasn't given Joey the kind of help he needs. And Plan C isn't going to give us the information we're looking for or help us solve the problem. Which leaves us only one option: Plan B. Why don't I call Ms. Lowell and see if she can bring Joey in early on Monday."

Joey was watching his late-afternoon TV shows on Friday. His mom approached him warily. "Joey, sorry to interrupt your TV show, but I need to talk about what's going to happen on Monday."

Joey didn't look away from the TV. "Later."

"Not later. This is more important than TV."

Joey ignored her.

"Joey, we need to talk about it," his mom repeated.

"What's the big deal?!" he snapped. "Why not after my show?!"

"What's the big deal? You get suspended from school for a week and you want to know what the big deal is?!"

Joey's eyes were glued to the television.

"Listen, Joey, you're going back to school on Monday and I need to make sure you don't blow it. I don't know how many chances you've got left, buddy."

The phone rang and Ms. Lowell went into the kitchen to answer it, making little effort to hide her agitation. "Hello."

"Ms. Lowell, it's Carl Bridgman. If this is a bad time . . ."

"Dr. Bridgman. Funny you should call. Joey and I were just talking about him coming back to school. Or at least trying to."

"That's exactly why I'm calling," said Dr. Bridgman. "I'd like to see if we can set the stage for him to do well when he comes back. I've had a conversation with Mrs. Woods and Mrs. Franco, and they've filled me in on the things that seem to be giving Joey the most trouble. I'm wondering if there's any chance of your getting Joey to school a little early on Monday. I'd like him to sit down with me and Mrs. Woods to come up with an action plan so he's less likely to get so upset again."

"What time do you want him?"

"Can you have him there about a half-hour early?"

"Yes, I think so. Anything I ought to know about your meeting with his teachers?"

"Well, we tried to get a handle on the skills Joey's lacking that might be setting the stage for his worst moments. But we pretty much decided that we're going to start off by trying to figure out why he gets confused on assignments, since that's what seems to have set him off the other day."

"Oh, OK. Um, Dr. Bridgman?"

"Yes."

There was a pause. "There's hope for him, right?"

"Hope? Yes, of course. I think we're going to get a good plan in place for him."

Joey's mom felt her voice catching. "He's not going to end up in jail someday . . . or some mental institution . . . right?"

Dr. Bridgman had heard this question from many parents before. He had a fairly standard answer. "Not if we do the right thing now."

"And you think we're doing the right thing?"

"Yes, I do."

"Thank you," she said as she placed the phone on the receiver.

"That's what we're here for," Dr. Bridgman said to himself.

Mrs. Galvin invited Dr. Bridgman into her office as he was leaving school on Friday afternoon. "Mr. Middleton is going to join us," she said.

Mr. Middleton entered the office just after Dr. Bridgman. "I found your comments about Joey very interesting yesterday," said the assistant principal.

"Oh, good," Dr. Bridgman sat down. "He's an interesting kid."

"Aren't they all," said Mr. Middleton.

"I was wondering," began Mrs. Galvin, sitting down behind her desk, "about the reentry plan for Joey. Actually, I think you called it a 'staying in school' plan. I must say, your ideas about problem kids are a little new to me. Where did you come up with them?"

"Oh, it's not me who came up with them," said Dr. Bridgman. "Developmental psychologists have been writing about the skills kids need for handling life's challenges for quite a while, but it can take a long time for what we've learned about kids' brains to translate into how we help them."

"Yes, I suppose it can," said Mrs. Galvin. "I'm very interested to hear about how what we know about Joey's brain is going to help him not threaten his classmates or hurt our assistant principal anymore. As you know, our standard practice is to have the student and his parents sign a contract agreeing not to do anything unsafe again. But I have the impression that you don't necessarily agree with what we usually do."

"I'm just not convinced that what's usually done is going to fix the problem," said Dr. Bridgman.

Mr. Middleton cleared his throat and shifted in his chair. Mrs. Galvin leaned across her desk toward Dr. Bridgman.

"Dr. Bridgman, I have to apologize," said the principal. "I don't really know very much about you. I don't even know where you worked before you came to our school system this year. Have you ever worked with kids like Joey?"

"I was at a middle school in an inner-city school system," said Dr. Bridgman. "I've worked with some very difficult kids."

"Difficult like Joey?" asked Mrs. Galvin, glancing over at Mr. Middleton.

"Oh, to be perfectly honest, Joey's not all that difficult."

"Mr. Middleton's jaw would beg to differ," said Mrs. Galvin stiffly. "I suspect the young lady Joey threatened to kill and her parents would beg to differ, too."

"Oh, I'm not saying . . ." started Dr. Bridgman. "It's just that, well, I'm not really comparing, but in my last few schools I've worked with some kids who were in pretty bad shape. A few brought guns to school because they didn't feel safe in the building. Some others pulled knives on their teachers. Several were pregnant, or had some pretty serious substance use problems . . . at some very young ages. Some couldn't come to school because they had to stay home to watch their younger siblings. And quite a few were already in trouble with the law—at ages ten and eleven— because they were involved in gangs or had to steal food or sell drugs to buy food. So I guess that's my way of saying that I've worked with a lot of troubled kids."

"Dr. Bridgman, in this school we have rules and we make sure that our students follow them," said Mrs. Galvin. "When students don't follow the rules, they are sent a very strong message. Believe me, I get sent a strong message by my superiors and by parents if I don't keep all the students in my school, and my teachers, and my assistant principal, safe. And I get sent a strong message if the students in my school don't learn what they are supposed to learn. If Joey is making my school unsafe or interfering with the learning that is supposed to be going on in this building, my job is to hold him accountable. I'm assuming that makes sense to you."

"It does," said Dr. Bridgman.

"Ah, good," said Mrs. Galvin, her posture relaxing. "So, why don't you draw up a reentry contract and have Joey and his mother sign it so we can get him back to class and back to learning."

"Getting him back to class isn't the problem," said Dr. Bridgman. "Helping him stay there without more incidents is going to be a problem. I don't think a reentry contract is going to solve that problem."

Mrs. Galvin stiffened again. "Dr. Bridgman, perhaps I'm not making myself—"

"Um, Dr. Bridgman," interjected Mr. Middleton, "is there something else you think would work better?"

"Don't get me wrong," said Dr. Bridgman. "If you tell me Joey and his mother have to sign a reentry contract, I'll have them do it. But I'd rather put my energy—and everyone else's—into doing something that will actually work."

"Yes, that's what I'm asking," urged Mr. Middleton. "What do you think will work?"

"Well, I've already met with him, and his mother, and Mrs. Woods and Mrs. Franco. So I think we have a pretty good sense about where we want to start."

"And where's that?" asked Mrs. Galvin.

"We're pretty sure that he gets set off when he doesn't understand an assignment or gets embarrassed, so we'll start by trying to solve those problems."

Mrs. Galvin had trouble hiding her skepticism. "Dr. Bridgman, in real life people get embarrassed, and they don't always understand tasks they've been assigned. But they don't threaten their classmates or run out of the school. Joey's going to have to learn how to deal with things not going according to his plan if he's going to succeed in the real world."

"Yes, exactly," said Dr. Bridgman.

"So we agree," said Mrs. Galvin.

"Well, we seem to agree on *what* he needs to work on," said Dr. Bridgman. "But I'm not sure we agree on *how* to do it."

"How do you think we should go about helping him do it?" asked Mr. Middleton.

"Mostly through Collaborative Problem Solving," said Dr. Bridgman.
The principal and assistant principal glanced at each other.

"Excuse me, what?" asked Mrs. Galvin.

"Collaborative Problem Solving," said Dr. Bridgman. "It's where we adults try to work with Joey to come up with solutions to the problems that are causing him difficulty."

"And how exactly does one do Collaborative Problem Solving?" asked Mrs. Galvin.

"Well, there are some specific steps," said Dr. Bridgman. "First, you make sure you understand the kid's concern or perspective about whatever is causing him difficulty. That's called the Empathy step. Then the adults make sure the kid understands their concerns. That's called Define the Problem. Then you invite the kid to brainstorm solutions so as to come up with a realistic, mutually satisfactory solution, one that addresses both concerns. That's called the Invitation. Probably sounds confusing, but it's pretty straightforward."

There was another long pause as Mrs. Galvin processed this additional information. "Dr. Bridgman, I've been in this business a long time. I've seen many fads come and go when it comes to disciplining kids. I hope you'll understand if I'm not all that enthusiastic about having the flavor of the month upsetting the apple cart in my school."

Dr. Bridgman paused. "Helping Joey learn how to solve problems and deal better with frustration isn't the flavor of the month. If we teach him those things, then he won't be upsetting the apple cart anymore."

"So this Collaborative Problem Solving is something you'll be doing with Joey so he doesn't blow up anymore?" asked Mr. Middleton.

"Well, yes, I'm certainly happy to get the ball rolling," said Dr. Bridgman. "But for it to really be effective, it's something Mrs. Woods and Mrs. Franco and those who spend the most time with him need to be doing."

Mrs. Galvin closed her eyes and sighed deeply. She glanced at her watch. "And you think my teachers, with everything else they have going on, have time to do problem-solving in a class of twenty-six students?" asked Mrs. Galvin.

"Oh, Collaborative Problem Solving ends up saving time," said Dr. Bridgman. "It certainly takes a lot less time than when we do things that aren't working and Joey loses it."

"And do Mrs. Woods and Mrs. Franco know how to do this?" asked Mrs. Galvin.

"Well, I've explained it. But I'll help them."

"And you don't think Joey needs to have our expectations spelled out for him in no uncertain terms?" asked Mrs. Galvin.

"Joey already knows he's supposed to do what Mrs. Woods says, not threaten to kill his classmates, and not run out of the building."

"And you don't think he needs to be taught that we won't accept that kind of behavior?" asked Mrs. Galvin.

"He already knows we don't accept that kind of behavior," said Dr. Bridgman. "If I may be so bold, I think it's a real shame that all Joey has ever gotten from adults is consequences that don't teach him the skills he lacks or solve the problems that continue to precipitate his challenging behavior."

"Well, that is a bit bold," chuckled Mrs. Galvin, finding herself becoming a bit more intrigued by the ideas and determination of the large man sitting in her office. "Especially since I'm one of those adults who've been using consequences on him."

"I'm sorry if my comments offend you."

Mrs. Galvin smiled. "No offense taken. I may be a bit stuck in my ways, but that doesn't mean I'm completely closed to new ideas. Isn't that right, Mr. Middleton?"

Mr. Middleton nodded. "She has a heart of gold."

"I'll tell you what, Dr. Bridgman," said Mrs. Galvin. "I don't know you very well yet, and I'm not completely comfortable with your way of thinking. But you're our school psychologist, not me, and I can tell you want to do the right thing by Joey and by my teachers. I'm willing to give you some rope on this one. I just hope it's not enough for you to hang us both."

"I can't promise that Joey won't blow up again," said Dr. Bridgman.

"Well, as I think about it now, I wouldn't have been able to promise that a reentry plan would have kept him from blowing up again, either," said Mrs. Galvin. "So we're even on that score. But what happens next?"

"Joey and Mrs. Woods and I are going to do some Collaborative Problem Solving."

*   *   *

Monday morning. Joey and his mother were seated at the kitchen table.

"How come we're going to school so early today?" Joey asked.

"Because Dr. Bridgman and Mrs. Woods want to talk with you to make sure you don't explode again."

Joey looked up from his bowl of cereal. "I don't want to talk about that."

"Look, Joey, you're not in trouble. They just want to help you."

"I don't need any help," Joey grumbled.

"Well, I think you're getting their help whether you want it or not."

Surprises were not Joey's forte. "How come you didn't tell me about this before?! I'm not doing it!"

Ms. Lowell was now regretting that she hadn't tried to talk with Joey about the meeting since her failed attempt on Friday.

Joey's brother, Jason, overheard the conversation and offered his two cents. "Hey, doofus, if you don't talk to them about it they'll toss your butt out of the school!"

"Jason, I don't need you—"

"Well, they will!" Jason interrupted. "Some of the kids were saying Joey doesn't belong in our school."

"Jason, go get in the car and let me talk to Joey," ordered Ms. Lowell. "Now!"

Jason flicked his brother's ear, said "Bye, doofus," and went out to the car.

"Loser," Joey muttered.

"Joey, honey, I know you don't want to talk about what happened," said Ms. Lowell. "But Dr. Bridgman wants to come up with a plan so you don't get so upset again."

"I don't need a plan. I can do it myself."

"Joey, I don't see the harm in letting him and Mrs. Woods help out with the plan. You liked Dr. Bridgman. And you kind of like Mrs. Woods, too. They're not mad at you. They just want to help."

Joey didn't respond.

"Can we please try?" urged Ms. Lowell.

"I don't want to."

"I know you don't want to. But can we please try?"

"Fine!" said Joey. "But I'm not saying anything!"

"That's fine," said Ms. Lowell. "But maybe you could at least listen to what they have to say."

Ms. Lowell issued a warning as she climbed into the car. "Jason, you give him a hard time in this car and you can kiss your PlayStation goodbye. For a month."

The three rode to school in silence.

At school, Ms. Lowell walked Joey to the door. "You want me to come in with you?" she asked.

"No," said Joey.

Dr. Bridgman had been waiting for Joey just inside and opened the door. "Hi, Joey," he said. "Welcome back."

Joey didn't reply.

"Let's go chat a little with Mrs. Woods."

Joey shuffled into his classroom with Dr. Bridgman, head down, and Mrs. Woods rose to greet him. "Hi, Joey, we missed you."

"Mmm hmm," said Joey, looking down at his hands.

Dr. Bridgman guided Joey to a table. "Have a seat, Joey. Let's talk. Mrs. Woods and I wanted to see if we could try to come up with a plan so that what happened last time you were in her class doesn't happen again. Do you think that's a good idea?"

"Mmm hmm."

"From what you told me, the reason you got so upset was because you didn't understand an assignment," said Dr. Bridgman, easing his way into the Empathy step. "And then you got embarrassed in front of the other kids. Is that about right?"

"Mmm hmm."

"I'm sorry I embarrassed you, Joey," said Mrs. Woods. "I didn't realize I was upsetting you."

Joey looked up. "I didn't mean to hurt anyone," he mumbled. "It was an accident."

"I know that," Mrs. Woods said softly.

Dr. Bridgman returned to Joey's concern. "Joey, you get confused about how to do assignments a lot, yes?"

"Yes," said Joey.

"Can you remember what was confusing about the social studies assignment the day that you got upset?" asked Mrs. Woods.

"It wasn't the same," said Joey.

"I'm not sure what you mean," said Mrs. Woods. She looked to Dr. Bridgman for help.

"Can you tell us what you mean that it wasn't the same?" asked Dr. Bridgman, trying to clarify Joey's concern.

"You told us you wanted us to do a report on the natural resources of the state we picked," Joey began, "and you said it should be just like the report we did on the population of the state . . . but the population is not the same thing as the natural resources. So it wasn't the same."

Mrs. Woods was still confused. "So, when I told you to write a report just like the one on the population, you couldn't do it because even though it was the same state, and the same kind of report, the topic was different?"

"It's not the same kind of report," Joey insisted. "It was about the natural resources, not the population. I didn't know how to do that. They're not the same thing."

Dr. Bridgman was intrigued. "What state did you pick, Joey?"

"Alaska."

"And the first paper you wrote was about the population of Alaska?"

"Uh-huh."

"And then you were supposed to write the same kind of report about the natural resources, but that was confusing for you because the population is not the same thing as the natural resources?"

"Yes. It's not the same."

Mrs. Woods was still a bit perplexed. "Joey, when I said 'the same,' I just meant the same *type* of report—you know, three or four paragraphs—even though the topics were different. Do you understand?"

"No."

Mrs. Woods tried to explain. "Topics are one thing . . . how I want you to show me what you've learned is different."

"You said it should be the same."

"Yes, I understand that was confusing for you," said Mrs. Woods. "But do you understand that I meant the same type of *report* and not the same *topic*?"

"Um, I guess, but . . ." Joey looked uncomfortable continuing.

"But what, Joey?" Dr. Bridgman encouraged.

Joey looked concerned. "I don't want to say anything that isn't, um, the right thing to say."

"If it helps us understand why you were confused, I bet it's OK," said Dr. Bridgman.

Joey looked at Mrs. Woods and took a deep breath. "You didn't say you meant the report and not the topic, and plus, there's more to write about the natural resources, so it couldn't be the same length, either."

"Joey, can it be the same type of report—you know, writing some paragraphs—even if one report is longer than the other?" asked Dr. Bridgman.

"She said three or four paragraphs," said Joey.

Mrs. Woods looked at Dr. Bridgman. "He's right, I did." Then she looked at Joey. "But, Joey, it would have been fine if you needed to write more than that. I just meant three or four paragraphs as a general guide."

"Do you understand what Mrs. Woods means by 'general guide,' Joey?" asked Dr. Bridgman.

"No."

Dr. Bridgman thought it might be best to move the Empathy step along. "So, Joey, you sometimes get confused about the directions on some assignments, especially if it's not exactly the same as something else you've done. Yes?"

"I think so."

"And that makes it hard for you to start working on the assignment, because you're confused about what to do, yes?"

"Uh-huh."

Dr. Bridgman added some reassurance before continuing with the Define the Problem step: "We're not saying you shouldn't get confused. And I think you've helped us understand why you get confused. Our concern is that, because you weren't working on your assignment, you were disturbing the other students around you."

"All I was doing was asking Blake what to do," said Joey. "But he wouldn't tell me. He told me to figure it out myself."

Dr. Bridgman continued with the Invitation. "I wonder if there's some plan you and Mrs. Woods could come up with to let her know you're confused, so you don't disturb the other kids around you. Do you have any ideas about that?"

Joey pondered the question. "I don't know."

"Take your time," said Dr. Bridgman. "If you don't have any ideas, Mrs. Woods or I might have some."

There was another pause. "You could explain the assignments I'm not going to understand ahead of time," said Joey.

"Joey, I'm not sure I'm going to know ahead of time which assignments you're not going to understand," said Mrs. Woods.

"Well, at least you don't have to embarrass me," mumbled Joey.

"You mean it would be good if Mrs. Woods and you figured out a way for her to explain things to you that isn't embarrassing?" asked Dr. Bridgman.

Another pause. "Yeah," said Joey.

Dr. Bridgman seemed pleased with the course the conversation was now taking. Mrs. Woods wasn't so sure. How could she figure out what was going to be confusing to Joey and then explain things without embarrassing him?

"Mrs. Woods, could you do that?" said Dr. Bridgman.

Mrs. Woods was still considering the feasibility of such an arrangement. "Let me make sure I understand. If there's an assignment or project that's going to be confusing for you, you want me to let you know ahead of time. Is that what you mean, Joey?"

"Yeah. And if I don't understand it you could explain it to me. Without everybody seeing us."

"I'm trying to think of when we would do that, Joey," said Mrs. Woods. "And I think I need a better idea of when things are going to be confusing for you. Do you have any ideas for how I could know that?" She looked to Dr. Bridgman again, hoping she'd made a proper Invitation. He smiled his approval.

"I could come in before school," said Joey.

Mrs. Woods was again considering whether this was feasible. "You could come early," said Mrs. Woods. "Can your mom bring you in early?"

"I don't know," said Joey, looking at Dr. Bridgman. "But she sometimes brings my brother early to work with Mr. Armstrong."

"So let's assume she can bring you in early," said Dr. Bridgman. "I'll check with her."

Dr. Bridgman could see the look of concern on Mrs. Woods' face. "I think Mrs. Woods still has some concerns. Yes?"

"Well, there is one more problem," she said. She looked at Joey. "I'm a little concerned about what will happen if I miss one. What if there's an assignment and I don't realize it's confusing for you and so I don't explain it to you before school? Or what if it's a day you couldn't come in early? What then?"

"Joey, is there some way you could let Mrs. Woods know you're confused that wouldn't embarrass you in front of the other kids?" asked Dr. Bridgman.

"I don't know," said Joey.

Mrs. Woods and Joey both looked to Dr. Bridgman for help.

Dr. Bridgman pursed his lips. "That's a tough one. Joey, what do you think would be the best way for you to let Mrs. Woods know if you're confused?"

"We could have a signal."

"What kind of signal?" asked Dr. Bridgman.

"I could scratch my nose. I saw that on TV once."

"That's an interesting idea," said Dr. Bridgman. "So if you wanted to let Mrs. Woods know you're confused, you could scratch your nose?"

"Yeah."

"Mrs. Woods, how would that work for you?" asked Dr. Bridgman.

"I think that would work fine," said Mrs. Woods. "Actually, if I see Joey not doing his work, from now on I'm going to assume he's confused. But the nose scratching would help, too. Now there's one more thing I'm not too clear about."

"What's that?" asked Dr. Bridgman.

"What's supposed to happen if I know Joey's confused but he doesn't want me to explain it right then, because that would embarrass him in front of his classmates?" asked Mrs. Woods.

"Ah, good question," said Dr. Bridgman. "What do you think, Joey?"

"I don't know," said Joey.

"That's kind of what happened the other day," said Dr. Bridgman. "We're trying to make sure we don't find ourselves in that same situation again, you know, by having you come into school early, and by having you scratch your nose. But we do need a plan for what to do if it does happen again. Any ideas?"

Joey began shifting in his seat. Mrs. Woods could see that he was starting to tire of the conversation. "I have an idea," she said. "Joey, let's see if you like my idea. If you don't like it we'll come up with something else. How about we keep some assignments in your notebook that we're sure you can do. If you get confused about something we're doing in class, you could take out one of the assignments you know how to do and do that instead until we have a chance to talk about the assignment that's confusing. What do you think?"

"What if the other kids notice that I'm not doing the right assignment?" asked Joey.

"I'll let them know that you're doing a special assignment for me," said Mrs. Woods. "Would that be OK?"

"I guess," said Joey.

"Well, we want to be sure the solution works for you, Joey. What do you think?"

"We could try it," said Joey.

"OK, then let's wrap this up," said Dr. Bridgman. "Joey, you did a great job in this meeting. Thanks for helping us come up with a plan."

"OK," said Joey.

"Let me just say what I think our plan is," said Dr. Bridgman. "Joey, you're going to try to come in early so Mrs. Woods can tell you about the assignments for the day and explain them to you if you're confused about anything. And if you still get confused about an assignment during class, you're going to give Mrs. Woods the signal so she knows you're confused. And if it's not a good time for Mrs. Woods to explain the assignment to you, you'll do some other work and she'll explain it to you later. Sound OK to both of you?"

Joey and Mrs. Woods nodded.

"Will I get a lower grade if I don't do one of the assignments I'm confused about until later?" asked Joey.

"No," said Mrs. Woods. "I know you try really hard to get all your work done. We'll find another time for you to do it."

Joey suddenly became conscious of the time. "Aren't the other kids coming in soon?"

"Yes, in about five minutes," said Mrs. Woods. "You'd prefer they not see us talking?"

"Yeah."

"Why don't you go back out to where the other kids are," said Dr. Bridgman.

After Joey had left, Dr. Bridgman checked in with Mrs. Woods. "How do you feel that went?" asked Dr. Bridgman.

"I'm still digesting," said Mrs. Woods. "It's the most he's ever talked about anything."

"Plan B has a way of doing that," said Dr. Bridgman. "Do you think the solutions we all came up with make sense?"

"We'll see," said Mrs. Woods, as she turned her thoughts to the impending arrival of all her students. "We'll see."

CHAPTER 5

Bumps in the Road

You've been given a lot to digest already, and there's much more to cover about Plan B, but you're ready for your first homework assignment (due date: your call, but preferably sooner rather than later). Complete the ALSUP for a specific challenging kid. Pick a specific unsolved problem as the focus of your first attempt at Plan B with that kid. Which unsolved problem should you pick? Perhaps one that is causing the kid's challenging behavior most often or setting the stage for his worst moments. Perhaps one that is causing significant disruption to the learning of the other kids. Perhaps one on which you think you have the greatest chance of early success. You'll get to the rest later. Arrange a good time for Proactive B. Give some thought to the words you'll use for the Empathy step. Be prepared to be flexible as you make your way through the Empathy step. Remember, your goal is to gather information and understand the concern that is setting the stage for challenging behavior. Also think about how you'll go about communicating your concern, and how the Invitation is a recap of the two concerns (the kid's and yours) that have been identified. Next, *go for it*. Do Plan B.

Then try to figure out what went wrong.

First attempts at Plan B often don't go very well. You're new at it; the kid's new at it, too. Creating a helping relationship and using Plan B effectively takes time, practice, and perseverance. So hang in there. It can take a while to get into what we'll call a "Plan B rhythm." If you ran into trouble, here are the common patterns that can interfere with successful implementation of Plan B.

YOU USED PLAN A
INSTEAD OF PLAN B

The most common reason adults didn't do Plan B is because they were busy doing Plan A. Sometimes that's because they had no intention of doing Plan B in the first place. But, more often, adults revert to Plan A because they got stuck somewhere in the midst of doing Plan B—frequently because they're not exactly sure what to say, especially as they begin trying to clarify a kid's concerns—and simply returned to something more familiar. Luckily, with the pressure for adults to be geniuses now removed, there's no need for you to figure things out all on your own. In other words, confusion and uncertainty are permitted. If you're uncertain about what the kid is trying to tell you, ask for clarification. He may be confused himself (again, this may be the first time anyone's ever asked him what his concerns are, so the information may not be on the tip of his tongue), in which case the Empathy step represents a great opportunity to get things sorted out.

Adults may also revert to Plan A in the midst of Plan B because they're more focused on their own concern than on the kid's concern. Now, maybe it's just human nature to be more focused on your own concern than that of another person. And many adults have had a lot of practice having their concerns ignored or dismissed in childhood and adolescence and are simply perpetuating the cycle. But it doesn't need to be that way. When you're using Plan B you're as focused on clarifying and addressing the kid's concern as you are on clarifying and addressing your own concern.

PERFUNCTORY EMPATHY

This problem was mentioned in the last chapter, but it's probably a good idea to spend more time on it. Perfunctory Empathy is the tendency to rush through the Empathy step as quickly as possible, which has the effect of preventing adults from understanding the kid's concern or perspective. Thus, instead of fully clarifying the kid's concern, a "low-quality concern" is entered into consideration. The problem: *Vague concerns lead to vague solutions.* If the kid's concerns are not well-specified, it's unlikely that the eventual solution will address his specific concerns.

Many adults find it hard to stay patient in the Empathy step. But the goal is not to get the conversation over within a nanosecond (again, a good reason to be using Proactive B rather than Emergency B). Problems that get solved in a nanosecond usually aren't durably solved. It's important to remember a crucial idea that was mentioned in the last chapter: You're not done with the Empathy step until you have the clearest possible understanding of the kid's concern or perspective. When you're in the Empathy step, you're in information-seeking mode.

Need an example of Perfunctory Empathy? Here goes:

ADULT *(using Proactive B): Tanya, I've noticed that you don't seem too enthusiastic about going out for recess lately.*

TANYA: *Yup.*

ADULT: *So what's up?*

TANYA: *I just don't want to go out.*

ADULT *(prematurely jumping into the Define the Problem step): OK, so you don't want to go out for recess. The thing is, I don't mind you staying in with me every once in a while, but sometimes I have things to do outside the classroom while the class is at recess, and so there wouldn't be anyone to watch you. Do you understand?*

TANYA: *Uh-huh.*

ADULT *(moving on to the Invitation): I wonder what we can do about the fact that you don't want to go out for recess and I can't always have you stay in with me? Do you have any ideas?*

You might be thinking that this example wasn't so awful. No, it wasn't awful, but the adult doesn't really understand Tanya's concern about going out to recess, so it's highly unlikely that Tanya's concern will be addressed.

You pretty much know whether you've done a good job of identifying and clarifying concerns when you arrive at the Invitation. If, in the midst of the Invitation, you find yourself summarizing concerns that are not yet specific enough, what should you do? Backtrack. Go back to the concerns that aren't specific enough and clarify further. Let's see what that would look like.

ADULT *(using Proactive B): Tanya, I've noticed that you don't seem too enthusiastic about going out for recess lately.*

TANYA: *Yup.*

ADULT: *So what's up?*

TANYA: *I just don't want to go out.*

ADULT *(prematurely jumping into the Define the Problem step): OK, so you don't want to go out for recess. The thing is, I don't mind you staying in with me every once in a while, but sometimes I have things to do outside the classroom while the class is at recess, and so there wouldn't be anyone to watch you. Do you understand?*

TANYA: *Uh-huh.*

ADULT *(moving on to the Invitation, then backtracking): So, I wonder what we can do about the fact that you don't want to go out for recess and . . . wait a second. I don't think I really understand why you don't want to go out for recess. Can you help me understand that better? Do you know why you don't want to go out?*

TANYA: *Um, kinda.*

ADULT: *Can you tell me what it is?*

TANYA: *Well, I'm not supposed to.*

ADULT: *Hmm. Sounds pretty important. How come you're not supposed to?*

TANYA: *Can't say that, either.*

ADULT: *Tanya, did someone tell you not to talk about these things?*

TANYA *(nods)*

ADULT: *Is it one of the kids in our class?*
TANYA *(nods)*
ADULT: *OK, I don't need to know who, but what did they say would happen if you told me?*
TANYA: *I would get hurt.*
ADULT: *So if you tell me why you don't want to go out for recess, you're worried that someone will hurt you?*
TANYA *(nods)*

Looks like there's more going on in recess than Perfunctory Empathy will reveal. Take your time. There are important concerns to be uncovered.

The adult tendency to rush through or pay short shrift to the Empathy step is aggravated by the fact that, as mentioned in Chapter 4, many kids don't know what their concerns are. Because kids are accustomed to having their concerns dismissed, it's possible they haven't given the matter much thought. They may need some help figuring out what their concerns are, and your best strategy here would be *educated guessing,* or what some might call hypothesis testing. Your powers of observation and recollection of past instances in which the child (or others) had a similar problem should serve you well here. Plus, there are a finite number of concerns or problems that might be associated with a given unmet expectation. For example, there are probably a half dozen or so concerns or problems that might be interfering with homework completion; the same number of concerns or problems that might make it hard for a kid to sit through circle time; and a similar number of concerns or problems that might be impeding a kid's ability to get started on class assignments.

Also, consistent with what you read a few paragraphs ago, bear in mind that your educated guesses are *tentative hypotheses.* You want to make sure it's the *kid's* concerns, and not your presuppositions, that are entered into consideration. If your educated guess is on the money or even close, kids will usually find a way to let you know. And they'll let you know if your guess is off base, too.

ADULT *(initiating Proactive Plan B): I've noticed that sometimes you have trouble sitting in circle time. What's up?*

CHILD: *I don't know.*

ADULT: *You don't? Take your time. There's no rush. Think about it a little. What's hard for you about circle time?*

CHILD: *I don't know.*

ADULT: *Well, I might have some ideas about that, but I want to hear your ideas first.*

CHILD *(shrugs)*

ADULT: *Well, I've noticed that you don't have too much trouble in the beginning of circle time, but it gets harder for you the longer you have to sit. Do you think that could be part of the problem?*

CHILD *(if we're lucky):* Yes.

ADULT *(reempathizing so as to get the kid's concern on the table):* *So it's very hard for you to sit in the circle for a long time. Is there anything else that's hard for you about circle time?*

CHILD: *I don't know.*

ADULT: *Well, sometimes it seems like you find it more interesting to talk to the kids sitting next to you about things that are different than what we're talking about in the group. Do you think that could be part of the problem, too?*

CHILD: *Um—no. I think what we're talking about in the group is interesting. I think I just start talking about other stuff when I have trouble sitting for a long time.*

ADULT *(same routine as above):* Ah, I think I understand. So if we did something about how long you have to sit, you'd find it easier to stick with whatever the group is talking about?

CHILD: *Right.*

Some adults also have a tendency to conclude that a kid's concerns aren't "accurate," but it's important to be open to the possibility that your own assumptions about the kid's concerns are inaccurate. There are basically two mistakes you can make:

1. assume the kid's concerns are on target when there's a chance they're not, or
2. assume the kid's concerns are not on target when there's a chance the kid has hit the nail on the head.

The first mistake is far preferable. The price of the second mistake is much higher. The worst-case scenario, and this is no tragedy, is that you and the kid agree to a solution that addresses the kid's stated concern (but not what turns out to be the primary or central concern) and the original solution doesn't resolve the problem. When you return to Plan B, you want to suggest that there might be more to the problem than was captured by the original concern and that other concerns may be coming into play:

ADULT: *Elena, remember when we talked about how it was really important to you to partner with classmates you get along with?*

ELENA: *Yes.*

ADULT: *And remember that we came up with a list of kids you felt OK working with?*

ELENA: *Uh-huh.*

ADULT: *Well, I've been pairing you with the kids you said you were OK working with, and I'm noticing that there are still a lot of times where you're not doing your work. I'm beginning to wonder if maybe there are some other reasons you're having difficulty getting your work done. Can we think about that a little?*

MISSING STEPS

Often, Plan B goes awry because the adult skipped one of the three steps of Plan B. As you might imagine, the most commonly skipped step is Empathy. If you skip the Empathy step, you won't engage the kid in the conversation, you won't identify and clarify his concern, and you won't reach a mutually satisfactory resolution to the problem you were trying to address. That's a lot of won'ts! But here's what missing Empathy might sound like, switching to a different kid:

ADULT: *Ahmad, I want to talk to you about how things have been going in our class.*

AHMAD: *What about it?*

ADULT *(skipping Empathy and jumping to the Define the Problem step)*: *Well, you're spending a lot of time socializing with Antoine and it's disrupting the learning of the other kids and I don't want to have to send you out.*

AHMAD *(responding as kids frequently do when their concerns are disregarded)*: *I don't care if you send me out.*

ADULT *(plunging into a halfhearted, frustrated Invitation, then throwing in the towel)*: *Look, I just wanted to see if we could figure out what to do about it. But if you don't care, then I guess you'll be spending a lot of time in the hallway until you change your attitude.*

That was quick, and it wasn't Plan B. Now, let's rewind the tape, add the Empathy step back into the mix, and see how it goes:

ADULT *(Empathy, Proactive B)*: *Ahmad, can we talk a little about how things have been going in our class?*

AHMAD: *What about it?*

ADULT: *Well, to be perfectly honest, I've noticed that you're not getting much work done, you're joking around a lot, making strange noises, and making it hard for the other kids to work. I'm just wondering what's going on.*

AHMAD: *I can't do it.*

ADULT *(clarifying)*: *You can't do it. What can't you do?*

AHMAD: *I just can't do it.*

ADULT *(still clarifying)*: *I hear ya. But I'm still not clear about what part you don't get.*

AHMAD: *I can't remember all these parts of the nervous system!*

ADULT: *Remembering all the parts of the nervous system is hard for you. So that's why you're cutting up a lot?*

AHMAD: *What's the point in my trying hard? I can't do it.*

ADULT: *Well, at least we have a better idea about what's getting in your way. Just one question: Why are you feeling so much pressure to memorize the parts of the nervous system so fast?*

AHMAD: *My mom said if I get anything below a C on my next report card, she's gonna ground me for a month.*

ADULT *(empathizing yet again): Ah, so you're feeling extra pressure.*

Now that we have a much better sense of what Ahmad's concern is, we can work toward addressing it.

Adults don't often skip the Define the Problem step. But, as mentioned in Chapter 4, this step can go awry because adults end up putting a *solution* rather than a concern on the table, often because they're not sure what their concern is.

RODNEY *(loudly): This test sucks!*
ADULT *(Empathy, Emergency B): Uh-oh. Sounds like someone's having trouble with the test. What's up, Rodney?*
RODNEY: *I can't do this much writing.*
ADULT *(putting a solution into play): I hear ya. I'm sorry the writing part is hard for you, but you really have to take the test.*

Well done on the Empathy step. But Define the Problem needs some work. And the timing wasn't the best, especially if the problem was predictable (and therefore grist for the Proactive B mill). But let's rewind the tape and see how it goes:

RODNEY *(loudly): This test sucks!*
ADULT *(Empathy, Emergency B): Uh-oh. Sounds like someone's having trouble with the test. What's up, Rodney?*
RODNEY: *I can't do this much writing.*
ADULT *(refined Empathy, then Define the Problem): I hear ya. I know writing is a little hard for you. The thing is, I need some way of making sure you've learned the material.*

Now *there's* an adult concern we could try to address. Is there a way for us to make sure that Rodney knows the material even though the writing part is hard? Undoubtedly. But realistic and mutually satisfactory solutions to this problem would never be contemplated if the adult wasn't able to be specific about his or her concern. For many adults, this is the hardest part of Plan B.

Of course, the other step adults frequently skip is the Invitation. It's fairly common for adults to successfully navigate the Empathy and Define the Problem steps and then veer off the cliff anyway by skipping the Invitation. For an example, let's go back to our friend Rodney.

> RODNEY *(loudly): This test sucks!*
> ADULT *(Empathy, Emergency B): Uh-oh. Sounds like someone's having trouble with the test. What's up, Rodney?*
> RODNEY: *I can't do this much writing.*
> ADULT *(refined Empathy, then Define the Problem, then veering): I hear ya. I know writing is a little hard for you. The thing is, I need some way of making sure you know the material. So just buckle down and do the best you can. I bet if you tried harder you'd be able to do it.*
> RODNEY: *I said I can't do this much writing!*

Rodney was actually hanging in there, right up until the veering part. Shall we rewind the tape again?

> RODNEY *(loudly): This test sucks!*
> ADULT *(Empathy, Emergency B): Uh-oh. Sounds like someone's having trouble with the test. What's up, Rodney?*
> RODNEY: *I can't do this much writing.*
> ADULT *(refined Empathy, then Define the Problem, then the Invitation): I hear ya. I know writing is a little hard for you. The thing is, I need some way of making sure you know the material. I wonder if there's some way for me to make sure you know the material even though the writing part is hard for you. Do you have any ideas?*

Very nice.

But, you may be wondering, what about Rodney's profanity? What you do about his profanity *at that moment* is your judgment call. In the above example, the adult decided that the use of profanity was not the most important issue to attend to at that moment, and made the judgment call that the best course of action was to get the test issue settled. Addressing the profanity issue at that moment might have pushed Rodney beyond the brink and set the stage for a major episode. At the very least, it probably would have ended his participation in Plan B. If his use of profanity is a concern the adult wants to address, that can be done later with a separate Proactive Plan B. Will the other kids get the idea that it's OK to use profanity in the classroom? Not if the adult addresses the profanity issue later with Proactive Plan B. And, of course, not if Rodney and his teacher are busy solving the problems that are setting the stage for his profanity.

You may also be wondering what to do if Rodney is unable to generate any solutions. As you've already read, resolution of the problem isn't solely Rodney's responsibility; it's a team effort. He may need some help thinking of solutions. That's where you come in. In the following (now Proactive) Plan B dialogue, the teacher and Rodney have returned to the writing problem:

ADULT: *OK, let's talk. You're having trouble with the writing part.*

RODNEY: *Writing sucks.*

ADULT: *What is it about writing that you're not so keen about?*

RODNEY: *It just sucks. It's too hard for me. It's too much.*

ADULT: *You know, I'm sorry we haven't talked about this earlier. I guess I just haven't had time to sit down and chat about this. I know writing is a little hard for you. Help me understand more about that. Why is it hard? What makes it feel like it's too much?*

RODNEY: *I don't know, man, like, one- or two-word answers, that's no problem, but when you want us to write more than that, it feels like a whole book!*

ADULT: *So that's when it feels like too much? Is that what you mean that it's too hard?*

RODNEY: *Yeah.*

ADULT: *So now let me ask a few more questions. When you're supposed to write more than a few words, when it feels like a whole book, is it that you're having trouble thinking of the words to write, or that writing down the words is hard, or something else?*

RODNEY: *Both of those things. Plus, I write slow, so even when I think of good words, by the time I get around to writing them I forget what I wanted to write.*

ADULT: *I understand. That is hard. And the help Mr. Morgan is giving you, does that help?*

RODNEY: *It helps while he's helping me! But it doesn't help when he's not helping me!*

ADULT: *OK. I think I understand why you're so frustrated about this. I'm glad we're talking about it. Here's the thing . . . I need some way of making sure you know the material, and I want to make sure you get some practice at writing so it's not always this hard for you. So I'm wondering if there's some way for me to make sure you know the material even though the writing part is hard for you. Do you have any ideas?*

RODNEY: *No. It's too hard.*

ADULT: *You don't have any ideas about what we could do?*

RODNEY: *I don't know.*

It looks like Rodney doesn't have any ideas on this one. Luckily, solving this problem is a joint venture.

ADULT: *Well, I might have a few ideas.*

RODNEY: *Like what?*

ADULT: *Well, for some assignments, I could get someone to write for you. Then I could be sure you know the material and you wouldn't get so frustrated about the writing being hard.*

RODNEY: *I guess that's OK.*

ADULT: *And then, just to make sure you won't need someone to write for you forever, we could pick a few assignments that you'd practice writing with Mr. Morgan. What do you think?*

RODNEY: *That could work.*

ADULT: *Well, there might be other ways to solve the problem. Any ideas come to you?*

RODNEY: *No.*

ADULT: *Let's keep thinking. I know you've been learning to*

keyboard with Mr. Morgan. Does that make writing less
frustrating?
RODNEY: *Not really. I'm slow at that, too.*
ADULT: *Maybe we should go with having someone write for*
you . . . for now. What do you think?
RODNEY: *OK.*
ADULT: *And if it doesn't work out so well, we'll talk again and*
figure out why and come up with something else.

Remember, any proposals you make in the solution department
are just that: *proposals.* If you're *imposing* solutions, Rodney may
refuse to participate. And he certainly won't learn how to come up
with solutions that are mutually satisfactory. The hope is that, after
seeing solution-generating modeled over multiple repetitions, Rodney
will get the hang of it.

DUELING SOLUTIONS

As you already know, Dueling Solutions is the tendency to get two
solutions rather than two concerns on the table in the first two steps
of Plan B (to be clear: getting multiple solutions on the table *once*
you've arrived at the Invitation step is perfectly fine, but only after
there are two well-clarified concerns on the table). As mentioned in
Chapter 4, if two solutions (the kid's and yours) are all you have
on the table after the first two steps of Plan B, you will simply engage
in a power struggle where each party is focused only on making sure
that their own solution wins out. That's not Plan B, nor is it going to
solve any problems in a mutually satisfactory or durable manner.

Hard as it is to reconcile two concerns, reconciling two solutions
is often downright impossible. People may try anyway by meeting
halfway (for example, agreeing that a child will work on her spelling
words for fifteen minutes as the midpoint between ten minutes—the
amount she wanted—and twenty minutes—the amount you wanted).
The reality is that meeting halfway will solve only a very small per-
centage of problems. Addressing two concerns in a realistic and mutually satisfactory manner typically requires much more thought.

STEPS OUT OF ORDER

Plan B doesn't go very well if you play roulette with the steps. If you start with the Define the Problem step (your concern), the kid's going to think you're doing Plan A (because that's what Plan A starts with). If you start with the Invitation, you have no idea what problem you're trying to solve because you haven't yet identified anyone's concerns. No, Plan B always starts with the Empathy step, continues with the Define the Problem step, and is capped off with the Invitation.

OVERRELIANCE ON EMERGENCY B

Hopefully, you're convinced that Proactive B is far preferable to Emergency B. Proactive B takes place under planned conditions, so you have time to prepare. Proactive B takes place under calmer, less heated circumstances so the participants are more capable of information-sharing and reasoned discussion. And Proactive B doesn't take place in front of the entire class, so the participants don't have the added pressure of being the center of attention and the work of the other kids isn't being disrupted.

Not that doing Proactive Plan B with the entire class doesn't have its benefits. There are lots of problems that affect all the kids in a classroom, and these problems are often best resolved by involving all the kids in the process. There are also advantages, especially when you get to the Invitation, to having other kids in the class try to help one of their classmates with a given problem in the context of Plan B. But most people are more comfortable doing Plan B privately before they venture into the full-class variant, which is described in Chapter 7.

And yet, having made the case for Proactive B, most adults who are new to Plan B find themselves starting the hard way, with *Emergency* B. Presumably this is because Proactive B requires reflection and advance planning (What unsolved problems are precipitating a kid's challenging behavior and when should I try to talk with him about one of them?). It's not that use of Emergency B is a catastrophe, it's just that you don't want to make a habit of it. If you're trying to solve the same problem every day using Emergency B, you're actually doing more Plan B than you need to, something called *Perpetual B*. Remember, the goal is to work toward durable solutions—getting the problem solved once and for all—a task much better suited to Proactive B.

Plan C is another option in emergent circumstances. Sometimes it makes sense to drop an expectation temporarily (Plan C), ensure the other kids stay focused on the task at hand, and then return to the problem—perhaps two minutes later, perhaps two hours later—under more ideal circumstances.

> RODNEY *(loudly): This test sucks!*
>
> ADULT *(Empathy, Emergency B): Uh-oh. Sounds like someone's having trouble with the test. You know what, Rodney, I had a feeling this might be a little hard for you. I should have discussed it with you before I passed it out. Why don't you hang tight for a few minutes while I get everyone started, and then we can try to figure out what's troubling you about the test. Sound OK?*
>
> RODNEY *(if we're lucky): Fine. So what am I supposed to do, just sit here?*
>
> ADULT: *Only for a minute or two. I'll be with you in just a sec.*

In some emergent circumstances, especially those involving safety, Plan A is an option. Plan A makes sense in situations in which safety is jeopardized and there's no viable option except to impose adult will (for example, if two kids are in the midst of a fistfight). But on many emergent safety issues, you do have the options of Plans B and C. Plan C would make sense when you think defusing the kid (by dropping the expectation that heated him up in the first place) is possible. And—believe it or not—even Emergency B could make sense. In the words of Harry Taylor, a corrections officer who works in a juvenile detention facility in the state of Maine, "If the kid's still talking, you're still in business."

Of course, if we're doing a good job of identifying the lagging skills and unsolved problems of kids at risk for unsafe behavior, if we're working together to communicate and prioritize, if we're systematically teaching those skills and solving those problems and keeping track of how things are going, if we're developing the types of helping relationships with at-risk kids that they so desperately need, then the likelihood of unsafe behavior will already have been dramatically reduced.

Q & A

Question: I'm having some trouble with the Empathy step. I'm still not sure what to say to get the ball rolling. For example, I have a kid who had a major blow-out the other day because he refused to leave the classroom for a fire drill. I did Plan A at the time—it wasn't pretty—but I want to do Plan B now to keep it from happening again. What should I say to get Plan B going on that one?

Answer: Your goal is to gather information so as to better understand why the kid became so upset over the fire drill so you can help solve the problem. So, generically, you could say something like, "I noticed that you became very upset during the fire drill the other day, but I still don't understand why. What's up?"

Question: You mentioned some of the most common unsolved problems in Chapter 2. Would they sound pretty much the same?

Answer: Yes. Here are some examples:

- "I've noticed that there's been some trouble on the school bus lately. What's up?"
- "I've noticed that you've been getting thrown out of the cafeteria a lot. What's up?"
- "I've noticed that you and Santiago haven't been getting along so well lately. What's up?"
- "I've noticed that you haven't been getting much done on your civil rights project. What's up?"
- "I've noticed that there hasn't been much homework coming in lately. What's up?"
- "I've noticed we haven't seen you in school much the past few weeks. What's up?"

- "I've noticed that some days you come into my class and you're really ready to sink your teeth into what we're doing. Other days you don't seem to be able to get much done at all. What's up?"

Question: Is it OK to have a specific behavior be the focus of Plan B? Like, for example, spitting? What would the Empathy step sound like then?
Answer: Yes. "I've noticed that the other kids have been getting mad at you for spitting. What's going on?" But then you'll need to drill a little (or a lot) to fully understand the who, what, where, when, and sometimes why of the spitting. Once you feel that you have enough information to understand the kid's concern or perspective, you'll enter your concern into consideration, and this will usually be related to safety, how the kid's behavior is affecting him or others, lost learning, or wanting the kid to be part of the community. Then you're brainstorming solutions that will address both concerns. Remember, solutions are weighed on the basis of whether they address both concerns and whether they're realistic.

Question: What if the kid doesn't follow through on his part of the solution?
Answer: This is usually a sign that the original solution wasn't as realistic and mutually satisfactory as you may have thought. By the way, kids are not the only ones who sometimes have trouble following through on solutions they've agreed to. Either way, you're back to the Plan B drawing board. If it makes you feel any better, in life most good solutions follow solutions that didn't pan out so well. The important thing is to figure out why the original solution didn't pan out and make sure that the next solution incorporates what you've learned.

Question: What if the kid says he doesn't care about your concern?
Answer: He gets ten points for honesty. Sounds like a kid who's had a lot of his own concerns blown off the table and is now responding in kind. Plan A begets Plan A; Plan B begets Plan B. The long-term answer to a kid not caring about your concerns is to care more about his. The short-term answer is to acknowledge that he doesn't care

about your concern, that there's really no way for you to make him care about your concerns, to let him know that you've begun trying very hard to take his concerns into account (hopefully, he's noticed), to point out that your goal is to find a solution that addresses his concerns and yours, and to underscore the fact that once the problem is solved it won't get in the way anymore.

Question: Don't adults' concerns trump kids' concerns?
Answer: If the adult's concerns are trumping the kid's concerns, then you're not doing Plan B, you're doing Plan A. Even if the adult's concern is really important, there's no reason to dismiss the kid's concern or to think that both concerns can't be addressed using Plan B.

Question: Don't adults' solutions trump kids' solutions?
Answer: Not if you want to solve a problem durably, meaning in a realistic and mutually satisfactory manner. If a kid isn't OK with a solution, or if it doesn't address his concerns, the problem is not durably solved and will resurface.

Question: In some of your examples, it looks more like the problem is being avoided rather than solved. Care to comment?
Answer: Don't confuse *avoiding* with *prioritizing* and *incremental problem-solving*. In some instances, you're choosing not to work on something (Plan C) because you have bigger fish to fry first. In other instances, you're agreeing to a solution that will move the process along incrementally while realizing that the problem is not yet completely resolved.

Question: What if the only solutions a kid can come up with are consequences?
Answer: Sounds like he's been trained by adults whose only solutions are consequences. You'll have to help broaden his range of options.

Question: What if the kid just keeps repeating his original solution?
Answer: He's probably having trouble thinking of other solutions or hasn't had much practice taking another person's concerns into

account. That's where you come in. But you may want to check out Chapter 6 for more specific strategies.

Question: What if the solutions a kid proposes are not realistic or mutually satisfactory?

Answer: This is covered in Chapter 6 as well. But briefly, he'll need some feedback along those lines. For example, "Hey, there's an idea. The only problem is, I don't know if it's truly realistic for us to assume that you'll be able to stay in your seat all the time. Let's see if we can come up with a solution that you can really do." Or, "Well, that's an option. The only thing is, if I let you walk around the room whenever you feel like it, *your* concern would be addressed—you know, that it's hard for you to sit in your seat for long periods of time—but *my* concern—that I don't want you to disturb your classmates—wouldn't be. Let's see if we can come up with a solution that works for both of us."

The Story Continues . . .

Mrs. Woods greeted each of her students as they filed into her classroom.

"Good morning, Sam." As always, she had much on her mind besides making sure her students felt welcome. The schedule for the day. Getting two of her students caught up on missing assignments. Separating two students who weren't working well on a project together. The frequent absences of another student and the need to call the student's mother. Fire drill at 9:15.

"Hello, Liz. I like your new shirt." Remembering that Mrs. Wagner is coming in to work with Liz on writing at 10:00. And that Mrs. Grady is coming in to observe Eddy today.

"Hi, William." Wondering if William's had breakfast today—he's a different kid when he hasn't had breakfast. "William, after you put your things down, I need to ask you a question. Hi, Raymond. Don't forget you're going with Ms. Hall at ten forty-five. We'll need to figure out how to get you the math materials you'll be missing." Needing to talk to Raymond about what's been going on between him and Kellen at recess lately.

"Welcome back, Joey." Hoping Joey remembers the plan. Hoping Bridgman knows what he's doing.

The day proceeded along and Mrs. Woods found herself anxiously focused on Joey, casting wary glances to see if he was using their new signal. On one of the assignments Mrs. Woods was concerned about, Joey plowed right into the material with no problem. On another, she saw him working on some old worksheets he'd taken out of his backpack. He was using their plan! When she drew near, he looked at her and began rubbing his nose. She smiled to acknowledge him. Joey looked back down at his work.

Mid-afternoon, Mr. Middleton stuck his head in the door to make sure everything was OK. Mrs. Woods gave him the thumbs-up sign. At the end of the school day, Mrs. Woods was so wrapped up in the hustle and bustle of getting her kids off to their rides and buses that she barely noticed Joey tugging on her sleeve.

"Oh, Joey, hi," she said. "What's up?"

Joey tried to look inconspicuous. "Should I take the work I didn't understand home with me tonight?"

"Oh, wow, Joey, that's great that you're following up with me," said Mrs. Woods. "But I don't want you to have to worry about homework you don't understand."

"Maybe my mom can help me with it."

"Tell you what. Why don't you and your mom give it a try and if you still have trouble I'll explain it to you when you come in early one morning. Sound OK?"

"OK." As quickly as Joey had appeared he was gone.

Dr. Bridgman breathlessly appeared at her door just as Mrs. Woods was leaving her classroom for the day.

"Tried to get here earlier," he puffed, "but I'm running way behind as usual. How'd it go today?"

"Uneventful," said Mrs. Woods. "It dawned on me as the kids were coming in this morning that there would be several assignments that might be confusing to Joey, but he did fine on one of them and on the other he used our plan."

"He used our plan?" asked Dr. Bridgman, both surprised and heartened by the news. "That was fast. You heading out?"

Mrs. Woods turned the lights off in her classroom. "Not out of the building, but out to a meeting. You know, he even came up to me at the end of the day and asked if he should do the confusing assignment at home tonight."

"Wow. They should all be this easy. 'Course, we're not out of the woods yet." Dr. Bridgman considered his words. "No pun intended."

"No pun taken," said Mrs. Woods with a smile as she began walking down the hall. "Did you have a chance to ask his mother about bringing him in early some mornings?"

"Not yet. I'm going to call her now. Do you want me to let you know if Joey will be in early tomorrow?"

"No, if he's there that's fine, if he's not I've got lots to do. You were saying that we're not out of the woods yet?"

"Well, it's good that he seems to be working with us, and good that we have a signaling system in place . . . and good that he used it," said Dr. Bridgman. "But we still don't really understand why he's so easily embarrassed and so hypersensitive about having the other kids know he's having trouble with something."

"I have a tough crowd in my class. They're very hard on one another."

Dr. Bridgman thought of a few ideas that might help on that count, but decided to hold off on making suggestions for the entire class until things were more settled with Joey. "Well, we're off to a good start with Joey."

Mrs. Woods paused outside the conference room door. "Wasn't as hard as I thought it would be. At some point in the day it suddenly dawned on me that what I'm doing with Joey isn't really any different from what I do on academics for every other kid in my class."

"A lot of teachers feel they have so much on their plates already that my adding one more thing . . ."

"Well, that's just the thing," said Mrs. Woods. "If this keeps working—and I know we don't know if it will yet—then we'll actually have taken something *off* my plate, not added more to it."

Ms. Lowell walked into the house after work and found Joey waiting for her at the kitchen table.

"I need you to help me with this" were Joey's first words.

Ms. Lowell placed a bag of groceries on the kitchen counter. "Sure, bud. How was school today?"

"Fine. But I need your help with an assignment I didn't understand. Mrs. Woods said you could help me with it and if you don't know how she'll help me when you bring me in early in the morning."

"When I bring you in early in the morning?" asked Ms. Lowell. What is this, she wondered, another punishment?

"Dr. Bridgman said I could meet with Mrs. Woods sometimes when you bring Jason to school early to work with Mr. Armstrong. So she can explain assignments that I don't understand. Dr. Bridgman is going to call you to ask you about it."

"So you didn't have any problems in school today?"

"No, and I used my signal."

"Your signal?"

"Yeah, when I'm confused about an assignment, I rub my nose so Mrs. Woods knows I'm confused." He pointed to some papers on the table. "This is the assignment I got confused on."

Joey's mother smiled as she sat down at the kitchen table. "Well, I think I'm the one who's a little confused. Sounds like you all came up with some interesting ideas at school today."

"Yeah, and I need you to help me with this assignment."

"OK, but give me a second," said Ms. Lowell. "You say Dr. Bridgman's going to be calling me?"

"But I don't know when," said Joey. "I need Mrs. Woods to explain assignments to me if I'm gonna get confused. Are you taking Jason early tomorrow?"

"Yes, Jason goes early every Tuesday and Thursday," said Ms. Lowell. "You can go early those days, too, if you want. In fact, I'll take you early *every* day if you want."

Dr. Bridgman called Joey's mother around five p.m.

"Hi, Dr. Bridgman," said Ms. Lowell. "You're working awfully late, aren't you?"

Dr. Bridgman sounded tired. "I'm not quite done yet. A few more phone calls to make. But there are a bunch of us still here."

"Sounds like things went well today," said Ms. Lowell. "You all came up with a signal, I heard."

"Yes, so Joey can let Mrs. Woods know he's confused about an assignment," confirmed Dr. Bridgman. "He told you about it?"

"Yes, about that and about coming in early. . . . I guess that's why you're calling."

"Sounds like Joey beat me to the punch. I heard you bring your other son in early sometimes to work with his teacher. Any chance you can bring Joey in early, too?"

"I told Joey I'd bring him in early every day if that's what he needs."

"Ah, good. I don't think he'll need to come early every day, but I'm glad to hear you can do it. I'd also like to get you in again to meet with Mrs. Woods and Mrs. Franco, just to coordinate efforts."

"Dr. Bridgman, there isn't much I wouldn't do to help Joey do well in school. Can you explain to me about the signal? How's that going to help?"

"Well, we were thinking that if Joey can let Mrs. Woods know he's confused, we'll kill a few birds with the same stone. None of us knows just how often he's getting confused, so that would be good information to have. And the way he's been letting her know he's confused up until today hasn't exactly been working very well. Plus, it's good for him to know she's working with him on this problem, you know, together."

"So you mentioned something about wanting to meet with me again."

"Right, yes. I want to make sure we get you working with Mrs. Woods and Mrs. Franco. I know it's hard for you to get off work."

"Oh, I'll get off work. I don't think I have a very good reputation at that school, but just give me some advance notice and I'll be there. So should I bring Joey in early tomorrow?"

"Yes, that would be great," said Dr. Bridgman.

"I, uh, hate to keep asking you for reassurance, but my other son, Jason, told me some kids were saying Joey didn't belong in the school. Are people talking about putting Joey in one of those special ed classrooms?"

"Not that I'm aware of," said Dr. Bridgman.

"So is Joey going to end up in one of those classrooms?"

"Not if things keep heading in the right direction," said Dr. Bridgman. "I've always found it's possible for a lot of kids, even kids who are a lot more challenging than Joey, to stay in their general ed classrooms, if we do the right thing."

"There are kids who are more challenging than Joey?"

"Well, let's just say that there are kids who do things that are more extreme when they get upset."

Mrs. Woods' husband arrived home from work to find his wife cooking and listening to classical music. "A good day," he whispered to himself. "Hi, honey," he said.

"Oh, hi," said Mrs. Woods.

"Good day at school today?" asked Mr. Woods.

"You know, the usual. My friend Joey's back."

"Joey. Oh, you mean the kid who hammered Middleton?"

"He didn't exactly hammer him. It was an accident."

"Ah, so it was an *accident.*"

"Well, it *was* an accident," said Mrs. Woods. "Anyway, our new school psychologist and I had a discussion with Joey this morning and we came up with a plan so Joey won't blow up anymore and . . . at least today . . . the plan worked."

"There's always tomorrow."

Mrs. Woods looked at her husband. "Thanks for your optimism."

"Realism's more like it," said Mr. Woods. "I mean, the kid isn't going to go from clocking Middleton and threatening to kill someone and making half the school chase after him to being an angel in one conversation."

"I didn't say he'd been transformed into an angel. Sorry I brought it up."

"No, no, don't be sorry, I'll be optimistic if you want me to."

"It's just that I had a bit of a transformation myself today," continued Mrs. Woods.

"A transformation?"

"Yes, sort of. I realized that Joey's not so . . . unusual. He's a regular kid with some challenges. He needs special treatment from me just like every other kid in my class. But the special treatment he needs from me isn't on academics, it's on other things, things I don't understand all that well yet."

Mr. Woods mulled this perspective. "OK, no crime in giving a kid special treatment if he needs it, I guess. Like if I have a product that isn't selling very well, I might highlight it in some way, you know, in the front window, or in a special display. Doesn't mean it's a bad product, just that it needs a little extra help. Like those new flashlights I was trying to sell. Went like hotcakes once I put 'em over by the front counter. That sort of thing."

Mrs. Woods appreciated her husband's attempt to understand her classroom. "Yeah, something like that."

"Now, I don't know if flashlights and difficult kids are exactly the same thing," Mr. Woods continued, thinking about things a bit more. "One's a good product that just needed a little help, the other's a bad—"

"Maybe you should quit talking while you're ahead," interrupted Mrs. Woods with a smile.

"So how do you know it was your little conversation that did the trick?" asked Mr. Woods. "Maybe it was the five-day suspension. Maybe the message finally got through."

"Joey's been suspended before. Lots of times. Never made a dent. Didn't keep him from blowing up in my class last week. But today, for the first time, I actually felt like I had the beginnings of a . . . a *relationship* with the poor kid. And I felt like he wasn't so scary."

"We'll see how far your new relationship goes once he's ticked off about something again. Hope your new relationship keeps *you* from getting the hurt jaw next time."

"Flashlights don't need a relationship. But kids do."

Mr. Woods took slight offense to this statement. "I vaguely recall having been involved in the raising of our kids. Had a relationship with 'em, too, if my memory serves me. But that's not why they behaved themselves. They behaved themselves because they knew what they had coming if they didn't."

"Ah, Plan A," said Mrs. Woods.

"What?"

"Plan A. It's when you make a kid do what you want or punish him. Plan A."

"Whatever you call it, our kids turned out OK."

"Our kids turned out OK because they had two parents who were willing to take the time to talk to them about things and help them when they had trouble. And isn't it possible we were just *lucky* that our kids were relatively easy?"

Mr. Woods relented. "I'm glad you had a good day. I hope you have more good days. And I hope you save poor Joey and that he never gives you another problem for the rest of the school year. How's that?"

Mrs. Woods smiled. "Much better."

The next day, Mrs. Woods was at her desk poring over her plan for the day when Joey appeared at the doorway for his first early-morning meeting. "Good morning, Joey. How are you today?"

"Fine," mumbled Joey.

"Come on in . . ." Mrs. Woods pointed Joey to a chair next to her desk. "How did the science assignment go last night?"

Joey laid the assignment on Mrs. Woods' desk. "My mom helped me."

"Oh, fantastic." Mrs. Woods looked at the assignment. "Looks good. Tell me, what parts did your mom help you with?"

"She explained it to me. She told me it was kinda like a homework assignment you gave us another time. But not exactly."

"Yes, I recall that we did do something similar for homework in science once. And that made it easier for you to do?"

"Yes," said Joey. "Once my mom explained that it was a little different."

It puzzled Mrs. Woods that something so simple was making things so hard for Joey. "You know, Joey, most of the assignments we do in class are similar to others we've done before. But they're all a little different, too. You know, kind of makes things interesting."

Joey mulled this revelation. "Not for me."

"Yes, in your case, I think that having things be a little different can be a little confusing, yes?"

"Yes."

"So, I was thinking . . . there are three assignments today that I thought might be a little confusing for you. They're all similar to others we've done, but they're not exactly the same." Mrs. Woods pulled out one of the assignments she thought Joey would find confusing. "Like here's this history worksheet. It's very similar to something we did on slavery a few weeks ago, but it's not exactly the same. Want to take a look?"

"OK."

Joey studied the assignment.

"Do you remember the worksheet we did on slavery a few weeks ago?" asked Mrs. Woods.

"No."

"Let's look in your history folder and see if we can find it," suggested Mrs. Woods. She retrieved Joey's history folder and began leafing through it. "Ah, here it is. You did really well on this assignment, too." She showed the completed assignment to Joey.

"Oh, yeah. That was easy."

Mrs. Woods returned to the new assignment. "Well, we're doing something similar in social studies today. But the matching part is a little different. I thought that might confuse you a little."

Joey examined the new assignment.

"Would you like to try some of the items?" asked Mrs. Woods.

"OK."

Mrs. Woods watched Joey doing several of the items. He looked up after a few minutes. "This is easy."

"Great," said Mrs. Woods. "Want to see the other things I thought would be confusing?"

"Yeah."

Mrs. Woods and Joey inspected the other assignments, comparing them to some past assignments and talking about the differences.

"I don't think you'll have any trouble with anything else we're doing today," said Mrs. Woods. "Of course, if you do, just give me the signal, or use our plan, like you did yesterday."

"OK."

"So, would you like to go join your classmates before they come in?"

"Yes," said Joey, beginning to head toward the door. He suddenly stopped. "Um, Mrs. Woods?"

"Yes, Joey."

"I . . . I think . . . we made a good plan."

"I agree."

"Mrs. Woods?"

"Yes, Joey."

"Am I going to get put in a special class?"

"A special class? What kind of special class?"

"I don't know. I heard my mom talking on the phone yesterday. She didn't know I was listening."

"Well, I'm not sure what kind of special class she was talking about," said Mrs. Woods. "But whatever she was talking about, I'm not letting you go so fast. You're a very important member of our class."

Mrs. Woods thought she saw a slight look of relief on Joey's face before he turned toward the door. She called after him, "See you soon."

That afternoon an argument erupted at recess between two students in Mr. Armstrong's class. The argument was still unresolved as the students spilled back into the classroom.

"What's going on here?!" demanded Mr. Armstrong, seeing that the argument was about to turn physical.

"She called me a whore!" shouted a girl named Ashlee. "She's lucky I didn't—"

"You are a whore!" retorted the other student, a hard-luck girl named Crystal who was a frequent flyer in the school discipline program. "Take your best shot. I'll take the life right out of you!"

Mr. Armstrong put his body between the two girls. "Both of you, out in the hall! Now! The rest of you, sit down and get to work!"

Out in the hall, Mr. Armstrong looked at Crystal. "Did you call her a whore?"

"Damn right," said Crystal.

"Crystal, you better calm yourself down, because you know I don't take well to swearing," said Mr. Armstrong. "You need to apologize to Ashlee. Then you need to apologize to me."

Crystal was indignant. "You don't even know what happened."

"I don't care about what happened right now, Crystal," said Mr. Armstrong. "'Whore' and 'damn right' are completely unacceptable. Apologize. Now. To both of us."

"Bullshit," muttered Crystal.

Mr. Armstrong had heard enough. "Ashlee, get back in the classroom. Crystal, we're going to visit Mr. Middleton."

When they arrived at the office, Mr. Armstrong pointed Crystal toward a chair. "Sit down!" he commanded. He looked at Mrs. Westbrook, the secretary. "Where's Mr. Middleton?"

"On the phone," said Mrs. Westbrook. "Shall I let him know you two are here?"

"I need to go back to my class," said Mr. Armstrong. "Let Mr. Middleton know that Crystal is doing her thing again today. Seems to me she needs to be reminded of what happens when she starts fights, calls other kids names, and forgets how to talk to her teacher."

"Will do," said Mrs. Westbrook, glancing warily over at Crystal.

Minutes later, Mr. Middleton came out of his office. "Crystal, what's going on?"

Crystal scowled. "I got nothin' to say. You wanna know what's going on, you better ask Captain Armstrong."

"Crystal, please, I don't have time to be a detective today. Come in my office and tell me what happened."

Crystal followed Mr. Middleton into his office. "OK, I shouldn't have called Ashlee a whore. So sue me. But Mr. Armstrong wouldn't even listen to what she said to me first. All he did was say I had to apologize."

Mr. Middleton sighed. "Crystal, how many suspensions and detentions have you had over the years for fighting and swearing?"

Crystal scowled again. "I thought you were supposed to keep track of stuff like that."

"Crystal, all I know is it's been a lot of times. And here we are again. When are you going to give it a rest?"

"I'll rest at home after you suspend me."

"Crystal, I don't want to suspend you. But you don't give me much choice. Can your grandma come pick you up?"

"Nope. She's sleeping. Night shift."

"Can your brother come pick you up?"

"Haven't seen my brother in weeks."

Mr. Middleton sighed again. "Crystal, what do you do when you're home suspended, anyway?"

Crystal smirked. "Hang out."

This is pointless, thought Mr. Middleton. "Crystal, I'm not going to suspend you out of school. I'm giving you in-school suspension for two days. I want you to go there now. I'll let Mr. Strickland know you're on your way."

"I don't want in-school suspension. If you're gonna suspend me, at least let me get out of this place."

Mr. Middleton shook his head. "Now, what good would that do? Have you sitting at home, or whatever you mean by 'hanging out.' No, I'd rather have you here."

Crystal rose from her seat. "Whatever."

* * *

The next two weeks went well for Joey in Mrs. Woods' classroom. He came early again on several days and he and Mrs. Woods continued to examine new assignments that were similar to but not exactly the same as others he'd completed. Once, Joey became slightly confused on an assignment Mrs. Woods hadn't reviewed with him in the morning, but the signal worked well. Indeed, after a few minutes of confusion, Joey was able to start working after recognizing how the assignment was slightly different from one he'd completed a few weeks earlier.

Two weeks into the plan, Mrs. Woods woke up feeling sick one morning. She asked her husband to call the school to arrange for a substitute and went back to sleep. The substitute teacher was an enthusiastic young man named Mr. Owens. He'd subbed a few times already at the school, but never in Mrs. Woods' class. It occurred to Mr. Middleton to let Mr. Owens know about some of the kids in Mrs. Woods' class, but he was distracted by a problem that had taken place between two students on a school bus and didn't get to Mr. Owens before classes began. Mrs. Franco, who had been involved in an early-morning meeting, didn't know her friend had called in sick until she stuck her head into the classroom just as Mr. Owens was introducing himself to the class.

Mr. Owens did his best to stick to Mrs. Woods' teaching plan for the day. Around mid-morning, he noticed a student working on something different from the rest of class. It was Joey, working on something he'd taken out of his backpack, sticking to the plan. The plan Mr. Owens knew nothing about.

Mr. Owens approached Joey's desk. "Um, that's not the assignment you're supposed to be working on," said Mr. Owens.

Joey looked up, mortified. The unexpected deviation from the plan left him at a loss for words. His face reddening, he went back to working on the materials he'd taken out of his backpack.

"Um, excuse me, but that's not what you're supposed to be working on," repeated Mr. Owens.

Liz, the classmate sitting next to Joey, tried to ward off impending disaster. "I wouldn't do that if I was you," she said. Mr. Owens noticed with dismay that several other kids were now focused not on their work but on him. Joey, looking around, saw them, too, and grew even more embarrassed.

"Thanks," he said with a pleasant smile, "but he's supposed to be doing what everyone else . . ."

Mr. Owens' insistence pushed Joey close to the edge. But this time he didn't jump out of his seat. He didn't scream. He didn't threaten to kill anyone. He just got out of his seat and walked quickly toward the classroom door.

"Hey, where are you going?!" called Mr. Owens, but Joey didn't even acknowledge the question as he walked out of the classroom.

Eddie, trying to help, yelled, "You better get after him! He'll run out of the school!"

Mr. Owens was torn between following Joey and leaving the class unmonitored. He decided on the slightly lesser of two evils and began rushing toward the door of the classroom.

Mrs. Franco was helping a student when she saw Joey in the hallway rushing past her door. "Oh, no!" she said under her breath. She dashed into the hallway, almost bumping into Mr. Owens. She started walking quickly down the hall after Joey with Mr. Owens in tow.

Mrs. Franco felt the urge to yell "Joey, get back to class, now!" but resisted the temptation. Instead, as she rounded a corner, she did her best Bridgman imitation and yelled, *"Joey, what's up?"*

Joey stopped dead in his tracks. He turned around and looked at Mrs. Franco and Mr. Owens.

"He . . . he . . ." Joey sputtered, pointing at Mr. Owens.

Through intuition, or sheer luck, or perhaps because she couldn't think of anything else to say, Mrs. Franco tried to empathize. *"He doesn't know the plan!"*

Joey looked as if he were about to cry. "He doesn't know the plan," Joey mumbled.

Mr. Owens made a move forward to grab Joey while he had the chance. Mrs. Franco, knowing the possible effect of that course, hissed, "Leave him alone!"

"You know him?" asked Mr. Owens.

"Why don't you go back to your class and I'll handle Joey," Mrs. Franco said without looking away from Joey. "And stick your head in my class and let them know there had better be silence in there when I come back."

When Mr. Owens was gone, Mrs. Franco walked slowly toward Joey, who was leaning against some lockers. "Joey?"

"Leave me alone."

"Joey, Mr. Owens didn't know the plan, did he?"

"He's a moron."

"I don't know if he's a moron, but—"

Without warning, Joey spun around and punched one of the lockers with all his might. Stunned, Mrs. Franco suddenly wasn't so sure about Plan B or anything else Dr. Bridgman had said. She had no idea what Joey would do next. "Joey, please don't hit the locker like that. I don't want you to hurt yourself."

"It doesn't hurt," Joey lied.

Mr. Armstrong stuck his head out his classroom door. "Everything OK out here?"

"I think we're OK."

Mr. Armstrong looked hard at Joey, then at Mrs. Franco. "You let me know if you need any help."

Mrs. Franco focused on Joey again. "I'm sorry Mr. Owens didn't know the plan. Mrs. Woods must be really sick today and probably didn't have a chance to tell him. But I think you did the right thing not to run out of the school."

Joey was silent.

Mrs. Franco struggled to think of what to say next. She tried not to think about the chaos that might be ensuing in her own classroom. Empathy, empathy, she thought. What would be empathy? "I bet you don't want to go back to class right now." Joey didn't respond.

Now what? Mrs. Franco's mind was racing. "Joey, your hand is bleeding. It must hurt really bad. Will you let me take care of it for you?"

Joey was suddenly acutely aware of the extreme pain in his hand. "Where?" He looked around warily. "I don't want anyone to see me walking with you."

"That would be embarrassing," empathized Mrs. Franco. "How about you walk over to the nurse's office? If anyone sees you, you could tell them you don't feel well. No one will know what happened. I'll go check in on my class and meet you at the nurse's office. What do you think?"

Joey pondered the proposed arrangement. "My hand really hurts."

"I can imagine. You hit that locker really hard."

"Am I in trouble?"

"Well, the locker doesn't look any worse than it did before you hit it."

"I'll go to the nurse's office, but don't walk next to me."

"No problem." Mrs. Franco waited for Joey to pass by before turning to follow several paces behind him. She ducked into her classroom on her way to the nurse's office. Her students were silent. "Kids, thank you for continuing your work while I was out of the classroom. I'm going to be a few more minutes. I'll be right back." Then she stuck her head inside Mrs. Woods' classroom, where things were a bit more chaotic and Mr. Owens looked frazzled. She glared at the students and they immediately fell silent. "You all will be very sorry, and I mean *very* sorry, if I have to stick my head in this classroom again today. You need to be on your best behavior for Mr. Owens or you'll have to answer to me. Mr. Owens, can you check in on my classroom in a few minutes?"

"Sure thing," said Mr. Owens.

"What happened to Joey?" asked Liz.

"Joey is fine," said Mrs. Franco.

"Is he suspended again?" asked Taylor.

"I do not think he is suspended again," said Mrs. Franco. "Now get back to work."

Before going to the nurse's office, Mrs. Franco knocked on Mr. Middleton's door. He opened the door a crack and she could see that a meeting was going on. She whispered through the crack in the door, "Joey got a little upset with the substitute." A wide-eyed look of concern came over Mr. Middleton's face. "But he's fine. Punched a locker hard. We'll be in the nurse's office if you'd like to join us. There's no adult in my classroom."

"I'll be right out," he said, closing the door.

In the nurse's office, Joey sat dejectedly on a cot, holding his hand, but the nurse wasn't there. "Your hand must be killing you," said Mrs. Franco.

"It hurts really bad."

"We should probably get you to a doctor."

"My mom's gonna go nuts."

"What happened in there?"

"He wouldn't listen to me. He embarrassed me in front of everyone. And I was just doing the plan. But he wouldn't leave me alone, so I just left."

"Mrs. Woods told me that you had come up with a plan."

"You sure I'm not in trouble?"

"Aw, Joey, I don't get to decide who's in trouble around here. But I think you did a lot better this time than the last time."

"You do?"

"I do."

Joey stiffened as Mr. Middleton came into the nurse's office.

Mrs. Franco looked at Mr. Middleton. "I was just telling Joey how much better I thought he handled things just now," she said.

"What happened?" he asked.

"Well, Joey was using a plan he and Mrs. Woods came up with if he didn't understand an assignment, but Mr. Owens didn't know the plan so he kind of insisted that Joey do what the rest of the class was doing and that was a little embarrassing. So Joey left the classroom, and he was pretty upset, but he and I talked about it a little and now we're talking about what to do about his hurt hand."

"I sent Mrs. Westbrook to watch your classroom," said Mr. Middleton, trying to digest this information. "What happened to your hand, Joey?"

"Joey hurt it on a locker," Mrs. Franco interjected quickly.

Mr. Middleton assumed there was more to the story but decided not to pursue it. "You walked out of the classroom, Joey?"

"Yes sir," Joey said quietly.

"Let's take a look at your hand," said Mr. Middleton. It was cut and already swollen. Mr. Middleton winced. "We probably should get that taken care of. Looks like you ran into a very angry locker."

"Yes sir," said Joey, glancing anxiously at Mrs. Franco.

"Joey, I'd suggest we call your mom and have her take you to the doctor to get your hand taken care of," said Mr. Middleton. "On Monday morning before school I want to sit down with you and Dr. Bridgman and Mrs. Woods if she's back," Mr. Middleton looked at Mrs. Franco again, "and Mrs. Franco, so we can talk about this a little."

"Yes sir. Am I suspended again?"

"Walking out of a classroom isn't something we'd usually suspend a student for. Only you and Mrs. Franco know what happened between you and that locker. But if Mrs. Franco thinks you handled things better this time, I'm going to take her word for it, for now. So I'm going to talk a little more with Mrs. Franco and Mr. Owens and we'll get together on Monday morning and get it all sorted out."

Joey's mother arrived at the school looking anxious. She found Joey and Mrs. Westbrook, the school secretary, waiting for her in the nurse's office.

"What happened?" she asked Joey.

"Nothing," mumbled Joey.

"Doesn't look like nothing. Did you hit someone?"

"Some*thing*," clarified Mrs. Westbrook.

"Great. What did you hit, Joey?" asked Ms. Lowell.

"A locker," Joey mumbled as he rose to leave the office.

"A locker," repeated Ms. Lowell. "Just for kicks, or were you mad about something again?"

Joey began leaving the office to head toward the car. "I don't want to talk about it."

"That's great, Joey. I'm missing work to take you to the doctor because you hit a locker and you don't want to talk about it."

Joey turned to face his mother. "I don't want to talk to *you* about it. All *you* do is yell at me and get all stressed out."

Ms. Lowell was trying not to yell. "All I do is yell at you? Joey, I sure as heck hope this isn't the straw that breaks—" She stopped herself. "Who are you going to talk to about it then?"

"Mrs. Woods. She understands."

Though a bit hurt at the idea that Joey was more comfortable confiding in someone else, Ms. Lowell quickly considered the upside of Joey's statement. "That's fine, Joey. You talk to Mrs. Woods about it. Was Mrs. Woods there when you hit the locker?"

Joey got into the car. "She's out sick today."

Ms. Lowell was beginning to get a grasp on what had transpired at school. "So why'd you hit the locker?"

"'Cuz Mr. Moron didn't know the plan."

"Who's Mr. Moron?"

"The sub."

"Who was there when you hit the locker?"

"Mrs. Franco. She said I handled things better this time."

"She said that, did she?" She looked at Joey's swollen, bloody hand. "Your hand must really hurt."

"Bad," said Joey, his eyes welling up.

CHAPTER 6

Filling in the Gaps

In the last chapter I encouraged you to embark upon your first Plan B adventure. Your inaugural foray into Plan B may have gone quite well. Or maybe it didn't go well but you were able to figure out why and are ready to try again. Or maybe you came away feeling it was an unmitigated disaster. You're entitled to your feelings, of course, but attempts at Plan B that don't go as well as hoped seldom qualify as disasters. It can take a while to get into a "Plan B rhythm." It can also take a while to counterbalance the many years a kid has been misunderstood, misinterpreted, and mistreated. Rather than perpetually putting out brush fires, you're trying to systematically chip away at the unsolved problems and teach the lagging skills that have been setting the stage for a kid's challenging behavior for a long time. Hang in there. All change is incremental. At the very least, you want to make sure that nothing happened in your first attempt at Plan B to *decrease* the kid's receptivity to your next attempt.

You've been given a lot to digest already. But now let's go into greater detail about additional considerations that can come into play when using Plan B.

STARTING WITH
UNSOLVED PROBLEMS

I recommended that, in your first attempt at Plan B, you focus on a specific *unsolved problem* rather than a specific lagging *skill.* You may have wondered, "If the kid is lacking skills, why start Plan B with a problem?" Good question. Here's the answer, or at least part of it. *When you're using Plan B to work on problems, you're simultaneously teaching skills.* In other words, by focusing on the *who, what, where,* and *when* of challenging behavior, you're simultaneously addressing the *why,* albeit in a somewhat indirect fashion.

There are a variety of skills that kids learn and practice by participating in Plan B, including (but by no means limited to) identifying, articulating, and clarifying their concerns; taking into account situational factors they may not have fully appreciated; understanding and taking into account the perspectives of other people; generating and considering alternative solutions; and working toward solutions that are realistic and mutually satisfactory. In fact, Plan B can be an effective way to teach and practice most of the skills on the ALSUP. To underscore this point, it might be a good idea to return to some of the skills that were highlighted and kids you were introduced to in Chapter 2 for some additional examples.

Would Plan B, for instance, be an effective way to help a kid better handle transitions? Let's see. Remember Kelvin, the fourth grader who has difficulty making transitions in general and has particular difficulty transitioning from choice time (playing a game with a friend) to the next activity (math)? Recall that he's also a black-and-white thinker who has difficulty taking another's perspective into account and moving off his original idea or plan. In the following dialogue, let's see if focusing on a specific unsolved problem (transitioning from choice time to math) helps us teach some of the skills Kelvin is lacking.

ADULT *(using Proactive B): Kelvin, I've noticed that sometimes it's hard for you to stop playing a game when it's time to move on to math. Have you noticed that?*
KELVIN: *Yup.*

ADULT: *So, what's up? Why is that hard for you?*

KELVIN: *You always make us end the game before we know who won.*

ADULT *(not quite understanding Kelvin's concern)*: *I always make you end the game before you know who won. That's true, sometimes I do make you end the game before you know who won. But I don't understand why that's hard for you.*

KELVIN: *How can the game be over if you don't know who won?*

ADULT *(still not quite comprehending)*: *So you need to know who won for the game to be over?*

KELVIN: *Yup. The White Sox don't stop playing till they know who won. The Bears don't stop playing till they know who won. The game isn't over until you know who won.*

ADULT: *So you feel very strongly that the game can't be over until you know who won. Is that the main reason it's hard for you to end the game and move on to math?*

KELVIN: *Yes.*

ADULT: *OK, I think I understand that. The thing is, you're a very important member of our class, and if you're still playing your game while the rest of the class is in math, you won't be part of our class. Plus, I want to make sure you learn the math. Know what I mean?*

KELVIN: *Yeah.*

ADULT: *So I'm wondering if there's a way for us to know who won the game but still have you be part of our class and learn the math. Do you have any ideas?*

KELVIN: *No.*

ADULT: *Well, let's take our time. I might have some ideas, but I'd rather wait until we hear if you have any.*

KELVIN *(sticking with his original plan)*: *I could keep playing and then come to math when the game is done.*

ADULT: *That's one idea. The thing is, if you did that, you still wouldn't be part of our class. And you wouldn't learn the math, either.*

KELVIN: *Yeah.*

ADULT: *Any other ideas?*

KELVIN: *We could save the game and I could come to math and then I could finish it later and see who won.*

ADULT: *You mean, we could save the game and you'd get back to it later to find out who the winner is?*

KELVIN: *Yes, but you'd have to put it up high somewhere so people wouldn't wreck it.*

ADULT: *Up high, like on a shelf somewhere?*

KELVIN: *Yeah, or else the game would get wrecked.*

ADULT: *I could do that. Kelvin, I think this idea could work. I mean, you'd know who won the game and could still be part of our community and learn the math.*

KELVIN: *Yep.*

ADULT: *Let's give it a try, and if, for some reason, it doesn't work as well as we think it will, we'll talk again and figure out some other solution. OK?*

KELVIN: *OK.*

On the basis of this one Plan B, was Kelvin's problem-transitioning from choice time to math durably solved? In this particular case, yes, the solution did end up solving the problem. In most cases, no, as the first solution seldom solves a problem durably. As you know, solving a problem durably usually requires a few visits to Plan B.

By focusing on this specific transition, was Kelvin "cured" of his difficulties making transitions in general? No. But Kelvin and his teacher worked toward solutions for other predictable problematic transitions in much the same way, and over time Kelvin's difficulty with transitions improved dramatically.

Did the work done on *predictable* transitions help Kelvin when he was faced with *unpredictable* ones? Because Kelvin and his teacher made a conscious effort to consider the transitions that occurred throughout a typical day and week and used Proactive Plan B to come up with a game plan for those that were likely to cause him difficulty, there weren't many unpredictable ones. Over time, they developed a general framework for thinking about and dealing with transitions ("Just because I need to move on to something else now doesn't mean I can't come back to it later, and if I start getting mad about needing to stop what I'm doing, I can talk to my teacher about it").

Plan B plus a helping relationship is a pretty powerful one-two punch.

Back to the original question: In focusing on the problem of moving from choice time to math, did this Plan B dialogue simultaneously help Kelvin with any of the skills he lacks (besides making transitions in general)? He did practice taking another person's perspective into account, moving off his original plan and considering other possible (mutually satisfactory) solutions, and considering situational factors that necessitated "grayer" rather than black-and-white thinking. So, yes, several skills were being addressed and practiced simultaneously. Of course, he needs more practice. Just like any other developmental delay.

Let's think about a few of the other skills that were highlighted in Chapter 2. Would Plan B be an effective way to help a kid (or an adult) *stay calm enough in the midst of frustration to think rationally* (separation of affect)? Remember, the main task presented to the human brain when faced with a frustration is to solve the problem that prompted the frustration in the first place. Plan B is a systematic, calm(er), thoughtful, (preferably) proactive approach to solving problems, and engages the kid in a process that ensures that his concerns will both be taken seriously and addressed. My experience is that Plan B eventually helps kids learn the skills they need to respond to life's frustrations with far more thought than emotion, and without as much help from adults.

How effective is Plan B at helping kids *keep track of their thoughts and approach problems in a more organized fashion?* Identifying lagging skills and unsolved problems helps kids and adults target the specific problems that need to be focused on and resolved. And, over multiple repetitions, the structured, systematic nature of Plan B provides a framework for incorporating the key ingredients necessary for working toward realistic, mutually satisfactory solutions to those problems.

Finally, an important skill Plan B teaches is *appreciating how one's behavior is affecting others.* Many kids who lack this skill receive continuous feedback on how their behavior is affecting others (e.g., "Rodney, the girls don't think that's very funny," "Luis, your noises are bothering everyone around you," "Akiko, if you call out without raising your hand, it's not fair to the kids who are raising their hands"), but somehow the feedback never quite seems to "sink in." How does Plan B teach this skill? The Define the Problem step focuses on the concern of the other party participating in Plan B with a kid. Often, this concern is related to how the problem or behavior is affecting either that individual or others in the kid's environment. For the problem to be solved, the way others are being affected must be taken into account and addressed. When you're using Plan B, the kid isn't merely on the receiving end of yet another dose of the same feedback. He's actually *working* on the problem. He's actually *thinking* about it.

By the way, there is another reason you'd want to kick off Plan B with an unsolved problem rather than a skill: It's easier. That's right, in general, it's easier to initiate Plan B with a specific problem than with a lagging skill. *But whether you initiate Plan B with an unsolved problem or a skill, what you're trying to resolve often shifts or is modified once you've achieved a clearer understanding of the concerns of the two parties.* Until these concerns are fully understood, the precise direction in which Plan B is heading is unknown. In the case of Kelvin, Plan B started by focusing on his difficulty transitioning from choice time to math, but it *ended up* focused on how he could be sure of knowing who won his game and still be a part of the class.

STARTING WITH SKILLS

As noted above, when Plan B is focused on resolving a specific problem or trigger, it is a rather indirect approach to teaching skills. There are some kids who will require a more direct approach to learning skills, especially (1) those skills related to participating in Plan B, and (2) those that are generally better taught in a more direct fashion. Let's tackle number one now and turn to number two after that.

The examples of Plan B you've read so far may have led you to believe that kids needs some pretty well developed language skills to participate in Plan B. Some kids, especially those who are sometimes called "low functioning" or "nonverbal," don't have the communication skills to identify and articulate their concerns and participate in generating solutions to problems. But that doesn't mean that Plan B isn't a viable option for these kids, though they will most certainly need extra help communicating their concerns and generating solutions to problems. Of course, there are some "high functioning" and "very verbal" people who have difficulty identifying and articulating their concerns and generating alternative solutions, so this section isn't solely applicable to the "low functioning" and "nonverbal" ones. General cognitive functioning is not the most important variable, communication is. Either way, there are skills to be taught.

Identifying and Articulating One's Concerns

Whether their communication skills are fairly intact or quite limited, kids who are having difficulty identifying and articulating their concerns need adults to help them develop a rudimentary vocabulary of concerns. For kids whose communication skills are fairly intact, the educated guessing/hypothesis testing strategy described in Chapter 5 should help. You may want to augment that strategy by creating a written list of the predictable concerns that reliably cause the kid to become frustrated so as to have a ready mechanism for pinpointing problems that might come into play (for example, bulky or itchy clothing, food that doesn't taste good, bothersome noises, being annoyed or bothered by a peer). The list of possibilities is endless but is usually confined to five or six reliable triggers for each kid. This should reduce the need for you to constantly guess quickly and accurately, and should eventually help the kid consider the possibilities and verbalize specific concerns more independently. I am reminded of the proud pronouncement a second grader made to his teacher: "I don't need my 'frustration list' anymore, now I'm good at knowing what's bothering me!" Of course, the ultimate goal is to help the kid resolve the concerns on his list through use of Proactive Plan B so they're not causing "emergent" frustration anymore.

In kids whose communication skills are more limited, developing a rudimentary vocabulary of concerns is still the goal. This may seem impossible for kids who are nonverbal, but your situational analysis should permit you to home in on triggers that are routinely frustrating the child and help you choose the vocabulary to be trained. If the child is unable to provide you with information about their concerns, you're going to be entirely dependent, at least for now, on your own observations and intuition. The initial goal may be to depict the child's common, predictable triggers or concerns in pictures so he can point to the concern that's causing problems at specific times. Over time, it may be possible to begin pairing pictures with specific words so that the child becomes less reliant on pointing at pictures and more proficient at using words.

One such kid—for what it's worth, his Full Scale IQ was in the mid-50s, and he had only rudimentary expressive language skills—was having great difficulty letting people know what was frustrating him, and this was precipitating some pretty extreme challenging behavior. However, through observation and past experience, the adults in his life were able to identify the concerns that were frustrating him most often: being hot, being tired, being hungry, thinking someone was mad at him, being surprised, and having difficulty with an academic task. The list of triggers was depicted in pictures on a laminated card, and the kid's teachers and parents familiarized him with their new communication tool. When the kid needed to let adults know there was a problem, or when he began exhibiting signs of frustration, the adults would ask him to point to the picture that best captured what was frustrating him. As the kid pointed at a picture, the adults would verbally confirm the problem (e.g., "Ah, you're hot"), thereby kicking off Plan B and, eventually, setting in motion solutions that had been agreed upon in earlier Proactive Plan B discussions. After multiple repetitions, the verbal prompts (such as "You're hot") provided the kid with the vocabulary he needed to eventually become less reliant on pictures and increasingly able to articulate a greater number of his concerns independently. As the kid's concerns became well-delineated and as specific words became part of his rudimentary vocabulary, the list was periodically modified so as to fit his evolving vocabulary and changing needs.

Naturally, when a kid has significant language delays or other cognitive impairments, it is crucial to give serious thought to which words or concepts are of the highest priority and need to be taught first. My usual vote is those words or concepts needed for pinpointing concerns, solving problems, and handling frustration, because the lack of this vocabulary causes the kids' most challenging moments and impedes their ability to learn much else.

You may have noticed that the CPS model doesn't place a strong emphasis on teaching kids a "feeling vocabulary." While it's useful for a kid to learn to let you know that he's "sad," "mad," or "frustrated," it's more important for him to let you know what concerns are causing him to be sad, mad, or frustrated in the first place. Otherwise, it won't be clear what problems need to be solved.

Specific concerns, such as "I'm hot," apply only to situations in which a kid is hot. You may find it useful to teach a "problem vocabulary" that can be applied across many situations. A variety of more generic phrases—for example, "Something's the matter," "I can't talk about that right now," "I need help," "I don't know what to do," and "I need a break"—are applicable to a wider range of circumstances and can be similarly taught through repetition (for example, saying "Looks like something's the matter" whenever it looks like something's the matter). Most kids need to be taught only the one or two phrases applicable to their specific requirements. We adults overestimate the linguistic skills we use to let people know we're frustrated, embarrassed, stuck, or overwhelmed; the truth is, most adults rely on only a few key phrases. By teaching kids a few of them, we're helping raise them to the same level as the rest of us.

GENERATING SOLUTIONS

With Plan B, kids are being asked not only to generate solutions but also to try to make sure that the solutions they generate take another person's concerns into account. Many kids become frustrated in response to this challenge—or simply shrug or stare blankly—so be prepared to lend a hand in helping them develop this skill.

Why wouldn't a kid be able to generate solutions to a problem? Given the variability in development of every other skill, we shouldn't expect less variability when it comes to thinking of solutions. Black-and-white thinkers often have difficulty envisioning solutions that differ even slightly from their original configuration. Disorganized thinkers often become overwhelmed by the sheer universe of potential solutions and need us to find ways to help them structure their thinking. Kids with delayed communication skills need us to help them find the words. And, of course, kids who get lots of Plan A thrown at them don't get much practice thinking about mutually satisfactory solutions (but get a lot of practice with solutions that are imposed by others and are not mutually satisfactory).

For kids whose communication skills are fairly intact but who seem unable to generate solutions, observing an adult proposing solutions in the Invitation step (as described in Chapter 5) often promotes imitation. But some kids, especially those whose communication skills are limited, will need something more basic and structured. Fortunately, the universe of Plan B solutions can be reduced to a framework of three categories:

1. ask for or seek help
2. give a little
3. do it a different way

These categories can be used to guide and structure consideration of possible solutions and, as with articulating one's concerns, can be taught and facilitated through repetition and the use of pictures. If the child is able to understand the general idea of each solution, then, after being oriented to the pictures, he should be able to point to the one he thinks would make the most sense for resolving a specific problem. The adults then provide a verbal prompt ("Ah, do it a different way") so as to confirm the kid's idea and encourage the use of words. Then the different ways in which things could be "done a different way" (so as to solve the problem) can be explored.

Do these suggestions represent the universe of possible ways to go about training these skills? No way. Your creativity, expertise, knowledge of a given child, and sense of the specific increments and doses of skills-training he can handle will be crucial. So long as you're recognizing that teaching the child skills, rather than relying exclusively on imposed solutions and punitive measures, is the key to helping him overcome his challenges, you're good to go.

Skill-Focused Plan B

Let's now turn our attention to other skills that might be better taught in a direct fashion. A kid wouldn't learn these skills through mere participation in Plan B, but Plan B is a good format for making the skills-training process more collaborative, thereby increasing the kid's investment and participation in learning the skills.

Let's say you were trying to help a kid who was lacking some basic social skills, like seeking attention in appropriate ways. In this instance, Proactive Plan B might sound something like this:

ADULT: *Sann, I've noticed that it's been a little hard for you to make friends this year. I was wondering if you have any ideas about that. You know, about why it's been a little hard for you to make friends.*

SANN: *Oh, I have plenty of friends.*

ADULT: *Well, let me put it a different way. I've noticed that some of the other kids aren't too crazy about some of the things you do. Like when you pull the girls' hair and run away.*

SANN: *Oh, they like that!*

ADULT: *How can you tell?*

SANN: *They laugh when I do it. Plus, it doesn't hurt.*

ADULT: *Well, Sann, this might surprise you, but several of the girls have complained to me about you pulling on their hair.*

SANN: *They have? Then why do they laugh about it?*

ADULT: *Sometimes people laugh when they think something is funny, but sometimes they laugh when something is making them uncomfortable. Because they're complaining to me about it, I think they might be laughing because they're uncomfortable.*

SANN: *Oh. OK.*

ADULT: *Sann, are you pulling on the girls' hair because you'd like them to notice you?*

SANN: *Um, kinda. But they don't want to hang out with me.*

ADULT: *I see.*

SANN: *Not just the girls. A lot of the boys, too.*

ADULT: *So a lot of the kids don't want to hang out with you. And that probably doesn't feel so great.*

SANN: *Well, it's not like I don't have a lot of friends.*

ADULT: *But it sounds like it bothers you a bit that some of the other kids don't want to hang out with you, yes?*

SANN: *Yes.*

ADULT: *Do you have any ideas about why some of the other kids might not want to hang out with you?*

SANN: *No.*

ADULT: *And you wish more kids were interested in hanging out with you, yes?*

SANN: *Yes.*

ADULT: *OK. I think I might be able to help you with that. Would that be good?*

SANN: *I don't know . . . I guess so.*

ADULT: *My concern is that some of the things you're doing so the other kids notice you actually make it less likely that they'll want to play with you. Do you know what I mean?*

SANN: *Not really.*

ADULT: *Well, you're pulling the girls' hair and running away because you want them to notice you. But the more you pull their hair and run away, the less they want to hang out with you, because your pulling their hair and running away is annoying to them. You with me?*

SANN: *Yes.*

ADULT: *So I wonder if there's some way we could help the other kids notice that you'd like to hang with them in ways that don't make them annoyed or uncomfortable. Do you have any ideas for how we could do that?*

SANN: *No.*

ADULT: *Well, let's think about it. Would it help if you and I practiced ways—you know, good ways—of letting kids notice that you want to hang with them?*

SANN: *I guess so.*

ADULT: *So I wonder how I could help you with that?*

SANN: *I guess you could teach me. I was in a social skills group once, but the kids were weird so I quit.*

ADULT: *You know, Mrs. Tobin, our guidance counselor, is thinking of putting together a lunch group of kids who need some help making friends. If you want I could tell her about you and see if she thought her group would work for you.*

SANN: *Nah. I don't want to do any more groups.*

ADULT: *OK, well that's only one idea. Do you have any others?*

SANN: *Could you teach me?*

ADULT: *Me? Well, I suppose that's a possibility. But I'm not exactly sure when I'd do that.*

SANN: *Well, I don't want to be in another group.*

ADULT: *You know, Sann, I'm not sure I'm the best one to be teaching you these things. But let me give it some thought. I'll do it if I can, but there might be someone better than me. Can you give me a few days to think about it?*

SANN: *OK. Or maybe Mrs. Tobin could teach me about it, but not in the group.*

ADULT: *There's an idea. Why don't I check with her about that, and if that solution isn't possible, we'll put our heads together again and see what we can come up with. Yes?*

SANN: *OK.*

ADULT: *Thanks for talking about this with me.*

SANN: *OK.*

Again, in the above dialogue, while Plan B wasn't being relied upon to teach the skills, it did provide a structure for approaching skills-training in a way that improved the prospects of a kid's participation in the process. In other words, approaching skills-training in this way helps the kid feel that learning skills is something that is being done *with* him rather than *to* him, thereby increasing the likelihood that he will actually think about the skills he's trying to learn and how to best go about learning them rather than being a passive recipient of adult ingenuity.

"DIFFERENTIATED DISCIPLINE"

Educators spend a lot of time talking and thinking about differentiating instruction for individual learners. Perhaps what you've read in this and preceding chapters has you thinking that reducing challenging behavior is no different, although the term *differentiated discipline* might be closer to the mark. When you're differentiating instruction, your expectations are pretty much the same for all students, but how you're helping them meet those expectations differs, especially for those who run into difficulty. The exact same principles apply when you're differentiating discipline.

In her excellent book, *The Differentiated Classroom: Responding to the Needs of All Learners,* Dr. Carol Ann Tomlinson describes the characteristics of teachers who are differentiating instruction. While Dr. Tomlinson's wisdom is primarily applied to academic challenges, let's look at how some of these principles extend to challenging behavior. I've added the parenthetical references to facilitate links.

Dr. Tomlinson writes that, in differentiated classrooms, teachers accept and build upon the premise that learners differ in important ways (both academically and behaviorally). These teachers do not force-fit students into a standard mold (or set of disciplinary procedures). They do not reach for standardized, mass-produced instruction (or disciplinary procedures) assumed to be a good fit for all students because they recognize that students (including the behaviorally challenging ones) are individuals. They accept, embrace, and plan for the fact that learners bring many commonalities to school, but that learners (and behavers) also bring the essential differences that make them individuals. They allow for this reality in many ways to make classrooms a good fit for each individual. They call upon a range of instructional strategies (including those that would be applied to the lagging skills and unsolved problems of challenging kids). They use time flexibly and become partners (collaborators, helpers) with their students to ensure that what is learned and the learning environment are shaped to the learner.

Why, so often, do we not extend these precepts to social, emotional, and behavioral challenges? Probably because many adults don't yet realize that such challenges occur because of *lagging skills and unsolved problems* and should be approached with precisely the same mentality, and in the same manner, as academic challenges.

Let's go back to the goals we wanted to accomplish through use of Plan B, summarized at the beginning of Chapter 5, and see if, by differentiating discipline, we're at least off to a good start:

- Ensure that your unmet expectations are pursued and that your concerns about a given kid's challenges are addressed. *Check.*
- Solve the problems precipitating a kid's challenging episodes durably and collaboratively. *Check.*
- Teach lacking thinking skills. *Check.*
- Reduce challenging behavior. *Check.*
- Create a helping relationship. *Check.*

Well done. So long as you understand that you're not quite done yet.

Q & A

Question: I understand the necessity of making sure that a challenging kid has the skills to participate in Plan B. But there are some kids who just won't talk to me, even though I think they have the skills to do it. **Answer:** While Plan B can run aground for any of the reasons described in this and the preceding chapter, adults often comment that they "never got past the Empathy step," frequently because "the kid didn't have a concern" or because "he denied there was a problem" or because "the kid wouldn't talk."

As you now know, there are a variety of factors that can interfere with a kid talking. But hopefully you're reasonably certain that you didn't use Plan A (in many kids, Plan A is a very effective conversation stopper), that your Empathy step wasn't perfunctory (some kids clam up instantaneously when adults dismiss or come to erroneous conclusions about their concerns), that your timing was good (Emergency B is generally not the ideal way to help reluctant talkers talk), that you used the steps in the proper order (are you sure you didn't start Plan B with *your* concern?), and that the kid has the skills to participate in Plan B.

What else would make it hard for a kid to talk? While many kids will begin talking simply because you're *not* using Plan A, some won't. Many start talking again because someone is finally trying to understand their concerns, but some don't. Some kids lost faith and trust in adults a long time ago. Some don't know what it's like to have an adult try to help in ways that aren't punitive. Some are so accustomed to having their concerns dismissed that they've just stopped talking. Some come to view adults as "the enemy." So you have your work cut out for you.

Some adults have an easier time forging relationships with challenging kids and drawing them out. They have a natural feel for how to approach these kids, are good at connecting with them about things that aren't related to school, and often use humor to help them feel more comfortable. But that doesn't mean that those who are less "natural" can't grow better at it.

It's important to remember that Plan B is not a robotic exercise and that the three steps of Plan B represent three *ingredients* necessary for the collaborative resolution of problems. So far, the official goal of the Empathy step has been to achieve the clearest possible understanding of the kid's concern or perspective related to a particular issue. But for kids who are reluctant participants in Plan B, there's a different goal—*just get the kid talking*—and this goal often requires a less direct approach, one in which, at least for the time being, you give thought to what the kid *will* talk about rather than what you *want* him to talk about.

Let's go back to two of the kids you met in Chapter 2 (and have been reintroduced to at a few points along the way), starting with six-year-old Cody. Recall that Cody was hitting his classmates a lot and that his teacher had tried talking with Cody about the hitting, but that Cody's response was to deny that there was a problem, shrug, or walk away. The teacher's attempts at Proactive Plan B on this issue usually began with "I've noticed that you've been hitting a lot lately. What's up?" But when that opening wasn't successful, she hypothesized that this was too direct and not conducive to drawing Cody out. She tried a more indirect approach, recalling that, on one of the few occasions on which Cody had said anything about the hitting, he had stated that the other kids had been teasing him. His teacher thought that Cody might be more likely to talk about being teased than about hitting. She began her next attempt at Proactive Plan B with teasing as the focus of her entry statement:

TEACHER: *Cody, I've noticed that you feel the other kids tease you a lot.*

CODY: *Huh?*

TEACHER: *I've noticed that you feel the other kids tease you a lot, and I'd like to hear more about that.*

CODY: *Why? Am I in trouble?*

TEACHER: *No, no, you're not in trouble. I was thinking maybe I can do something so they tease you less.*

CODY: *You can't.*

TEACHER: *Hmm. Sounds like you don't feel anyone's helped you with it before.*

CODY *(shrugs)*

TEACHER: *Has anyone ever tried?*

CODY: *Tried what?*

TEACHER: *To get the other kids to tease you less.*

CODY: *I don't know.*

TEACHER: *Would it be good if we could get you teased less?*

CODY: *Whatever.*

TEACHER: *I'd like to try, but I'm going to need you to help me know what's going on.*

CODY: *There's nothing you can do. I don't want to talk about this anymore.*

TEACHER: *OK. But if you think of something I can do to help, I'd like to try. I'm pretty good at helping kids not get teased, but I'm going to need your help.*

What a disaster, yes? Actually, no. Believe it or not, the teacher left this attempt at Plan B more optimistic that Cody would eventually talk about this problem, and she turned out to be right. Plan B eventually focused not only on Cody being teased by the other kids but also on ways he could deal with it more effectively—without hitting. What were the key ingredients? Convincing Cody that she wasn't his enemy, that it wasn't horrible to need someone's help, and that she truly cared about his well-being. It took awhile, but in the process she found that Cody did have concerns, knew there was a problem, and would talk.

Elena is the thirteen-year-old seventh grader who can be defiant in response to even simple requests, refuses to do any work when she's partnered with a classmate she doesn't like, skips class, and refuses to remove her iPod when asked. But you may recall that she doesn't exhibit these behaviors in every class. In fact, she's a totally different kid depending on what class she's in. One of the teachers with whom she has the most difficulty attempted to do Plan B with Elena, but Elena responded, "I'm not talking to *you* about anything!" Upon hearing of this in a meeting, one of the teachers who had a half-decent relationship with Elena volunteered to attempt Plan B. Rather than start the Empathy step with "I've noticed you won't do any work unless you're partnered with someone you like," or "I've noticed you don't like to switch seats when I ask you to," it went like this:

TEACHER: *How are you getting along with Mrs. Oliver these days?*

ELENA: *Why, what'd she say?*

TEACHER: *Nothing, really. I just get the feeling she's not your favorite.*

ELENA: *No, seriously, what did she say? I know she said something. She hates me.*

TEACHER: *How come she hates you?*

ELENA: *I don't know, she just does. What did she say?*

TEACHER: *She just told me she tried to talk with you about something and you wouldn't talk to her.*

ELENA: *Why would I talk to her? All she does is get on my case.*

TEACHER: *So her getting on your case makes you not want to talk with her.*

ELENA: *Why would I want to talk with her? She doesn't listen.*

TEACHER: *What was she trying to talk to you about?*

ELENA: *I don't know . . . something about how come I don't do work in her class.*

TEACHER: *So maybe it's better if you talk about that with someone who you feel is better at listening and isn't on your case so much.*

ELENA: *Yeah, probably.*

Elena was talking. It turned out that Elena had a lot to say and had legitimate concerns. But it took someone who had a decent relationship with her and a less direct approach to discover it. Once Elena started talking and her concerns were clarified, and once all her teachers learned how to do Plan B, Elena also started talking with the teacher she said she'd never talk to.

Question: I was doing Plan B with a kid in my class and things seemed to be going well for a few weeks but then deteriorated again. What happened?

Answer: It could be that the solution you and the kid agreed on wasn't as realistic and mutually satisfactory as it originally seemed. That's a fairly common occurrence, and it means that there is some additional problem-solving to do. It could also be that your initial success was due more to the quick burst of relationship-enhancing that occurs with Plan B. Durably solving problems takes longer, and teaching skills longer still. Unfortunately, it's when initial Plan B solutions fail to stand the test of time that adults are most prone to discard their improved relationship with a challenging kid and head back to the Plan A hills. Don't forget, Plan A wasn't working very well for a long time. The ingredients Plan B brings to interacting with and helping kids are reliable but not magical.

In fact, once people start using the CPS model with a kid, they discover that there's an impressive, perhaps overwhelming, pile of accumulated problems that have been precipitating challenging behavior for a long time. Remember, you won't be able to solve them all at once. Work toward solutions for one or two problems at a time, then move on to other problems once those initial problems are solved, all the while watching for whether the solutions to the initial problems are standing the test of time. After a while, you'll have made quite a dent in the pile of problems and the kid will have the beginnings of some new skills. Keep returning to the pile as necessary.

Question: Aren't there some challenging kids who need meds?

Answer: Yes, though nowhere near as many as are actually *on* meds. Overmedicating kids flows from an overemphasis on diagnoses, the ease with which medications are prescribed, a lack of awareness of the true factors underlying kids' challenging behavior, the failure to achieve a comprehensive understanding of a kid's challenges, and a lack of knowledge of Plan B. That said, there are some kids for whom psychotropic medication is an indispensable component of treatment and whose participation in Plan B is impossible without medication. It's crucial to differentiate between the things psychotropic medicine does well and the things psychotropic medicine does not do well lest, as is commonly the case, medicine be prescribed for things medicine does not do well. Medicine is effective at reducing hyperactivity and poor impulse control, improving attention span, enhancing mood, reducing obsessive-compulsive behaviors and general anxiety, reducing tics, inducing sleep, and helping volatile, aggressive kids be less reactive. Medicine does not teach skills.

Question: What if school staff thinks a kid needs medication and the parents don't agree?
Answer: First, you'll want to assume that the parents have legitimate concerns about medicating their child. You'll want to hear as much as possible about those concerns (that would be the Empathy step). Then you'll want to describe the specific difficulties the child is having that you feel would be well-addressed by medication (that would be the Define the Problem step). Then start brainstorming to arrive at solutions that address the concerns of both parties (the Invitation), if necessary (and with parents agreeing that it's a good idea) bringing in additional expertise and collaborating with professionals who may already be working with the child. "Medication yes" versus "medication no" is just dueling solutions.

Question: You said it was going to take awhile to become skilled at Plan B and solve the problems on my trigger list and teach some of the skills on the ALSUP. What do I do in the meantime while I'm waiting for Plan B to work?
Answer: You're *reducing your use of Plan A* because you now understand that Plan A heightens the likelihood of challenging behavior in challenging kids. Thus, you've eliminated many of the challenging behaviors that could have been set in motion through your use of Plan A. And because you now understand that the kid can't handle all the expectations on his radar screen, you've *increased the use of Plan C,* thereby eliminating some expectations and reducing challenging behavior even further. While Plan B is the process by which you're pursuing

the expectations that remain, teaching skills, and helping the kid solve problems, it's not the only ingredient in the mix.

But it depends a little on what you mean by *working*. What a lot of people mean by *working* is that the problem-solving process has reached its ultimate destination: the problem has been durably solved. But there are a lot of "workings" on the way to the ultimate destination, and it's important not to lose sight of them. At the micro level, Plan B is working if a kid is willing to stay in the room with you to talk about an unsolved problem. It's working if the kid actually talks (if he doesn't, then Plan B is working if you've started pondering why he's not talking so that he eventually does talk); if the adults finally achieve a clear understanding of the kid's concern or perspective; if the kid listened to your concern; if you and the kid are contemplating solutions together; if you agree on a solution and begin to enact it. And it's working if the kid is willing to return to Plan B if the first solution doesn't stand the test of time. At the macro level, Plan B is working if your relationship with the kid is improving. It's all good, even though solving the problem durably is your ultimate destination.

That said, there are certainly times when you'll need what might be called interim interventions while you're on the way to solving a problem. For example, even though Kelvin's teachers were aggressively trying to solve the problems that were precipitating his challenging episodes, they didn't make enough progress early on to circumvent a lot of these episodes. Specifically, they had to find a place for him to cool off and collect himself if he became agitated and had to develop a plan for him to seek help from adults. Once they started making inroads on the problems that were setting the stage for his challenging episodes, his use of his cooling-off spot and frequency of seeking help were dramatically reduced.

Question: In the research literature, training cognitive skills in kids with challenging behavior often hasn't fared very well. How is CPS different?
Answer: In the research literature (and in real life) cognitive skills training has often been conducted outside the environments in which a kid is having the greatest difficulty and by people the kid isn't having difficulty with—for example, in the office of a guidance counselor, prin-

cipal, or mental health professional or in a researcher's lab. Skills taught in these artificial environments often haven't generalized to the environments in which the kid was having difficulty. In addition, the training has often been done in a rote, circumscribed fashion using skills-training modules or curriculum that were not tailored to the specific lagging skills or unsolved problems of individual kids, so the skills weren't learned. The CPS model is designed to be applied by those who are in the environments in which a kid is having his greatest difficulties, and the artistry of the model is how it is tailored to individual kids.

Question: I'm having trouble imagining doing Plan B with kids younger than ten years old.
Answer: Plan B is frequently successfully implemented with kids as young as three years of age. The key variable is developmental skills, not chronological age. I've worked with three-year-olds who were able to participate in Plan B more readily than many of the seventeen-year-olds with whom I've worked.

Question: Does CPS help with kids on the autism spectrum?
Answer: It's often assumed that the CPS model has no application to these kids, and that well-known applied behavior analysis methodology is really the only option. I beg to differ. "Autism spectrum" doesn't say anything about the kid's general cognitive functioning, and unless you're ready to throw in the towel on teaching the kid lagging skills or helping him learn to solve problems—and hopefully you're not—then CPS may well have a role to play. The most common obstacle is communication skills.

As described earlier in this chapter, you'll want to focus first on helping the kid develop the skills to communicate his concerns (often through pictures or hand signals) in a very rudimentary manner, and if the kid is unable to provide much information about his concerns, then your powers of observation and intuition will be crucial. Of course, because your powers of observation and intuition aren't infallible, you'll need to continue observing and intuiting so you can recognize if you've hit the nail on the head with your hypotheses about the kid's concerns. Then you'll want to focus (if it's feasible) on help-

ing the kid express those concerns verbally and watch closely to see
if there is some mechanism for the kid to participate in generating
solutions.

Question: Are there kids Plan B won't help? Who need to be placed
in programs outside of public schools?
Answer: There are kids who might, despite our best efforts, need to
be placed in such programs. But it would be interesting to see how the
numbers of those kids would change if more schools were incorporating CPS into their practices for assessing and addressing the needs of
kids with behavioral challenges. In several current projects, researchers
are examining the degree to which implementation of the CPS model
reduces not only challenging behavior but also special ed costs and
referrals, the use of suspension, detention, and expulsion, and place-
ment of kids in programs outside of their home schools.

The Story Continues . . .

On the Monday morning after Joey's run-in with the sub, Mrs. Woods,
Mrs. Franco, Dr. Bridgman, and Mr. Middleton gathered in the assistant
principal's office. Joey was asked to wait outside for a few minutes.

"Mrs. Woods, how do you feel?" asked Mr. Middleton.

"Not completely up to par, but I'm here," said Mrs. Woods.

Mrs. Franco looked sympathetically at her friend. "She should have
stayed home another day."

"Mrs. Woods, I talked with Mrs. Franco and Mr. Owens about what
happened in your classroom on Friday," said Mr. Middleton. "It seems
that we didn't do a great job of letting poor Mr. Owens know about the
plan you had worked out with Joey. I'm going to apologize to Joey for
that. I assume your plan had been working up until then?"

"Joey and I have been meeting some days before school to go over
assignments that I think might be confusing for him," said Mrs. Woods.
"He's been very good so far about coming to school early to meet with
me, and he's been using a signal we've developed to let me know if I've
missed any."

"Good," said Mr. Middleton. "But walking out of the classroom and pounding his fist into a locker is not acceptable behavior around here, and Joey needs to know that. Now, I thought we should meet because I wanted to respect the fact that you all have been working together to help Joey control himself. And I wanted to involve you in the discussion about what we're going to do about what happened on Friday. I know that Mrs. Franco feels Joey handled himself reasonably well on Friday—I can't say that's my perspective exactly, but I wanted to get everyone's input."

"Well, whether what happened on Friday was an improvement or not, it tells us we have more work to do, especially in the communicating department," said Dr. Bridgman. "And I also think that we should probably start talking with Joey about why he gets embarrassed so easily in front of the other kids and about what we can do to keep that from happening."

Mr. Middleton considered this perspective. "OK, of course, we still have the matter of our school discipline code to consider. And what our school discipline code says is that Joey should be receiving one detention for leaving the classroom without permission and in-school suspension for destruction of property."

"It says that, does it?" asked Mrs. Franco.

"Yes, it does," said Mr. Middleton. "Why?"

"You want my honest opinion?" asked Mrs. Franco.

Mr. Middleton smiled. "Mrs. Franco, I've learned that under most circumstances you're going to give me your honest opinion whether I want it or not."

Mrs. Franco returned the smile. "Well, no offense, but I don't think much of our school discipline code. I'm the one who ran after him when he left the classroom and I'm the one who was out in the hall with him. And I'll admit I was scared when he hit that locker. But I could see how hard he was trying to hold it together, and I think punishing him for trying hard is not the message we want to be sending him."

"Of course, telling him it's OK to leave the classroom and slam lockers is not the message we want to be sending, either," said Mr. Middleton.

Dr. Bridgman cleared his throat. "We have other options besides Plan C—where we're doing nothing about what happened and maybe giving Joey the impression that what he did was OK—and Plan A, where we're punishing Joey for what happened. Don't forget about Plan B."

Mr. Middleton leaned forward in his chair. "Tell me more."

"Joey knows that leaving the classroom and punching a locker aren't OK," said Dr. Bridgman. "But he still doesn't know what to do when he's embarrassed in front of the other kids, and he didn't know what to do when Mr. Owens didn't know the plan. But detentions aren't going to teach him those things. If we do Plan B with Joey, we'll work on solving those problems, especially the embarrassment one, because it comes up a lot."

"And what message are we sending the other kids if we don't do what the school discipline code says we're supposed to do?" asked Mr. Middleton.

"What message are we sending the other kids if we continue to apply an intervention that isn't working?" asked Dr. Bridgman.

Mr. Middleton smiled slowly. "Dr. Bridgman, that's a good question. Mrs. Woods, Joey spends most of his time with you. What do you think?"

"For one thing, I think I wish I hadn't gotten sick," said Mrs. Woods. "But I'm torn. I don't think giving him a detention is going to accomplish anything, but I also understand that we can't send the wrong message to the other kids."

"I think we need to do what's best for Joey," said Dr. Bridgman. "I don't think the other kids care whether we follow the school discipline code. I think they want us to do whatever it takes for Joey to have better control of himself."

"But if we don't stick to the discipline code, what's to stop the other kids from just walking out of class and hitting a locker?" asked Mr. Middleton.

"The other kids aren't behaving themselves because of the discipline code," said Dr. Bridgman. "They're behaving themselves because they *can*. They've been watching Joey get punished for a long time. What they want us to do is *help* him. We don't teach every kid academics the exact same way, especially if they're struggling. I don't think we should apply a rigid algorithm of punishments to a kid if he's struggling, either."

"So you think we should just stick with Plan B and skip the detentions," said Mr. Middleton.

"I think we should get Joey in here and discuss it with him," said Dr. Bridgman. "He'll probably be harder on himself than any of us would be."

Mr. Middleton looked at Mrs. Woods and Mrs. Franco. "What do you think?"

"I like it," said Mrs. Franco.

"Sounds fine," said Mrs. Woods.

Mr. Middleton rose and invited Joey into his office. Joey glanced nervously at the four adults as he sat down. "Joey, as I told you, we thought it would be a good idea to talk about what happened on Friday. Remember?"

"Yes sir."

"First off, how's your hand?"

Joey looked down at his bandaged hand. "Nothing got broken."

"Ah, good. Those lockers hit awfully hard, don't they?"

"Um, yes sir." Joey failed to recognize Mr. Middleton's attempt at humor.

"Joey, I want to apologize for the fact that Mr. Owens didn't know about the plan you had developed with Mrs. Woods. We should have let him know what was going on. But I'm sure you know that it's not OK to leave the classroom without permission. And it's not OK to hit lockers, either. We'd like to hear your ideas about what to do next."

Dr. Bridgman wasn't sure Joey understood what Mr. Middleton was asking for. "Joey, I think what Mr. Middleton is saying is that we'd like to talk about what we might do to try to make sure that what happened Friday doesn't happen again."

Joey wasn't accustomed to being asked for his opinion, so his first proposal was something he'd heard adults say to him many times. "I could try harder."

"Ah, that would be good, Joey," said Mr. Middleton. "According to our school discipline code, I should be giving you detention for leaving the class without permission and in-school suspension for hitting the locker. But your teachers and Dr. Bridgman feel that punishing you might not be fair since it's not your fault Mr. Owens didn't know the plan and Mrs. Franco, here, feels you tried really hard not to get upset."

"I don't really mind doing in-school suspension," said Joey. "I haven't been in there yet this year."

Dr. Bridgman smiled. "Well, Joey, I suppose you could do in-school suspension. But I'm wondering . . . besides the fact that Mr. Owens didn't know the plan, is there anything else we should know about why you left the classroom?"

"I don't know."

"Well, let's think about it a second," said Dr. Bridgman. "We're in no rush."

Joey tried to think. "I don't know."

"I know the last time you got upset in the classroom you were embarrassed. Were you embarrassed this time?" asked Dr. Bridgman.

"Yes. Everybody was looking at me."

"Here's what I'm thinking," said Dr. Bridgman. "You and Mrs. Woods have a really good plan in place to help with confusing assignments. And it's working . . . when Mrs. Woods isn't sick. Luckily, she's not sick too often. But I'm thinking that we don't have a plan yet for what to do when you get embarrassed. In fact, we don't really know much about why you get embarrassed. So I'm thinking me and you and Mrs. Woods might need to have a conversation about that, just like we did about the confusing assignments. Then we could have a plan for helping you with embarrassment, too. What do you think?"

"OK."

"Mrs. Woods, are there any good times today that we could do that?" asked Dr. Bridgman.

Mrs. Woods looked at Joey. "Well, if it's not too embarrassing for you, we could do it during lunch . . . you could have lunch in the classroom with me today."

"What do you think, Joey?" asked Dr. Bridgman.

Joey didn't like this idea at all. "Um, well, the other kids . . ."

"I think you'd like to pick a different time," smiled Mrs. Woods.

Joey looked relieved. "Yes."

"Can you stay after school today?" asked Mrs. Woods. "No one will be around."

"Yes."

"I have some other meetings this afternoon," said Dr. Bridgman. "So if you want me there . . ."

"I think Joey and I could try to work on this one on our own," said Mrs. Woods. "Sound OK to you, Joey?"

Joey nodded.

"Sounds like a plan," said Mr. Middleton.

Joey had a lingering concern. "Am I getting detentions . . . or in-school suspension?"

Mr. Middleton rubbed his jaw. "You know what, Joey, for now, because I'm seeing that you and Dr. Bridgman and your teachers are working hard on making sure these episodes don't happen anymore, I think I'm going to hold off on the punishment. I won't be able to do that every time . . . and I need you to try very hard not to leave the classroom or slam lockers with your fist anymore. Understood?"

"Yes sir."

Mr. Middleton stood up. "OK, then, let's get you and your teachers and Dr. Bridgman on your way, and I'll check in with you all to find out how we're doing."

On their way out of Mr. Middleton's office, Mrs. Woods pulled Dr. Bridgman aside. "Do you have a minute?"

"Sure, what's up?"

"I realize I don't know what I'm doing yet, but I tried Plan B with one of my other students last week."

"You did? Fantastic!"

"Well, I don't know how fantastic it was. We didn't get very far."

"How come?"

"I'm not really sure. I was hoping you could tell me what I did wrong."

"Sure. What's the kid's name?"

"Consuelo. Very quiet kid . . . looks like she's scared of her own shadow. I was thinking that since Plan B seems to be doing Joey some good, maybe I should try to do the same thing with her . . . you know, to try to help her participate a little more in class."

Dr. Bridgman smiled. "Mrs. Woods, if everyone was as receptive to Plan B as you've been, I could retire."

"I don't think you're in much danger of tapping into your retirement funds just yet."

"So what happened?"

"I told her I'd noticed that she didn't participate much in class discussions and I was wondering if she could tell me why. But she didn't know. So I kept going with the second step, Define the Problem. I told her I thought she probably had a lot of good ideas and that it would be great if the other kids in the class could hear them. And then I asked her if she could think of ideas for how we could solve that problem. But she didn't have any ideas."

"Well, it sounds like you did the three steps of Plan B. But you may have rushed through the Empathy step before you actually got Consuelo's concern on the table, so it wasn't clear what problem you were trying to solve."

"Yes, right, that's what I thought," said Mrs. Woods. "But, like I said, she didn't know what her concern was."

"Yes, exactly."

Mrs. Woods wondered if Dr. Bridgman understood her dilemma. "So what should I have done?"

"You should have guessed."

This answer took Mrs. Woods by surprise. "Guessed?"

"Yes, if she doesn't know what's getting in the way of her participating in class discussions, we'll have to help her figure it out. Luckily, there are only a finite number of reasons she might not be participating in class discussions. Do you have any hypotheses about why it's hard for her?"

"I know she's had language therapy in the past. I was thinking maybe she wasn't sure what to say, or doesn't understand what the other kids are saying. But I didn't know if I should go putting ideas into her head."

"Oh, if she's having difficulty putting her concerns on the table, it's perfectly fine to hypothesize. So long as you're open to the possibility that your hypotheses may be off base."

"So I could have said something like, 'Is it because you're having trouble understanding what the other kids are saying?'"

"Yeah, that would be great," said Dr. Bridgman.

"Guess I'm still trying to figure out what all the Plan B rules are." Mrs. Woods smiled.

"No rules, really. Just some rules of thumb. But now you're ready to go back and try to help Consuelo figure out what her concerns are. Then you guys can get the problem solved."

"So if my first guess is wrong? Should I just keep guessing?"

"Sure, if you have other hypotheses."

"Well, like I said, she's scared of her own shadow. So maybe she's just really nervous or afraid of what others will think of what she says."

"Good hypothesis."

Mrs. Woods seemed pleased. "Thanks, Coach."

"Sure thing. Oh, by the way, I was talking to Joey's mom on the phone the other day. I'd still like to see if we can find another time to meet with her. I think it would be good for us all to sit down with her to tell her what we're trying to do with Joey. She wants to help out."

"That would be fine. Maybe she can take Joey's place at one of our meetings before school. That is, if Joey'll give up his time."

"Good idea. I'll run that by her. Maybe you can run it by Joey when you see him."

Joey stayed after school for the conversation he'd scheduled with Mrs. Woods earlier in the day. Mrs. Woods, still feeling the lingering effects of her illness, suddenly realized she hadn't really noticed Joey for most of the day. No signals. No problems.

"Joey, you've been very quiet today," said Mrs. Woods. "Everything OK?"

"Well, there weren't any assignments that I got confused about. So I guess I didn't need you today."

Mrs. Woods smiled. "No, I guess you didn't need me today. Of course, there are other things we could be working on besides you not knowing what to do on an assignment."

"Like what?"

"Well, remember what Dr. Bridgman said about how you sometimes get embarrassed in front of your classmates?"

"Oh, yeah," said Joey, looking uncomfortable.

"I was thinking maybe we could try to figure out what it is that you're getting embarrassed about."

"OK."

"So, what do you think?"

"About what?"

Mrs. Woods wondered if understanding Joey's concerns was always going to be this hard. She tried to hide a deep breath. "I was wondering if you had any ideas about why you get embarrassed so easily in front of your classmates."

Joey pondered the question. "I don't know."

"Take your time. There's no rush."

"See, I, uh, I've been getting in trouble at school for a long time."

Mrs. Woods tried not to respond too quickly, hoping Joey would elaborate. She was not so lucky. "You've been getting in trouble in school for a long time."

"And, see, I'm, uh, I'm kinda . . . tired . . ."

Mrs. Woods nodded her encouragement.

Joey shrugged. "I don't think I know how to say it."

"I think you're doing fine."

"It's just, I'm tired of . . . of being the kid who always gets into trouble. I'm tired of being the kid who doesn't know how to do assignments. I'm tired of being different." Joey paused. "I want to be normal. For once."

Mrs. Woods suddenly felt great tenderness for this student of hers. "I'm not sure what to say, Joey. I'm sorry you feel that way. I'm sorry you don't feel normal. I really am."

Joey felt the need to reassure his teacher. "That's OK. I'm kinda used to it."

"It's not OK for you not to feel normal, Joey," Mrs. Woods gently insisted.

Joey was silent.

"So help me understand something," said Mrs. Woods, returning to Plan B. "I understand that you're tired of feeling different. And that you're tired of not feeling normal. But I'm not sure I understand how that makes you feel so embarrassed in front of the other kids."

"'Cuz I know what they think of me. I know they're looking at me like I'm some . . . some kind of *freak*. Like I'm messed up or something. So when I don't know how to do an assignment, and I'm trying hard not to get upset, and then I get upset anyways, I know that's what they're thinking. It just makes me . . ."

"More upset," said Mrs. Woods, finishing Joey's sentence.

"Yeah. So, anyways, I don't think there's anything you can do to help me with any of this."

"I wouldn't be so sure about that. How do you know the other kids think you're messed up?"

"Well, they tell me I'm stupid," said Joey, "and call me names."

"What names?"

"Like 'head case.' Or 'moron.' And other ones I can't say to you."

"I see what you mean," Mrs. Woods said grimly. "Tell me, do *you* think you're a head case? Or a moron?"

"I know there's something the matter with me."

"And you think something's the matter with you because . . ."

"Because I'm the only one in the class who goes nuts, and needs shrinks, and medicine." Joey looked at Mrs. Woods. "Still think you can help me?"

"Joey, I'm wondering if there's anything I could do to help you not think there's something the matter with you . . . and to help you worry a little less about what you believe the other kids are thinking."

"Huh?"

"What I mean is, well, now that I'm getting to know you, I don't think you're messed up at all. So, now that *I* know that, I wonder how I could help *you* know that?"

Joey wasn't quite following. "I don't know."

"I don't, either. I'd like to think about it some more. How 'bout we talk about it again next time we meet?"

"OK."

"Good, then," said Mrs. Woods, who, despite her fatigue, had a fresh look of determination. "By the way, is it OK with you if I meet with your mom during one of our morning meetings? She'd like to know more about how to help you, too."

"Instead of me, you mean?"

"If that's OK . . ."

"Are you gonna tell her about the stuff we talk about?"

"If there's anything you don't want me to tell her, just let me know."

Joey considered this. "I guess it's OK for her to know."

"And you don't mind me taking one of our mornings to meet with her?"

"No, that's OK. Only one, right?"

"Right. Joey, I'm glad you told me what was embarrassing you. I think it's something we can work on. And now at least you know that there's one person in our class who doesn't think you're a head case or a moron."

"Who?"

"Me."

Mrs. Franco stuck her head inside Mrs. Woods' classroom a few days later. "You ready to go? I'll walk out with you."

"No, not quite," said Mrs. Woods. "You go ahead."

"What're you doing?" asked Mrs. Franco.

"Practicing," said Mrs. Woods.

"Practicing? Practicing what?"

"Doing Plan B with Consuelo. Tried it already, but I got sidetracked. So I asked Dr. Bridgman what I did wrong. He gave me a few ideas. So now I'm practicing."

Mrs. Franco sat down. "Cool. What's the Plan B about?"

"Well, you know what a quiet kid she is. Nothing the matter with being quiet, of course, but I sure would like her to participate more in class. So I need to find out what's getting in her way."

"You're really taking this Plan B stuff seriously, aren't you?"

"This is going to sound a little sappy, but in a way I feel like I've been less connected to my students for a long time. And now, I feel like I have a way of connecting with them again. Not only connecting with them, *helping* them. Like with Joey . . . I've been having some very interesting conversations with him. I feel like I know him much better than I did just a few weeks ago. I'm not scared of him anymore. Turns out he's been feeling pretty bad for a long time about how the other kids have been treating him. Kind of explains a lot."

"Wow," said Mrs. Franco. "Of course, it's not like we never talked to the kids before Dr. Bridgman arrived."

"Yeah, but Plan B is different than just talking to a kid. I think a lot of adults who think they're talking *with* a kid are really talking *at* the kid. Plan B helps you talk *with* the kid."

"So now you're trying the same thing with Consuelo?"

"Trying. But not just Consuelo. I've got big plans for two or three others in my class."

"And you're doing this yourself?"

"Well, I can ask Dr. Bridgman for help when I need it. But I want to become good at it myself."

"You're brave. So you really think there's something to it, huh?"

"It just makes sense to me. Of course, the proof's in the pudding. Doesn't matter how much Plan B I do if I have nothing to show for it in the end."

Mrs. Franco hated to miss out on a good thing. "Well, you and I usually think alike. I wonder if I should be doing Plan B with some of my kids." She paused. "You know, I bet I'm not the only one who'd like to know more about how to do Plan B. I was talking to Christine Estrada, the new seventh-grade teacher—you know I'm her mentor this year—boy, is she overwhelmed. Always has that 'deer in the headlights' look. Says she's spending so much time on behavior problems that she has no time left to teach. But the last time we talked, she wondered if there was a way we teachers could get together just to talk about stuff that goes on in our classrooms, you know, maybe exchange ideas."

"Interesting concept," said Mrs. Woods. "When would we do that?"

"Well, that's the thing. We talk about how to improve ourselves as teachers all the time in this school. But it's always about academics. How come we never talk about improving how we handle our tough kids?"

Mrs. Woods sighed. "Your guess is as good as mine. By the way, I've emailed Joey's mom to try to arrange a meeting to talk about him some more. You free next Tuesday morning before the kids get here?"

"That should be fine."

"Good. It seems like she really wants to work with us."

Later in the week, Mrs. Woods asked Consuelo to join her for lunch. After some small talk, Mrs. Woods plunged into Plan B. "Consuelo, remember the other day when I was asking you about why you didn't participate very much in our class discussions?"

Consuelo nodded and took a bite from her sandwich.

"You know, we never really did figure out why you don't participate very much," continued Mrs. Woods. "So I thought we could talk about it some more."

"OK," said Consuelo.

"When I asked you if you had any ideas about why you don't participate, you said you didn't know. I was wondering if you maybe gave it some thought and had some ideas now."

"No. I don't think so."

This time Mrs. Woods was prepared. "I might have some ideas about it. Would you like to hear them?"

"OK."

"Well, I was wondering if maybe it was hard for you to understand some of the questions I'm asking you to respond to. Do you think that could be it?"

"You mean, am I having trouble, um, understanding what you want us to talk about?" Consuelo pondered this possibility. "I don't think that's the problem."

"OK. Another possibility is that you're having trouble following along with what the others kids are saying. Could that be it?"

"I don't think so."

"Are you worried about what the other kids will think of what you're saying?"

"No, I don't . . . I don't care about that."

"Do you have ideas for what it is that you'd like to say?"

"Um, sometimes. But I . . . I don't know what to say."

"You mean you don't know how to say it?"

Consuelo nodded.

"Ah, I was thinking that could be it," said Mrs. Woods. "So the words aren't coming to you so easily."

"I think so," said Consuelo slowly. "Like, um, sometimes, I kind of have an idea . . . of what I want to say, and, you know, I'm not sure how I could say it."

Mrs. Woods nodded her encouragement.

"And I know it takes me a long time to say stuff," Consuelo slowly continued, "and the other kids are, you know, they have their hands up and stuff, and they have things they could say. And I just think, you know, it's better if they talk instead of me."

"I understand," said Mrs. Woods softly.

Consuelo nodded and took another bite out of her sandwich.

"So, if I'm hearing you right, you sometimes aren't so sure of how you can say what you want to say, and the other kids having their hands up doesn't make it any easier."

Consuelo nodded and kept chewing. Having satisfied herself that she now had a decent understanding of Consuelo's concern, Mrs. Woods continued with the Define the Problem step. "The thing is, I bet you have some very interesting things to say, and if you don't say them, then we never get to hear them. And I'd really like to hear what you have to say."

Consuelo was listening intently.

"I wonder," Mrs. Woods began the Invitation, "if there's a way for us to give you the time you need to say what you want to say, without you worrying about what the other kids want to say, so we can hear your ideas."

Consuelo considered the question. "I don't know."

Mrs. Woods recalled Dr. Bridgman's response when Joey didn't immediately think of a solution to a problem. "Well, let's think about it a little. There's no rush."

Consuelo thought for a few more moments. "I don't know how to say it."

"Take your time, Consuelo. I really want to hear your ideas."

"Maybe, well, maybe you could tell the kids not to raise their hands ... when I'm trying to talk ..." She hesitated.

Mrs. Woods nodded.

"And you could tell them, I mean, you could give me more time to talk."

"Let me make sure I understand what you mean," said Mrs. Woods. "If I told the other kids to keep their hands down when I call on you, and if I tell them that you need some extra time to gather your thoughts, then you'd have an easier time telling us your ideas. Yes?"

Consuelo smiled. "Yes."

"Consuelo, I think that's a great idea. I can do that if you think it would help."

"But don't call on me, don't call on me, you know, if my hand's not up."

"No problem. But do you think you'll start raising your hand if you know I'm going to make sure you have time to say what you want to say?"

Consuelo nodded. Mrs. Woods made a mental note to talk to Dr. Bridgman about seeing if Consuelo might qualify for additional language therapy. But she felt as though their plan was a good start.

"Consuelo, I sure do wish I'd talked with you about this at the beginning of the school year," said Mrs. Woods. "I just didn't know how to, well, I didn't know ..." Mrs. Woods smiled. "Look at me, now I'm having trouble saying what I want to say!"

Consuelo smiled. "I understand."

CHAPTER 7

Meeting of the Minds

We have now arrived at an important question, one that is often a major concern for teachers and parents: *What about the other kids in the classroom?* This question could be asking several different things. It could mean, How are we going to reduce the negative impact of the challenging kid on the learning and safety of his classmates? Of course, everything you've read so far in this book provides the answer to that question. Or it could mean, Is there anything we can do with the classmates to help them view the challenging kid differently and possibly even help him? This is the question we'll focus on in this chapter, with a big assist from the community-building literature.

One of the most detrimental side effects of challenging behavior is how it causes classmates to view and treat a kid. Over time, challenging behavior can take its toll on peer relations—kids who are aggressive are often avoided, kids who lack social skills are frequently ignored or rejected, kids who get in trouble a lot are teased or ostracized—and challenging kids ultimately find themselves on the outside looking in. These patterns often set the stage for kids with behavioral challenges to become alienated from their peers and teachers and begin gravitating toward other kids who are similarly alienated.

But what if there was a level playing field? In other words, what if all the kids in a classroom appreciated one another's strengths and limitations and recognized that they were all on the hook for helping one another overcome their respective challenges? What if they all understood that social, emotional, and behavioral challenges are no different from other challenges confronting kids in the classroom, such as reading, writing, math, catching a ball, public speaking, test-taking, memorizing, spelling, and so forth? What if challenging kids were not solely in the position of *needing* help but were also in a position to *provide* it? Kids with behavioral challenges aren't the only ones in a classroom who can benefit from Plan B. If we operate on the assumption that every individual in every classroom has something to work on, then they *all* need Plan B. Why save it just for the challenging ones? Furthermore, if Plan B is being applied to everyone in the group, it won't be viewed as something that negatively distinguishes the "bad" kids. It will be the norm.

In addition, Plan B can be applied to unsolved problems affecting the group as a whole (or specific subsets of the group). Now, the thought of doing Plan B with an entire class often causes some apprehension, especially if one is still feeling a little shaky about using Plan B. And it's true, full-class Plan B can be more daunting, since there are more concerns and perspectives to keep track of, organize, and address. On the other hand, in some ways full-class Plan B is easier. First, Plan B meshes well with the community-building strategies we're about to consider, strategies that have become common practice in many classrooms. Second, many kids in a classroom may have similar challenges. While these challenges could be approached by doing Plan B with each individual kid, it can also be fruitful (and sometimes more efficient) to tackle shared challenges with the entire class and arrive at a solution that works for more than one kid. Third, some problems—general classroom conduct, teasing, bullying—do affect and involve the entire class, and are sometimes best resolved by engaging the entire class in Plan B. Fourth, in some instances, twenty-five brains are better than two when it comes to considering the range of potential solutions that could be applied to a problem. Some kids may have already overcome a challenge with which a classmate is currently struggling, and may be able to offer the wisdom that comes with experience. Fifth, if you want to teach yearlong lessons in democracy, empathy, problem-solving, and consensus building, and give kids lots of opportunities to practice, frequent class-wide Plan B is a good way to get there. And sixth, Plan B is an excellent way to help two kids resolve a conflict or problem together, initially with the adult as a facilitator and eventually independently.

Let's think a little about community building in general and then move on to how the addition of Plan B to community building can make for quite a combination.

Community Building

You may already be familiar with some of the excellent resources for general community building in a classroom, including *Beyond Discipline: From Compliance to Community* by Alfie Kohn, *Tribes: A New Way of Learning and Being Together* by Jeanne Gibbs, *Teaching Children to Care: Management in the Responsive Classroom* by Ruth Sidney Charney, and Open Circle Curriculum: Reach Out to Schools Social Competency Program, based at the Stone Center at Wellesley College. The goal of this chapter is not to provide an exhaustive review of community building, but rather to point out how the added ingredient of Plan B can make community building that much more productive.

To begin, here's my definition of good teaching (you may be interested to know that the definition of "good parenting" is the same):

**Good teaching means being responsive
to the hand you've been dealt.**

It goes without saying that each group of kids is different. The task with each group is to get a handle on its collective strengths and limitations and work toward building a community where each member feels safe, respected, and valued. But that takes time and concentrated effort. It doesn't happen by itself. And it looks different every year. That's what it means to be responsive.

It also goes without saying that every individual in a classroom is different. As you know, the best way to get a handle on each individual kid is to determine his or her strengths, lagging skills, and problems to be solved, and then start teaching each kid skills and helping them solve problems.

The ultimate challenge is to be responsive in both ways—to the group and to the individuals in it—simultaneously. This is hard to do, and is perhaps the hardest for teachers who have adopted the mentality, "I don't adjust my style of teaching to my students, my students adjust to my excellent style of teaching." The problem for such teachers and some of the kids they teach is that their style of teaching works well enough for the groups and individual kids who can adjust, but doesn't work well at all for the groups and kids who can't.

But even without this mentality, there are times, especially when a challenging kid is disrupting the classroom process and interfering with the learning of others, when the two ways of being responsive seem to be at odds. At these times it is not uncommon for teachers to feel that the dual agenda cannot be achieved and to begin the process of deciding which way of being responsive must be abandoned to salvage the other. In too many classrooms, the group wins out and individual challenging kids get lost.

The thinking goes something like this: "This kid is disrupting my class and interfering with the learning of the other kids. Despite my best efforts, I haven't made much progress in keeping that from happening. While I'd love to be able to help him, I do have the rest of the group to worry about. I also have a curriculum and high-stakes testing to worry about. If I can't help him, at the very least I need to minimize his negative impact on the rest of the group." At this point, the teacher begins to consider actions that will segregate a kid from his classmates (seating him in an isolated spot inside or outside of the classroom, or sending him to the assistant principal). Of course, such actions only serve to further distance the problematic student from the peers who could have offered assistance.

The reality is that the two ways of being responsive are inextricably linked. You can't do one without the other. Well, you could try, but it doesn't work very well. The things a teacher does to be responsive to an individual kid actually enhance the group . . . and the things a teacher does to be responsive to the needs of the group actually set the stage for the work to be done with individual kids. If, with an individual student, we use Plan B to teach skills and solve problems, the larger group will benefit because the student will learn the skills, the problems will eventually be solved, and the group will have had the opportunity to learn and benefit from the transformation.

If we actively promote a sense of community in the group, then the members of that group learn that they must be concerned not only with themselves but also with the well-being of other individuals in the group and with the group as a whole. Community members learn that they can and are expected to help one another. Everyone has gifts, everyone has things they're trying to improve. When you have a gift, you lend a hand to the members of the group who need help. When you need help, you know you can rely on the group for assistance. When a community member overcomes a challenge, the community overcomes a challenge. Avoiding, ignoring, rejecting, teasing, ostracizing, bullying, withdrawing, being aggressive: These are all signs of problems that a community has yet to solve.

The community should hold regular meetings to discuss and resolve these problems. In some classrooms these meetings take place several times each day (for example, first thing in the morning and at the end of the day). Taking into account the pressures imposed by high-stakes testing, can the time required by such meetings be justified? There are data to suggest that such programs actually improve test scores.[1]

What is the role of the teacher in the community? As articulated by Jeanne Gibbs, the teacher is a colearner and facilitator, rather than a giver of information. Teachers don't have all the answers, and there is no one right solution to the problems facing the group. The best solutions are the ones the members of the group develop and own. In the words of Carol Ann Tomlinson: "The teacher is the leader, but like all effective leaders, she attends closely to her followers and involves them thoroughly in the journey. Together, teacher and student(s) plan, set goals, monitor progress, analyze successes and failures, and seek to multiply the successes and learn from the failures."

Now, let's think in more specific terms about what Plan B adds to the community-building process.

Plan B for Every Kid

Should you use Plan B with kids who do not have significant social, emotional, and behavioral challenges? You'll find no downside in doing so, especially if you're interested in engaging any kid in a process that ultimately helps him overcome problems he's experiencing at school and teach him the skills he lacks. Potential topics for Plan B include difficulty with homework completion, disorganization, difficulty getting to school on time, difficulty getting to school at all, difficulty with a particular academic task, difficulty participating in class discussions, difficulty staying awake, fear of public speaking . . . the list is endless.

What would Plan B look like with an "ordinary" kid? No different from how it would look with a challenging one. Same three steps. Same process. Same goals. Can you get away with imposing your will on an "ordinary" kid to solve a problem? Probably, but why would you want to?

But, as you read above, another good reason to use Plan B with these "ordinary" kids is that *you want it to become the norm*. Plan B shouldn't be something that distinguishes kids with behavioral challenges from other members of the group. Plus, the minute the "ordinary" kids catch wind of Plan B, they're going to want to know why their challenging classmates are being treated differently. If Plan B is applied to everyone in the group, they're not being treated differently. Of course, there's nothing terrible about different kids in the same group being treated differently. Which brings us to another important mantra:

Fair does not mean equal.

Unfortunately, many teachers feel pressure to treat every member of the group exactly the same, most especially as it relates to behavior. Yet there is no classroom where every kid is treated exactly the same. In every classroom, kids are treated differently based on their unique needs (recall our discussion about differentiated instruction and differentiated discipline). Because every kid in a classroom has different needs, treating them all exactly the same would mean no one's needs were being met.

Adults long ago came to grips with the "fair does not mean equal" principle as it applies to academics (and the kids followed). The next seismic leap for our society is to apply the same mentality to social, emotional, and behavioral challenges. The kids will follow again. In fact, a lot of them are ahead of the grown-ups already.

Kids are keen observers of the world, and often question what they observe. Kids are bound to notice the obvious—that fair does not mean equal—and are likely to have some questions about it ("How come Joey gets to meet with you before school and I don't?" "How come Daniel gets to sit at a desk during morning meeting and the rest of us don't?" "How come Max gets extra time on tests?" "How come Kendrick gets to use a laptop to write stuff down?"). But, as noted by Carol Ann Tomlinson, children seem to accept a world in which we are not alike. They do not quest for sameness, but they do search for the sense of triumph that comes when they are respected, valued, and nurtured.

There are some key themes that can be incorporated into a classroom culture to move things in this direction:

> *"In our classroom everyone gets what they need," and*
> *"In our classroom, we help each other."*

Let's get a little more specific:

KID: *How come Daniel gets to sit at a desk during circle time?*

ADULT: *Well, as you know, Daniel has a hard time sitting on his mat during morning meeting. So the desk helps him have an easier time of staying in the group and helps him be able to participate better.*

KID: *How come I don't get to sit at a desk?*

ADULT: *Oh, I didn't know you were having a hard time sitting on your mat during morning meeting. Are you having a hard time with that?*

KID: *No.*

ADULT: *See, letting Daniel sit at a desk is our way of making sure he gets what he needs from us in our classroom. It's our way of helping him. Just like we've been helping you with your reading.*

KID: *What if I started to have trouble sitting on my mat?*
ADULT: *Well, then we'd figure out how to help you with that,
too.*

Plan B Between Two Kids

Plan B can be applied to interactions between two kids, with the
teacher in the role of facilitator. As always, you'll want to make sure
the circumstances under which Proactive Plan B is taking place are as
optimal as possible, that the concerns of the two parties are well clarified, and that the solutions are realistic and mutually satisfactory.
Let's see what the three steps would look like in this context:

ANNA (*in a conversation with her classroom teacher, Mr.
Bartlett): I don't want to be Zach's partner on the slavery
project.*
MR. BARTLETT: *You don't? How come?*
ANNA: *I just don't want to.*
MR. BARTLETT: *Sounds like there's a problem I should hear
about. What's up?*
ANNA: *I worked with him on a project last year. He always wants
things his way and then he doesn't do his share of the work.*
MR. BARTLETT: *Hmm. So he always wants his way and doesn't
do his share of the work. I didn't know that.*
ANNA: *Well, now you know.*
MR. BARTLETT: *Have you tried talking to him about it?*
ANNA: *Yes! Last year I told him we needed to come up with an
idea that we're both happy with and that he needed to do his
part, but he doesn't listen.*
MR. BARTLETT: *Is this something you'd like my help with?*
ANNA: *Yes, I want you to let me do the project with someone
else.*
MR. BARTLETT: *Well, that would be one way to handle things.
But my concern is that a big reason I'm having our class do
some projects in groups is so you learn how to work together,
even with kids you don't work very well with. If I assigned
you to another partner, you wouldn't learn how to do that.*

ANNA: *I don't want to be his partner!*

MR. BARTLETT: *I know, and I think I understand why, unless there's more to it than what you're telling me.*

ANNA: *No, that's it. Can't I just be partners with Kelly or Sabrina?*

MR. BARTLETT: *Well, that's part of the problem. They already have partners, and you already work very well with them. If we can get your concerns about Zach addressed, do you think you two could work together?*

ANNA: *Maybe. I mean, no. Anyway, it'll never happen.*

MR. BARTLETT: *Well, that could be true, but maybe we could help him do a better job of hearing your ideas and do his share of the work.*

ANNA: *How?*

MR. BARTLETT: *I'm not sure yet. I think we need to talk to Zach about it. Do you want me to talk to him myself or do you want to be part of the discussion?*

ANNA: *I want you to talk to him. But I don't want him to think I was trying to get him into trouble.*

MR. BARTLETT: *I think he knows enough about how our classroom works to know that you aren't trying to get him into trouble. But I was thinking that you might have some good ideas for solutions. So maybe it would be helpful if you were part of the discussion, even if I do all the talking at first.*

ANNA: *Fine.*

MR. BARTLETT: *Should we try to find a time for you and me and Zach to talk things over?*

ANNA: *OK.*

Next discussion, with Zach, Anna, and Mr. Bartlett:

MR. BARTLETT: *Zach, as you know, in our classroom, when something is bothering somebody we try to talk about it. As I mentioned to you yesterday, I thought it might be a good idea for me and you and Anna to talk together about the project you guys are supposed to be doing together.*

ZACH: *OK.*

MR. BARTLETT: *Anna has some concerns about what it's going to be like doing the project with you. It sounds like you guys worked on a project together last year, yes?*

ZACH: *Yup.*

MR. BARTLETT: *I don't know if you knew this, but Anna came away from that project feeling like you weren't very receptive to her ideas and feeling like she did most of the work. So she wasn't too sure she wanted to do this project with you.*

ZACH: *She doesn't have to do the project with me. I can find another partner.*

MR. BARTLETT: *Yes, she was thinking the same thing. But I was hoping we could find a way for you guys to work well together. What do you think of Anna's concern?*

ZACH: *I don't know. That was a long time ago.*

MR. BARTLETT: *Do you remember how you guys figured out what to do on last year's project?*

ZACH: *No.*

MR. BARTLETT: *Do you remember Anna doing most of the work?*

ZACH: *Sort of. But that's because she didn't like the way I was doing it so she decided to do it herself.*

ANNA: *That is so not true. I did most of the work because you wouldn't do anything.*

ZACH: *Well, that's not how I remember it.*

MR. BARTLETT: *It sounds like you both have different recollections about what happened last year and why it didn't go so well, so maybe we shouldn't concentrate so much on what happened last year. I don't know if you would ever agree on that. Maybe we should focus on the concerns that are getting in the way of you working together this year. Anna, your concern is that Zach won't listen to any of your ideas. And you're both concerned about Anna having to do all the work. I wonder if there's a way for you guys to make sure that you have equal input into the design of the project, without Anna having to do all the work in the end. Do you guys have any ideas?*

ANNA: *This is so pointless. He won't listen to my ideas.*

MR. BARTLETT: *Well, I know that's what you feel happened last year, but I can't do anything about last year. We're trying to focus on this year and on coming up with a solution so that you and Zach have equal input and put in equal work.*

ANNA: *Can you sit with us while we're figuring out what to do? Then you'll see what I mean.*

ZACH: *Then you'll see what I mean.*

MR. BARTLETT: *So, Anna, you're saying that maybe if I sit in on your discussions I might be able to help you guys have a more equal exchange of ideas?*

ANNA: *That's not really what I meant.*

MR. BARTLETT: *I know, but I'm thinking that it might not be a bad idea for ensuring the equal exchange of ideas. What do you think?*

ZACH: *I think we can work together.*

ANNA: *Fine, sit in on our discussion and help us have equal input.*

MR. BARTLETT: *Only if that works for you guys.*

ANNA: *It only works for me if I have to work with him.*

MR. BARTLETT: *I'm not saying you have to work with him. I'm saying I'd like you to give it a shot so the other kids don't have to break up their pairs. We can entertain other options if that solution doesn't work for you.*

ANNA: *What other solutions?*

MR. BARTLETT: *I don't know. Whatever we come up with. Can you guys think of any others?*

ZACH: *We could do the project by ourselves, you know, alone. She could do one and I could do one.*

MR. BARTLETT: *Well, that would probably work for you guys, but it wouldn't work for me. One of the goals of this project was for kids to learn to work together. I think it's an important skill.*

ANNA: *Why don't we try to work together, with you helping us, and if that doesn't work we can do our own projects.*

MR. BARTLETT: *Zach, does that solution work for you?*

ZACH: *Sure, whatever.*

MR. BARTLETT: *I need to think about whether it works for me. You guys'll try hard to work together with me helping you?*

ANNA: *Yes.*

ZACH: *Yes.*

MR. BARTLETT: OK, *let's go with it. We're working on the project again tomorrow. I'll sit in on your discussion with each other and see if I can help make sure the exchange of ideas is equal and the workload is equal. Let's see how it goes.*

Plan B in Groups

Discussions are a common occurrence in many classrooms, but mostly on topics that have an academic orientation and a right or wrong answer. What does Plan B add to a group discussion? To begin with, three steps. But beyond the three steps, Plan B will help the class focus on issues that are above and beyond academics, learn to listen and take into account one another's concerns, and recognize that there are no "right" answers, only solutions that are mutually satisfactory.

When doing Plan B with a group, the first goal is to achieve the clearest possible understanding of the concerns and perspectives of each group member related to a given problem. Eventually, kids come to recognize the need to thoroughly clarify one another's concerns. Naturally, the group needs to stay totally focused on concerns before moving on to solutions. Adults should add their concerns to the mix as well. You may find it useful to record the concerns for later reference.

Once the concerns have been well clarified, the group is on to the next challenge: finding a solution that will address those concerns (the Invitation). As hard as this can be when Plan B involves two individuals, it's harder, but also productive, when it involves an entire group. When exploring potential solutions, be sure to encourage participation and to gather all the ideas. Record these as well; a list will make it easier to gauge the degree to which each solution addresses the various concerns. Stress the fact that the solutions that will stand the test of time are those that address all the concerns. The definition of an ingenious solution remains the same: It must be realistic and mutually satisfactory.

Group problem-solving is no harder and messier than having problems that never get solved or having problems that "go underground" because there is no mechanism for solving them. It is also one of the best ways to give kids an incredible, yearlong lesson in true democracy.

You will find that it's important, early on, for the group to establish some expectations for communicating, listening, and taking turns, and for you to remind the group of those expectations if they aren't being met. Kids aren't always great at listening to one another in the first place, and sometimes become less so when they are verbalizing concerns about important problems. But these skills can be taught.

In group Plan B, the teacher is, once again, the facilitator. The teacher helps the group decide what problems to tackle first, keeps the group focused and serious (group members will eventually take on these responsibilities as well), and ensures that the exploration of concerns and solutions is exhaustive. The teacher's stance in helping the group sort through concerns and solutions is generally one of neutrality. There are no good or bad concerns, no such thing as "competing" concerns, only concerns that need to be addressed. Likewise, there are no right or wrong solutions, only those that are realistic (or not) and mutually satisfactory (or not).

In his book *Beyond Discipline: From Compliance to Community*, Alfie Kohn writes:

> It sounds easier than it is, this business of holding class meetings. Sometimes participants can't agree on a solution. Does that mean we carry the item over to the next meeting—or have we done something sufficiently constructive just by raising the issue and airing our ideas and feelings? Sometimes students don't participate. Shall we break into pairs to talk, or write down our individual responses, and then come back together to share our new proposals? Or might people be getting something of value from the discussion even when they don't contribute? Sometimes students snicker unkindly at someone else's idea, or don't pay attention, or let a couple of their peers effectively take over a meeting. These are not problems for the teacher to solve alone; they are issues to be folded back into the meeting and dealt with by its members.

Once the kids become accustomed to Plan B, in those (hopefully rare) instances in which Emergency B is necessary, the teacher can often turn for help to what is often the great untapped resource in the classroom: the kids. The teacher isn't the Lone Ranger. Everyone has the skills.

If you're wondering what group Plan B looks like, be sure to read "The Story Continues" section in this chapter.

SPECIAL EDUCATION CLASSROOMS

Thus far, we've focused exclusively on general education classrooms, but everything you've read in this and the preceding chapters is equally applicable to special education and self-contained classrooms, especially those specifically geared toward kids with behavioral challenges. Such classrooms may serve anywhere from a handful to a dozen challenging kids, depending on the school and school system, and are populated by kids whose needs exceed what can be delivered in general education. Some kids are better served in smaller settings. But many are placed in special education classrooms because no one in general education has the wherewithal to pinpoint and teach their lagging skills and work toward resolving their unsolved problems. Many special education classrooms rely heavily on consequence-based programs that, as you now know, don't teach skills or solve problems, and may actually exacerbate the kids' difficulties.

But the task is the same. You'll need a completed ALSUP for each kid so the who, what, where, when, and why of challenging behavior are well identified and understood. You'll need to get your priorities squared away so you and each kid know what you're working on together. You'll need Plan B to help teach lagging skills and solve problems. And you'll want to create a classroom culture in which kids are helping each other. If all that sounds like a lot of work, think about how hard you're probably working right now *without* those ingredients.

Oh, about that reward-and-punishment program. There's an excellent chance it's unnecessary. In many of the settings in which the CPS model has been implemented—general and special education schools, inpatient psychiatric units, and residential and juvenile detention facilities—adults came to the awareness that it was the application of the contingency management program that was setting kids off most often and causing many serious challenging behaviors. They recognized that both adults and kids were far more focused on rewards and punishments than on the skills the kids were supposed to be learning. They learned that providing structure and maintaining order in a classroom has a lot more to do with teaching skills and solving problems than rewards and punishments.

Q & A

Question: Our school system has been implementing Positive Behavioral Supports (PBS). It seems like there are some similarities between PBS and CPS. Is that true?

Answer: First, we'd better figure out what you mean by "positive behavior supports." Because PBS isn't well-defined in special education law, it can mean different things to different people. For some, PBS means you're "just trying really hard not to punish kids." But PBS can also refer to an approach to intervention put forth by George Sugai, Bob Horner, and their colleagues,[2] and yes, there are some similarities, along with some fundamental points of divergence.

The two models are certainly similar in their emphasis on proactive, preventive intervention and in the belief that children with challenging behavior should be treated with the same level of interest and importance as children with academic challenges. However, in assessing the function of a kid's challenging behavior, PBS is still largely oriented toward the "first pass" definition of function: namely, that the behavior is "working" for a kid by helping him avoid or escape something or by helping the kid get something he wants, such as attention or peer approval. As you know, the CPS model focuses on the "second pass" definition of function in positing that the primary function of challenging behavior is to communicate that a kid is lacking the skills to respond adaptively to specific problems. Thus, while PBS allows for the possibility of lagging skills as an explanation for challenging behavior, it places a strong emphasis on using environmental reinforcers to train replacement behaviors. The CPS model places a strong emphasis on adult-child problem-solving as the primary mechanism for teaching lagging thinking skills and helping kids solve problems.

But perhaps the most striking difference between the two models is that PBS doesn't involve collaboration between adult and kid; it is an adult-driven model. There is no major emphasis on collaborating with kids to identify their concerns (only a major emphasis on identifying *adult* concerns) and no emphasis on enlisting the kid in coming up with a mutually satisfactory action plan, rather, the *adults* come up with the action plan.

Question: Response to Intervention and PBS are very strongly oriented toward the use of empirically supported treatments. Do you share this orientation?

Answer: Studying treatments to ensure their effectiveness and favoring those treatments that are supported by research is very important. But people aren't robots; even treatments that are empirically supported have high rates of nonresponders. So we can't take adult intuition and wisdom out of the mix in selecting interventions that are best matched to the needs of individual kids and to those individuals responsible for implementation. Scot Danforth and Terry Jo Smith nicely articulated this perspective in their book, *Engaging Troubling Students* (2005): "Social science (research) provides an important source of knowledge for practitioners . . . yet (such) research does not stand above other kinds of available knowledge. . . . It is only one of many useful sources of guidance for teachers attempting to take ethical and practical action."

Question: It seems like CPS is similar in some ways to Developmental Discipline, as delineated by the Child Development Project (CDP). Yes?

Answer: In their focus on development and skills and lack of emphasis on behavior and punitive interventions, there are certainly some major similarities between the two models. However, the CDP project uses attachment theory as a jumping-off point and CPS does not.

Question: How about Restorative Justice?

Answer: Lots of similarities there. Both CPS and the Restorative Justice model eschew traditional, punitive disciplinary procedures. Both are collaborative and place a strong emphasis on relationships and community building. The restorative discipline model (see *Restorative Discipline for Schools: Teaching Responsibility; Creating Caring Climates,* by Lorraine Stutzman Amstutz and Judy Mellett) posits that "harmers" will choose more adaptive options when they come to understand, through dialogue and conversation with those harmed, the pain they have caused by their misbehavior. The CPS model believes that challenging kids will evidence more adaptive behavior when the lagging skills setting the stage for challenging behavior are taught and the problems precipitating challenging behavior are solved.

Question: And Nonviolent Communication?
Answer: Lots of similarities there, too. Marshall Rosenberg's Nonviolent Communication (NVC) paradigm places a heavy emphasis on empathy, clarifying concerns and feelings, and ways in which people communicate with one another that interfere with empathy and compassion. While the precepts of NVC and CPS are congruent, CPS places a significantly stronger emphasis on identifying and teaching lagging cognitive skills.

Question: Any others?
Answer: Thomas Gordon's *Teacher Effectiveness Training* model shares many important themes with CPS as well, again without the emphasis on lagging cognitive skills and unsolved problems.

Question: Any similarities to the Love and Logic program?
Answer: Only on the surface. The Love and Logic program does place an emphasis on empathizing with kids, but the empathy utilized in this program is primarily of the emergent and perfunctory variety, isn't aimed at gathering information or understanding kids' concerns, and is typically a prelude to Plan A. The problem-solving that takes place between kids and adults in this program isn't aimed at reaching mutually satisfactory solutions. And the *Love and Logic* program relies heavily on adult-imposed consequences.

Question: How does CPS differ from other crisis management programs?

Answer: Many crisis management programs are just that—crisis *management* programs. While it's good to know how to defuse and deescalate a crisis, and Emergency Plan B is useful along these lines, CPS places significantly greater emphasis on crisis *prevention*. No other learning disability is handled in crisis mode, and a crisis is clearly not the best time to address the lagging skills and unsolved problems underlying social, emotional, and behavioral challenges.

The Story Continues . . .

Several weeks after his meeting with Joey and his teachers, Mr. Middleton sat at his desk poring over detention slips. Five more from Mr. Armstrong . . . four of them for Crystal. "The man's trying to break his own record," he said to himself, sighing. "We need to talk." He decided to pay a visit to Mr. Armstrong at the end of the day.

"Can I talk to you for a second?"

Mr. Armstrong was packing up his belongings. "Well, I'm kind of in a rush. My son has a hockey game."

"Ah, fun. I'll walk with you. I saw that Crystal had four more detention slips."

Mr. Armstrong looked up from stuffing a few final papers into his backpack. "Bill, I don't tolerate disrespect. Someone should have nipped that stuff in the bud with her a long time ago. If my son ever acted the way she did, he'd remember what happened next for a long, long time." Mr. Armstrong zipped up his backpack and started walking toward the hallway. "Why, is there a problem?"

Mr. Middleton walked with Mr. Armstrong into the hallway. "I'm starting to wonder whether all these detentions and suspensions are ever going to get the job done."

Mr. Armstrong stopped walking. "Sometimes a kid has to hit rock bottom before she starts to get it. You don't get through to kids like Crystal by going soft. Haven't we learned that about her already?"

"I don't know what we've learned about Crystal. I do know she's been at rock bottom for a long time now. What is it that you're trying to get through to her?"

"That there are certain ways you act, certain ways you treat people, especially people in authority. That there are other people in the world besides Crystal. How's she going to live in the real world if she doesn't learn those things?"

"I'm a little worried about how she's going to live in the real world if all she gets from us is one suspension and detention after another."

"Why? How else are you going to teach her that stuff? Her grandma's not going to do it."

"You know, this Bridgman fellow, he's got some pretty interesting ideas."

Mr. Armstrong scowled. "Oh, I've heard about Dr. Bridgman's ideas. The man's probably never been in a classroom. Crystal doesn't need cajoling, she needs someone who doesn't back down." Mr. Armstrong stopped and glanced at his watch. "Look, I need to get to hockey. Anyway, Crystal already told me she's dropping out as soon as she can . . . just like her brother. Best I can tell, she's started dropping out already. She's only been here three days in the last two weeks. So none of this will matter eventually anyway."

A few days later, Ms. Lowell, Mrs. Woods, and Mrs. Franco met before school as planned.

"We appreciate your coming in," said Mrs. Woods. "We know how hard it is for you to get off work."

"Well, my supervisor tries to be understanding when it comes to Joey," said Ms. Lowell. "But she's given me a lot of time off over the years . . . I think even she is starting to wonder if things will ever get better with Joey."

"Well, let's get down to business then," said Mrs. Woods. "You have quite a son."

This compliment took Ms. Lowell by surprise. "Oh, geez, I don't get to hear that very often. Joey's really taken a liking to you. He says he'd rather talk to you than me!"

Mrs. Woods smiled. "I don't know if that's the desired outcome. But we do have some very productive conversations. He seems to have pretty good ideas for how to solve problems, once we figure out what the problems are."

Ms. Lowell looked at Mrs. Franco. "And he really appreciated how you handled the whole thing with the substitute and the locker."

"I could see how hard he was trying to hold it together," said Mrs. Franco. "But it did get a little rocky there."

"'Rocky' and Joey seem to go together," said Ms. Lowell.

"Well, that's why we wanted to meet with you," said Mrs. Woods. "I know you and Dr. Bridgman spent some time when you first met with him talking about skills Joey might be lacking. We thought it might be good for us to understand more about what things are like at home. You know, if he gets upset at home over the same things he gets upset about here."

"Oh, he gets upset at home all right," said Ms. Lowell. "His brother bugging him, things not going his way, the word 'no' . . . it doesn't take much."

"We don't really see those things setting him off here," said Mrs. Woods. "Of course, his brother's not in his class. But it's being confused on assignments and being embarrassed in front of the other kids—and thinking he has messed up—that seem to be coming into play most often here."

"Well, his brother gets some credit for making him feel bad about himself," Ms. Lowell admitted. "The name calling can get pretty intense. On the other hand, his brother's had to live with Joey's temper, and getting more of my attention, all these years. So there's probably some resentment."

"It sounds like you all have had quite a time of it," said Mrs. Woods.

"I won't lie to you, it hasn't been fun," said Ms. Lowell. "But you two don't need to hear about all that."

"The more we know, the better," said Mrs. Franco. "A lot of parents don't seem too eager to show their faces around here."

"I used to be one of them," said Ms. Lowell. "To be perfectly honest, it's hard to walk into a place where you feel like people are blaming you for your kid's problems. But I haven't been feeling that way lately."

"Would you like to hear about some of the things we're working on with Joey right now?" asked Mrs. Woods.

"Well, I know about the plan you two came up with," said Ms. Lowell. "But I don't know how you came up with it."

Mrs. Woods explained about the three Plans and the three steps of Plan B, concluding with, "Plan B helps you talk *with* kids instead of talking *at* them."

"That's what I do with Joey," said Ms. Lowell. "I talk at him. I think he stopped listening to me a long time ago." Ms. Lowell paused. "So who's going to help me do Plan B at home?"

"Maybe Dr. Bridgman," suggested Mrs. Woods. "But I'm happy to keep you informed on what we're doing here."

"I haven't done Plan B yet myself," said Mrs. Franco. "But I'm starting to think maybe there are a few kids in my class who need me to learn how, too."

Ms. Lowell looked at her watch. "I don't want to push my boss too far. Plus, I guess the kids are coming in soon. I don't think Joey would be too enthusiastic about having his classmates seeing me sitting here."

Mrs. Woods nodded. "I think you're right. But if your boss would agree, would it be possible for us to do this every month or so? I'm thinking it would be good for us to have some face time every once in a while, you know, in addition to email."

"Don't you worry about my boss," said Ms. Lowell. "I'll be here."

A few days later, as she sat at her desk thinking about Joey and some of the other challenging kids in her class, Mrs. Woods had a bit of an epiphany. Like many other teachers in the school, she used a ticket system for rewarding good behavior and punishing inappropriate behavior in her classroom. At the beginning of every week, each student in her class started with ten tickets. Tickets were taken away for inappropriate behavior and at the end of each week, students exchanged their tickets for small rewards. But as she thought about this system and the kids who lost tickets most often, she realized that while the system was "working" for the kids who reliably behaved themselves, it wasn't working at all for the kids who had trouble behaving themselves.

She walked over to Mrs. Franco's classroom. "Have you ever noticed that the ticket system doesn't work?"

Mrs. Franco looked up from revising a lesson plan. "How do you mean?"

"I mean that the kids who don't have any trouble behaving themselves don't ever lose any tickets and always get rewards. But the kids who do have trouble behaving themselves always lose a lot of tickets, and don't get very many rewards, but they still have trouble behaving themselves."

"Never really thought about it," said Mrs. Franco. "But I guess you're right."

"So if I'm right, why are we still doing it?"

"Oh, I bet there's a bunch of stuff we do around here that nobody really gave much thought to."

Mrs. Woods pressed the issue. "Is it written anywhere that we have to do a ticket system in our classrooms?"

"Good question. But do you really care?"

"Well, I'm not looking to break any rules. But I don't like to waste my time doing things that aren't working."

Mrs. Franco began taking the conversation more seriously. "I'm with you. But I wonder if the kids who are behaving themselves would stop behaving themselves if we took away the ticket system."

"I know what Dr. Bridgman would say," said Mrs. Woods. "He'd say the kids who are behaving themselves aren't behaving themselves because of the tickets; they're behaving themselves because they can."

"But it's not like the ticket system is harming the well-behaved kids."

Mrs. Woods pondered this statement briefly. "I'm not so sure about that. Why would we want to take kids who are already motivated to behave themselves and convince them that the only reason they should behave themselves is for some goody that we give them?"

"Hmm. Of course, if we take away the tickets, we still have the problem of what to do with the kids who aren't behaving themselves."

"Yes, exactly the problem we have right now, with or without the tickets. Anyway, I have some ideas about them."

"Really? What are you going to do?"

"I'm going to Plan B 'em. Every one of 'em. I'm going to figure out what's getting in the way of them behaving themselves and then I'm going to help them fix it. One kid and one problem at a time."

"You've got it bad."

"Got what bad?"

"You've got Plan B bad."

"Yeah, I've got it bad, all right," said Mrs. Woods. "And I can't wait to start helping these kids solve the problems that have been getting in their way for years. No one's ever done anything about it except continue doing something that isn't working. Isn't that incredible?"

Mrs. Franco was again thinking about the kids in her class who desperately needed Plan B. "Yes, it is." She hesitated. "Can I ask you a favor?"

"Of course."

"I've been thinking about trying Plan B with some of the kids in my class. Can you, uh, practice Plan B with me a little?"

Mrs. Woods smiled. "The blind leading the blind? Happy to."

"And if you're going to dump your ticket system, I'm going to dump mine," said Mrs. Franco. "Can't let you get into trouble all by yourself."

The following week, Mrs. Franco walked over to Mrs. Woods' classroom for her initial Plan B coaching session. "You ready for me?" she asked Mrs. Woods.

"Maybe you should be asking if you're ready for *me*," Mrs. Woods laughed.

"You're the only person in this building who knows anything about Plan B besides Dr. Bridgman, and he's too busy, so you're all I've got," said Mrs. Franco.

"Well, I'll do my best. So, do you know who you want to do Plan B with?"

Mrs. Franco rolled her eyes. "Travis. From what I can gather, he's absolutely brutal to a lot of the kids in my class."

Mrs. Woods had Travis for math. "I've heard. And I've heard he's been like that for a long time."

"Proof that our school antibullying program is working really well," said Mrs. Franco sarcastically. "Best I can figure, our antibullying program has simply sent him underground. Now he's just better at hiding it."

"So you want to talk to him about how he's treating some of the other kids."

"It's probably the biggest problem I have going in my classroom right now. And the kid won't give me the time of day. I mean, he does his work and he's not a behavior problem—not while he knows I'm watching him, anyway, and I watch him like a hawk—so I've never really had to talk to him about anything."

"Well, should we look at the ALSUP to see what we think might be contributing to him treating the other kids the way he does?"

This idea took Mrs. Franco by surprise. "Bullies have lagging thinking skills?"

"I guess so. Otherwise why would they be bullying?"

The two teachers reviewed the items on the ALSUP. They concluded that Travis wasn't very good at taking another's perspective, wasn't very good at appreciating how his behavior was affecting others, and didn't seem to have the best repertoire of basic social behaviors. They also wondered about possible cognitive distortions. They considered the situations in which Travis was having his greatest difficulties, and noted that recess, lunch, and on the school bus were times during which Travis' interactions with his peers were especially problematic, all times when he wasn't being closely supervised. Then they reviewed the three steps of Proactive Plan B and role-played how the conversation would go.

"This is so strange!" said Mrs. Franco after they'd finished practicing. "I mean, I knew I was a Plan A teacher, but I didn't realize how Plan A I was!"

"I didn't realize how Plan A I was, either. But your Plan A isn't a mean-spirited Plan A. It's—let me think of how to say this—it's an *energetic* Plan A."

"Oh, I've got energy all right. I always figured if I was demanding and enthusiastic and energetic, I'd get a lot out of my kids and eventually the enthusiasm and energy would rub off."

"It probably did rub off on a lot of 'em. And your energy *is* an asset. Your kids love you. They're scared of you, but they love you."

"Yes, but that's the point. Do I really want them working hard and behaving themselves because they're scared of me? Or because they know I'm watching? How reliable is that? Especially since I'm not going to be their teacher forever? But this Plan B business, it's really focused on something very different."

"You ready to give it a whirl with Travis?" asked Mrs. Woods.

Mrs. Franco looked uncharacteristically uncertain. "I think so. You sure you don't want to sit next to me while I'm doing this?"

Mrs. Woods smiled, then realized her friend was serious. "I guess I could sit next to you if you think it would help. But in hindsight, I'm kind of glad Dr. Bridgman wasn't sitting next to me after the first Plan B with Joey. I think it helped my relationship with Joey that Dr. Bridgman wasn't there. And it made me realize that I was the one who had to learn how to do Plan B."

"I guess you're right. Can't have you holding my hand forever. What's the worst that can happen?"

Two days later, Mrs. Franco asked Travis if he would stay in from recess so they could chat. Normally she'd have simply told him to stay in from recess. But this time, trying to stay far away from Plan A, she was a bit more tentative and simply mentioned that she'd like to chat with him and that recess might be a good time to do it.

Travis was underwhelmed by Mrs. Franco's new approach. "What do you want to talk about?"

Mrs. Franco was taken slightly aback by Travis' response. She had imagined that her kinder, gentler approach would be met with a kind, gentle response. "Oh, I just want to chat a little about how things are going with the other kids. You're not in trouble or anything."

Travis remained less than receptive. "I don't care if I'm in trouble. Why does it have to be during recess?"

Mrs. Franco was trying hard to stay in Plan B mode. "Well, it doesn't have to be during recess. Is there a time that would be better for you?"

"Never would be better for me."

Travis' response prompted Mrs. Franco to revert back to standard operating procedure. "Travis, you're staying in from recess so we can talk. End of conversation."

Travis slid down into his seat, crossed his arms, and sulked as he watched the rest of the class depart for recess.

When all the kids were gone, Mrs. Franco tried again. "Travis, I've been hearing some interesting things about how kids in our class are getting along with one another. How do you think that's been going?"

"Fine," he pouted. "Can I go out to recess now?"

"In a few minutes, Travis. The thing is, I've heard it's not going fine, and I was wondering if you had any thoughts about what's going on."

"What did you hear?" Travis asked defensively.

"Well, to be perfectly honest, I've heard that there are times when you're giving some of the other kids a very hard time. But I wanted to get your take on things."

"They can say what they want. Can I go out to recess now?"

This isn't going so well, thought Mrs. Franco. "Travis, I was really hoping we could talk about this."

"This wasn't my idea."

"No, staying in from recess to talk was my idea. We could have talked at another time, but you didn't seem interested in discussing it."

"And I'm still not."

Mrs. Franco was getting frustrated. "Tell you what, Travis. Since you don't seem interested in talking about this, we'll go with my plan. The next time I hear about you treating one of the other kids in an unkind manner, you're staying in from recess for an entire week. No questions asked. Am I making myself clear?"

"Whatever," grumbled Travis, his face turning red.

"Whatever is not the answer I'm looking for."

"Fine."

"Fine what?"

"Fine, I heard you. Can I go out for recess now?"

Mrs. Franco mustered one final try. "Travis, you've never acted this way with me before. What's going on here?"

"You're bugging me. Can I go out for recess now?"

"Go ahead. We're not accomplishing anything this way. Just don't forget what happens if I hear one word about you treating other kids poorly." Travis left the room.

Well, that went swimmingly, thought Mrs. Franco. That's why Plan B should be left to the experts.

Mrs. Franco wandered into Mrs. Woods' classroom at the end of the day.

"Hey, there she is," said Mrs. Woods. "My Plan B trainee. How'd it go?"

"It didn't," reported Mrs. Franco, slumping into a chair.

"You haven't talked to him yet?" asked Mrs. Woods.

"Oh, I tried. But I was the only one doing most of the talking. What a disrespectful little . . ."

"Uh-oh. Doesn't sound like it went very well."

"I knew I should have had you sitting next to me. I don't know what I did wrong."

"I messed up a few times before I sort of had the hang of it. What happened?"

"I asked him to stay in from recess so we could chat. He didn't like that idea, so I asked him if there was a time that would be better. He said never would be better. So I *told* him to stay in from recess. So then he's mad. Then I try talking to him about how he's giving the other kids a hard time and he basically wouldn't talk. In fact, he was rude. How come 'rude' and 'disrespectful' aren't on the ALSUP?"

"Hmm. I guess Dr. Bridgman would say kids who are rude and disrespectful are lacking the skills to be polite and respectful. Or they're already so mad that polite and respectful go out the window."

"The thing is, he's never been that way before. Of course, I've never tried to talk to him about anything before."

Mrs. Woods was thinking about what went wrong. "Well, there might be something to that. He's not *usually* rude and disrespectful, but he *becomes* rude and disrespectful when you try to talk with him about how he's giving the other kids a hard time. What we don't know is *why*."

"You sure we shouldn't be asking Bridgman about him?"

"Well, we could ask Bridgman for help. But I don't know if we need his help." Mrs. Woods paused. "I think you need to try again."

"No way!" Mrs. Franco shook her head. "Fool me once . . ."

"Oh, come on," urged Mrs. Woods. "That is not the Denise Franco I know talking."

"I don't know what I'm doing!"

"I didn't, either."

"But I don't even know what I did wrong!"

"Well, maybe you didn't do anything wrong. Maybe it's a really touchy issue for him. Maybe he really doesn't want to talk about it. Maybe he got the impression you think it's his fault how things are going with the other kids. Or maybe you did get off on the wrong foot by telling him he was staying in from recess to talk."

"I tried being nice about it. But I guess I did kind of force him to talk to me. So now what?"

"Well, if you want to, you should probably check out our hypotheses with Travis," said Mrs. Woods. "You know, try to figure out why he wasn't very interested in talking with you. We should probably practice the Empathy step a little more, too. I think you may have skipped it."

Mr. Middleton, who had been walking down the hall, saw the two teachers talking and popped his head in the door. "You two sleeping here tonight?"

"No thanks," said Mrs. Franco, "I've had enough for one day."

Mr. Middleton plopped into a chair, looking tired. "I think I know how you feel."

"Tough day?" asked Mrs. Woods.

"Two all-out fistfights in the eighth grade today," said Mr. Middleton. "Not one . . . *two*. Five suspensions."

Mrs. Woods grimaced. "That's a tough group. We had them two years ago."

"Well, the little darlings aren't as adorable now as they were then," said Mr. Middleton.

"Don't recall them being adorable back then, either," said Mrs. Franco.

"So give me some good news," said Mr. Middleton. "How's my friend Joey doing? I haven't heard a thing about him since our meeting."

"Joey's doing great," said Mrs. Woods, gently tapping her knuckles on her wooden desk. "I'm really enjoying working with him."

"Music to my ears," said Mr. Middleton. "I really admire how you've taken the ball and run with it. I just wish more people in this school would do the same. Everyone thinks I'm Mr. Fix-it."

"A lot of people in this school still think discipline is your concern, not theirs," said Mrs. Franco. "So it's kind of convenient that you're the assistant principal."

"Convenient, maybe," said Mr. Middleton. "Efficient, not at all. I'm never there to see what happened in the first place. People just expect me to back them up when they're doing things that aren't working. By the time problems get to me—and it's the same problems and the same kids every week—it's already *after* the fact. There's nothing incredible I can do after the fact. If I've learned anything from Dr. Bridgman, it's that the best time to do something about a problem is *before* it comes up again, and the best person to solve the problem with the kid before it comes up again is the person the kid's having the problem with in the first place." He looked at Mrs. Woods. "Like what you're doing with Joey."

"It's not just Joey," said Mrs. Franco. "She's working on a bunch of others, too."

Mr. Middleton was impressed. "Wow. Did you ever know you were such a trailblazer?"

"I'm not a trailblazer." Mrs. Woods looked embarrassed.

"Don't praise her," warned Mrs. Franco. "She can't handle it. She's even got me trying it, though I'm apparently a very slow learner."

Mr. Middleton lowered his voice. "I must admit, I've been experimenting with Plan B in my office. With the door closed, of course."

The two teachers smiled. "I think Mrs. Woods should tell everyone about what she's doing with Plan B in one of our faculty meetings," said Mrs. Franco.

Mrs. Woods shot a dark look at her friend. "No way."

"That's a great idea," said Mr. Middleton. "I have some teachers in the eighth grade who need to hear about this stuff."

"I think Dr. Bridgman is the person to be talking about Plan B in a faculty meeting," said Mrs. Woods.

"Well, maybe on the technicalities," said Mr. Middleton. "But you're the one with classroom credibility. I'm serious. I want more people to hear about this. I'm tired of putting out brushfires."

Mrs. Woods was now considering the possibilities. "You know, we're not having the same fistfights they're having in the eighth grade. But our kids in the sixth grade don't treat one another very well."

Mrs. Franco looked at Mr. Middleton. "Yeah, that was the topic of my first foray into Plan B territory. It was ugly."

"That's why I've been trying it with the door closed," said Mr. Middleton. "But I'm getting better."

"She'll get better, too," said Mrs. Woods. "But I'm not sure doing Plan B with individual students is the only way to go. I was talking to Dr. Bridgman the other day about whether I can do Plan B with my entire class. He gave me a few tips . . . and a book to read. And I'm starting with how the kids treat one another. What do you think?"

Mrs. Franco was impressed. "I think you are a trailblazer. As for me, I'll throw a party if I can just figure out how to get Travis to talk to me."

"That's probably wise," said Mrs. Woods. "But I think I'm ready to give it a shot with the whole gang."

Mr. Middleton looked energized by the conversation. "Let me know how it goes. Then you can tell the rest of us all about it."

A few days later, Mrs. Woods held her regularly scheduled Friday community meeting with her class. On this particular Friday, she announced her agenda to the class at the beginning of the meeting. "Kids, I wanted to see if we could talk about something a little different today. It's something we've never talked about before." She was a little nervous as she moved forward into her first full-class attempt at Empathy. "I was thinking about how we're all treating one another in our class."

She was greeted with silence and twenty-six blank stares. "I guess you need a little more detail than that. I've noticed that sometimes we're having some trouble treating one another kindly, just getting along with one another, and I was wondering if anyone had any ideas about what was going on." She decided a little reassurance might help. "You're not in trouble, I just wanted to know if anyone had noticed the same thing. If it's a problem, we could talk about how to solve it."

Now there were fewer blank stares and some uncomfortable shifting in seats. But still no raised hands. Finally, Taylor had a question. "You mean, like, teasing each other?"

"Yes, teasing is one of the things I've seen that I was thinking some kids might not be so happy about."

Now some of the kids were exchanging knowing glances.

"Like, do you want us to tell you who's teasing people?" asked Taylor.

"Well, that's not exactly what I was shooting for," said Mrs. Woods. "I was more interested in getting some ideas about ways people are being treated by their classmates that they're not too happy about."

"Isn't teasing kinda normal?" asked Alberto. "I mean, kids tease each other all the time."

"That doesn't mean the kids getting teased are happy about it," snapped Taylor.

"Let's not forget our community meeting rules," reminded Mrs. Woods. "I don't think we'll get very far if we don't raise our hands and listen to what each of us has to say."

"I think there's a lot of teasing going on," said Samantha. "And I don't like having people pull my hair without my permission, either."

"Who in our class has permission to pull your hair?!" shouted Alex.

The class burst out laughing. Mrs. Woods began to wonder if this topic was too much for them to handle. She raised her voice over the laughter. "Excuse me." They quieted. "I can already tell this is an important subject for many of you, and we are going to have to pay very close attention to our rules of communicating to be able talk about it. I hope we can do it. Can we do it?"

The kids nodded.

"Maybe we should make a list of the ways people are being treated that they're not happy about," suggested Samantha.

"We could do that," said Mrs. Woods. "Do you guys think that would be a good idea?"

This question was met with a mix of nods, blank looks, and smirks.

"Samantha, if you don't mind, maybe you could keep our list for us. Then, if we get to it today, maybe we should make a list of people's suggestions for what we could do about those things," Mrs. Woods proposed.

"You mean, like punish people?" asked Taylor.

"Well, I suppose we could talk about punishing people," said Mrs. Woods. "But I was hoping we could think about ways in which we might be able to help one another. Although maybe we should wait to talk about solutions until we know more about the problems. So far we know that people are not happy being teased or having their private space invaded without their permission. Although Alberto made a very good point that a lot of kids get teased, so it may seem kind of normal. But then Taylor made the point that teasing often doesn't feel good to the person who's being teased. What do you guys think?"

Consuelo cautiously raised her hand.

"Yes, Consuelo," said Mrs. Woods. "Consuelo, before you start, I need to let the rest of the class know something. It is very hard for Consuelo to participate in our discussions if people raise their hands while she's speaking. So I'd like to ask everyone to keep their hands down until she's done. Consuelo, go ahead."

"I, I learned, I learned in Sunday school, that there is good teasing and bad teasing," Consuelo said slowly. "Good teasing is when the person, the one who is being teased, thinks it's funny, and bad teasing . . . bad teasing is when the one who is being teased lets the person who is teasing them know they don't like it."

There was a brief silence after Consuelo finished.

"Can I ask a question?" Shawn said. "How come we're not supposed to raise our hands when Consuelo is talking but it's OK for us to raise our hands when other people are talking?"

"Excellent question, Shawn," said Mrs. Woods. "We have all kinds of different learners in our class. Everyone has some things that they're really good at, and everyone has things they're working on. One of Consuelo's challenges is that it's a little hard for her to say the ideas that she has in her head."

"Is that why she's so quiet?" asked Susie.

"Consuelo, would you like me to answer that question or would you like to?" asked Mrs. Woods.

"You can," said Consuelo.

"Yes, I think that's part of the reason Consuelo is a little quiet," said Mrs. Woods. "One of the things Consuelo needs from the rest of us is more time to collect her thoughts, and one of the ways we can let her know we're giving her more time is by keeping our hands down while she's talking."

Liz raised her hand. "Why don't we just add that to one of our rules of communicating? Then we could all have time to collect our thoughts. I don't like it when everyone's waving their arms when I'm talking, either."

"That's certainly an idea we could talk about," said Mrs. Woods. "But right now I was really hoping we could stick to the topic of things people are doing that are making their classmates unhappy. Does that sound OK?"

Another mix of nods and stares.

"Are there any other things people want to add to our list?"

"There are some kids in the eighth-grade class who like to boss people around," volunteered Duane. "And if you don't do what they say, they say they're going to kick your—I mean beat you up."

The kids snickered.

"Thank you for saying it that way," said Mrs. Woods. "I've heard that there's some bullying going on during recess and on the buses. Does anyone feel they're being bullied by anyone in our class?"

"Maybe a little," said Blake.

"Should we add it to our list?" asked Mrs. Woods.

The kids nodded their approval.

"This is dumb," announced Kellen.

"What's dumb, Kellen?" asked Mrs. Woods.

"Talking about bullies," said Kellen. "It's stupid."

"I'm not sure what you mean, Kellen," said Mrs. Woods. "What's stupid about talking about bullying?"

"If someone's bullying you, you got to show that person they can't push you around," said Kellen. "Survival of the fittest, man."

"That's an interesting take on things," said Mrs. Woods. "What do you all think of Kellen's idea?"

The kids looked reluctant to comment. Samantha, as usual, was undaunted. "I think if bullying is making people in our class feel bad, then we should be talking about it. I don't think it's stupid at all."

Some of the kids nodded their approval of Samantha's point of view.

"Well, those are both interesting points of view," said Mrs. Woods. "To be perfectly honest, I was hoping we might be able to find ways of dealing with bullying that didn't involve bullying the bullies. But it's something we'll need to keep talking about."

The discussion continued for another ten minutes. Then, with only a few minutes of community meeting time left, Mrs. Woods decided it was a good time to give the class an idea of what was up next.

"We've made a list of the ways that kids are treating each other in our class that are making classmates unhappy. Something we haven't talked about yet is *why* kids are treating one another these ways. The next time we meet we should probably talk about that. If you guys want to think about that before our next meeting, that would be fine. Oh, one more thing. I was thinking it might be a good idea for us to meet more often . . . like maybe three times a week instead of just one. What do you think?"

Consuelo raised her hand. "I think it's a good idea. We have a lot of things we need to work on."

With a new meeting schedule in place, Mrs. Woods and her students continued their discussion two days later in their next community meeting.

"OK, we've made a list of the ways that kids are treating one another that are making classmates unhappy," Mrs. Woods began. "Something we haven't talked about yet is why kids are treating one another these ways. Does anyone have any ideas?"

Again, mostly blank stares. But not Samantha. "Maybe they think it's funny."

"Possibly so," said Mrs. Woods. "Now, in our last meeting, Consuelo said something about teasing that I thought was interesting. She said it's not teasing if the person being teased thinks it's funny, but it is teasing if the person being teased doesn't like it. What do you guys think of that idea?"

"I think it's true," said Austin. "I told my mom what we were talking about the other day and she said sometimes people are mean to each other because they're not sure how to be friends with people."

"Smart mom," said Mrs. Woods. "Do you guys think that happens sometimes?"

Many of the kids nodded.

"I think some people just like being mean," said Duane.

"Interesting possibility, Duane," said Mrs. Woods. "But why would someone *like* being mean?"

"I don't know," responded Duane. "Maybe they don't know how to be nice."

"Ah, so maybe they don't *like* being mean, they just don't know how to be nice," said Mrs. Woods.

"Maybe," said Duane.

"Should I be making a list of these ideas, too?" asked Samantha.

"I think that probably makes sense," said Mrs. Woods. "I'm glad we're talking about this. You guys have some very good ideas. Are there more?"

"Maybe they're just in a bad mood that day," said Shawn.

After a few more ideas, Mrs. Woods moved on to the Define the Problem step. "Looks to me like there are lots of reasons kids might do things that make their classmates unhappy. Here's my concern. If we're trying to help one another in our class, and we're trying to make sure everyone gets what they need, and if we want our class to be a safe place for everyone to learn . . . well, we should be trying to help people with these things, yes?"

The kids nodded.

"So the next time we meet," she continued, "we should probably start talking about ideas people have for how we can make sure that these things on our list don't happen so much anymore, and talk about ways in which we could help one another. Good idea?"

The kids nodded their approval.

"If you want to, between now and our next meeting, you could start thinking about how we might be able to do that. You could even discuss it among yourselves. Then we'll make a list of everyone's ideas when we meet again and come up with a plan."

Plan B continued at the next community meeting.

"Well, we have our list of things that cause people to do things that make others unhappy," Mrs. Woods began. "And we know we want to make sure that members of our community who are having difficulty with these things get our help if they need it. Let's start talking about how we could be helping one another with these things. Anyone have any ideas?"

"Aren't bullies supposed to get punished in our school?" asked Taylor.

"Yes, they are," said Mrs. Woods. "But I don't think it's working too well. There's still a lot of bullying going on. It makes me wonder if that's really the best way to solve the problem." Mrs. Woods pointed to the list. "I'm not sure if punishing people fixes any of these things on our list. I don't know if it would help someone who thinks mistreating people is funny, I don't see how it would help someone who doesn't know how to make friends, or someone who doesn't know how to be nice, or someone who's in a bad mood, or someone who's been mistreated themselves so they don't know any better, or someone who's mad because they aren't popular. What do you think?"

"What else *is* there to do besides punish them?" asked Taylor.

"Well, let's think about that," said Mrs. Woods. "In fact, maybe we should take these problems one at a time. If someone thinks mistreating people is funny, and we wanted to help them with that problem, because it would be better for them and better for all of us, how could we help them?"

"We could tell them we don't think it's funny," said Samantha.

"But you would have to tell them nicely, instead of getting all mad at them," Eddie added.

"We could tell *you* what they're doing," suggested Taylor.

"These are very good ideas," said Mrs. Woods.

"Should we be writing them down?" asked Samantha.

Mrs. Woods smiled. "Samantha, you are very good at reminding me that we need to do that."

"These are wimpy ideas," said Kellen. "If someone's bugging you, you tell 'em to quit. And if they don't quit, you *make* 'em quit." This idea drew knowing nods of approval from a few of the kids.

"How would you do that?" asked Mrs. Woods.

"Like I said the other day," said Kellen. "Survival of the fittest."

"Ah, yes, you did mention that the other day," said Mrs. Woods. "So we should probably talk about it some more. I think you're talking about fighting, yes?"

Kellen smirked. "Whatever it takes."

"But why have a fight if you don't need to?" asked Mrs. Woods. "What if some of these other solutions people came up with worked instead?"

"Where I come from, if you tell somebody what they did wasn't funny, *you* get hit," said Kellen. "Me, I hit first, ask questions later."

More scattered nods of approval.

"Maybe that's why there's so much fighting where you come from," said Tina, a girl who shared Kellen's bus. "I'm sick of all the fighting. As far as I can see, it doesn't fix anything."

This comment drew nods of approval as well.

Mrs. Woods tried to empathize. "Kellen, it must feel terrible . . . worrying about getting hit all the time."

"It is what it is." Kellen shrugged.

"My concern is that if the only thing people do to keep from getting hit is to hit first, then the fighting never ends," said Mrs. Woods.

Kellen and his classmates pondered this observation.

"Kellen, have you ever been hit by someone in our class?" asked Mrs. Woods.

Kellen looked around at his classmates. "I don't think so."

"Maybe, if you think it's a good idea, you could think of our class as a safe place for trying out some new ways of dealing with people who you're having a problem with. Maybe some of the ideas we're talking about now will work for you."

Kellen was skeptical. "What if they don't?"

Mrs. Woods rephrased the question for the entire group. "What do you all do when the first solution you try doesn't fix a problem as well as you thought it would?"

Joey raised his hand. "You try to think of other solutions that might work better."

"So what are some other ideas for what you can do if someone is mistreating you and they think it's funny?" asked Mrs. Woods. "So far, we have telling them you don't think it's funny and telling me. Any other ideas?"

"You could just tell them to stop," said Duane.

"You could just ignore them and hope they go away," Shawn suggested.

"That doesn't work," said Austin. "If they think it's funny, they just keep doing it."

"Well, remember, Austin, right now we're just trying to think of as many possible solutions as we can. Some of our solutions might not work as well as some others. But we also have to remember that we've never really tried working on this problem as a group before. It's possible that some of the solutions you think wouldn't work so well would work okay if we were trying them together."

"You could ask them why they're bugging you," volunteered Tina. "Maybe they just want you to notice them."

The solution-generating continued. Eventually, the class agreed to post the solutions, begin using them, and put extra effort into responding to feedback they received from one another.

"We'll have to see how our solutions are working as time goes on," said Mrs. Woods to conclude the community meeting. "We have a lot more work to do, but I think we're off to a good start. In our next meeting we should probably tackle one of our other problems. I think you all did an incredible job of working on this together."

"Mrs. Woods, how come we never talked about this kind of stuff in other grades?" asked Samantha.

"You know, Samantha, I'm wondering the same thing myself," replied Mrs. Woods.

The following Monday, Mrs. Franco slid a sheet of paper onto Travis' desk while the class was doing a writing assignment.

> *It looks like recess is not a good time for us to talk. But I'd still like to discuss something with you. When would be a good time? Please check one:*
> *____ Before school*
> *____ During lunch*
> *____ After school*
> *____ Some other time I didn't think of (please write here)____*

On his way to lunch, Travis handed back the note. He had endorsed the "Some other time I didn't think of" option and, in the space provided, had written in the word *Never.*

Mrs. Franco shook her head when she read his response. Later that afternoon she handed Travis another note.

Why don't you want to meet with me?

As Travis left the room at the end of the day, he handed Mrs. Franco his response. She waited until all her students were gone before opening the note.

Your just going to tell me what I'm doing wrong and tell me your going to punish me and I don't need your help.

Mrs. Franco gave Travis another note as he entered the classroom the next morning.

I'm not going to tell you what you're doing is wrong. And I'm not going to punish you. I just want to hear your ideas about how things are going with the other kids.

Travis did not immediately respond to this latest correspondence. But two days later Mrs. Franco found a note on her desk at the end of a school day.

Why me?

She hurriedly penned a response and gave it to Travis the next day.

Because I'd like to know more about how people in our class are getting along, and I think you probably have some good information that would help me.

At lunch, Mrs. Franco received Travis' reply:

After school on Friday. For three minits.

She responded:

See you then.

After school that day, Mrs. Franco triumphantly showed Mrs. Woods the latest note from her new pen pal.

"Wow," marveled Mrs. Woods. "He's actually going to meet with you."

Mrs. Franco grimaced. "Now I know how actors must feel before a performance. I think I have stage fright."

"What are the three key words?" asked Mrs. Woods.

Mrs. Franco seemed puzzled. "Break a leg?"

Mrs. Woods laughed. "Empathy, empathy, empathy."

"Right, empathy, empathy, empathy."

On Friday, Travis stayed behind as promised. Mrs. Franco took a deep breath and took the plunge. "Travis, I know you didn't really want to talk with me. So I appreciate you doing this."

Travis didn't acknowledge this, and Mrs. Franco continued, starting with some reassurance. "Like I said, I'm not going to tell you that you're doing anything wrong and I'm not going to punish you. And I won't try to help you with anything if you don't want me to. I don't even know if there's anything you need help with. But I have a feeling kids in our class aren't getting along so well sometimes, and I thought maybe you had some ideas about what's going on."

"I don't know what you mean."

"You don't know what I mean when I say kids aren't getting along so well?"

"Yeah."

"Well, I've noticed that there's a lot of name-calling going on and kids picking on each other and just not being very nice to one another. Have you noticed that?"

"That's normal. That's just how kids treat each other."

"Oh. Does it bother you that kids treat each other that way?"

"No. It's just normal. It doesn't bother anybody."

"Well, now that's the thing. Some of the kids have told me that it does bother them . . . all the name-calling and picking."

Travis smirked. "They must be wimps."

"I wonder why it bothers them. Do you have any ideas about that?"

"Nope. It's just how kids treat each other."

"I guess there are just some kids who do mind it and some kids who don't. What do you think?"

Travis was losing patience with this conversation. "I guess. Are we almost done?"

"Yes, sure, almost. Just a few more questions. Tell me, does anyone call you names and pick on you?"

"Used to. All the time. But then I got good at it so they don't do it anymore."

"Interesting. So kids used to pick on you and call you names a lot?"

"Yeah. Like when I was in the first grade."

"Did you mind when they treated you that way?"

"Yeah," Travis started but then caught himself. "I mean, not really. Anyways, I was just a little kid then."

"But then you got good at it so they quit."

"Yep. My father says the best defense is a good offense."

"Yes, I've heard that expression before. I've just always wondered if it's really true, I mean, besides in football. Because then there's always someone getting picked on."

Now Travis was a bit more interested in the conversation. "Well, the trick is to make sure *you're* not the one getting picked on. That's what my father says."

"Let me see if I understand what you're saying," said Mrs. Franco, trying to get Travis' point of view on the table. "Other kids used to give you a hard time and you didn't like it very much, although you were just a little kid. But then you got good at giving other kids a hard time so now they don't give you hard time anymore. And giving kids a hard time isn't that big of a deal because it's the way kids treat one another these days. Do I have it right?"

"Yup. We done?"

Mrs. Franco wondered if she should take a stab at the Define the Problem step. "Yes, I think we're about done." She decided to forge ahead. "But here's my concern. Some kids don't like being picked on or being called names, so there are some kids in our class who are feeling pretty bad right now. Like you used to."

"That's their problem. They just need to get good at it like I had to."

"Does it bother you that there are kids in our class who feel the same way you used to?"

"No."

"So, since we're out of time, I'd like you to think about something. I know you don't care that there are kids in our class who are feeling bad right now about being picked on. But I'm still wondering if there's anything we can do so that *no one* in our class is getting picked on—not you, not them, not anybody. Then nobody would feel bad."

"I don't know."

"Well, let's both think about it a little. Maybe you'll come up with something. Or maybe I'll come up with something. What do you think?"

Travis was already finished with the conversation. "Um, I guess."

"I really appreciate you talking about this with me, Travis. I know you didn't want to, but it's been really helpful for me to understand things better."

"Sure."

"See you later."

"Uh-huh," said Travis as he turned to leave the room.

In one of her morning meetings with Joey, Mrs. Woods decided to follow up on something they had talked about previously. "Joey, I was wondering if we could get back to talking about you thinking you're messed up."

"OK."

"Besides getting confused on assignments, and getting upset about it, what makes you think you're messed up?"

Joey pondered the question briefly. "I can just tell."

"Did you know that you're not the only one in our class who gets confused about assignments?"

"I'm not?"

"No, other kids get confused, too."

"I never saw anyone get confused."

"I spend a good part of my day explaining things that your classmates are confused about."

"You do?"

"I do. You've never noticed that?"

"Nope."

"And I get confused about things sometimes, too."

"You?"

"Me."

A slight look of recognition came across Joey's face.

"So," continued Mrs. Woods, "you can think you're messed up if you want to. But if the reason you think you're messed up is because there are things you get confused about, then *I'm* messed up, too."

Joey smiled, but the smile faded. "Yeah, but you don't go nuts the way I do. You don't have to go to doctors the way I do. Neither do any of the other kids."

"Ah, the other part of being messed up."

Joey looked down at his hands.

"Here's what I'm wondering," said Mrs. Woods. "We're helping you understand why assignments are confusing for you . . . and what to do about it, yes?"

Joey looked up. "Yes."

"And our signal is helping you not get upset when you do get confused?"

"Yes."

"I wonder if you'll still think you're messed up if we're successful at helping you not get confused and helping you not get upset when you do get confused."

Joey looked at his teacher. "I don't know."

"I guess we'll find out." Mrs. Woods had another thought. "Is it messed up that you and I have our morning meetings?"

"Kinda. I mean, no one else has to do it."

"I see what you mean. Well, we don't have to keep meeting so often. In fact, I could use the time to plan what I'm doing with the class for the day."

Joey looked grim. "But I like meeting with you in the morning."

"Well, I like our morning meetings, too, Joey. I was just thinking maybe you might not want to have to come in and meet with me as often."

"I don't mind coming in. I don't even care if the other kids know. Some of 'em know anyways. So if there's a day you need to plan something, you could just tell me. I could just sit there and do something else."

"That would work. You know, Joey, what you just said wasn't messed up at all. In fact, it was very considerate."

"It was?"

"Yes. In fact, I'm wondering if I need to start pointing out to you all the things you do that *aren't* messed up."

Joey was unenthusiastic about that idea. "You don't need to do that."

Mrs. Woods recovered quickly. "How about I let you know in ways that no one else would notice?"

Joey's face brightened. "OK."

Mrs. Franco was eager to discuss her second attempt at Plan B with Mrs. Woods. But a week had elapsed and no opportunity presented itself. Then she bumped into Dr. Bridgman after school one day. "Dr. Bridgman!"

"If only I were always greeted with such enthusiasm," he mused.

"I did Plan B! Sort of."

"Sort of Plan B is better than no Plan B at all. Who'd you do it with?"

"Kid named Travis in my class. A real bully, from what I can gather. But clever about it, although now I'm wondering if clever is the best way to describe him. Anyway, he wouldn't talk to me the first time I tried Plan B. But Lori—you know, Mrs. Woods—helped me figure out what I did wrong and he actually talked to me the second time."

"Outstanding. So what's the 'sort of' part?"

"Well, we never really talked about any solutions. It didn't get that far."

"Hmm. So he wouldn't talk to you the first time but he did talk about it the second time. That's progress. A lot of times Plan B doesn't make it through all three steps in the first go. Did you get any useful information about his concerns?"

"I think so. He said he got bullied when he was in the first grade so he decided to become good at it so he wouldn't be the one getting bullied anymore. He seems to be getting some interesting guidance from his father, something about the best defense being a good offense. So he's not very sympathetic to the kids who are getting bullied now."

"Interesting. You did get some useful information. What did you tell him your concern was?"

"That we had some kids in our class who were feeling pretty bad about being bullied. He didn't care. What do you do if a kid doesn't care about your concern?"

"Well, I usually assume that kids who don't care about our concerns have spent a lot of time having their concerns disregarded. We may have to convince him that we care about his concerns before he starts caring about ours."

Mrs. Franco considered this perspective. "Wow. I never really thought about it that way before. I guess we spend a lot of time forcing kids to take our concerns into account without returning the favor."

"Then we wonder why they won't talk to us," observed Dr. Bridgman. "They'd be a whole lot more receptive to addressing our concerns, without being forced, if we were equally receptive to addressing theirs. Of course, that's why the first step of Plan B is Empathy. We want the kid to know we really are invested in taking his concerns into account."

"I get it. But I still don't get what I should do if he doesn't care about the other kids in the class feeling bad."

"Well, he doesn't have to care deeply about the other kids to work on trying not to make them feel bad. He just needs to take your concern about the other kids into account."

"So I should just go back to Plan B and see what solutions we come up with?"

"Exactly. And keep me posted."

The next day, Mrs. Franco wrote a note to Travis asking if they could talk again. She noticed him lingering when his classmates were on their way out to recess that afternoon. He waited until the last kid was just out of sight. "You don't have to give me notes anymore if you want to talk to me."

This news took Mrs. Franco a bit by surprise. "Oh, OK."

"How many more times do I have to talk to you?"

"Um, I'm not exactly sure."

"What do you want to talk about?"

"I just wanted to finish the conversation we started the last time. You know, about how kids are treating one another."

"How 'bout after school today?"

"That'll work."

Travis beat a path for the door.

"Thanks, Travis," Mrs. Franco called after him.

During the day, Mrs. Franco thought she saw Travis looking at her a few times. After the class was dismissed at the end of the day, Travis reappeared at the door. He announced his time line. "I only have five minutes."

That's more than the last time, Mrs. Franco thought, suppressing a smile. "Five minutes it is. Shall we get down to work?"

Travis nodded.

"So, last time we talked, I learned that you got bullied in the first grade and had to learn how to bully kids so they didn't bully you. I think you said the best offense was a good—no wait, it's the other way around—the best defense is a good offense."

Another impassive nod from Travis.

Mrs. Franco continued. "I understand that you don't want to get bullied. The thing is, no one else in our class wants to get bullied, either, and we have some kids in our class who are feeling pretty badly about how they're being treated."

Travis nodded yet again.

Mrs. Franco had arrived at the Invitation. She took a deep breath. "I'm wondering if there's a way for us to make sure you don't get bullied—so you don't feel bad—and also make sure the other kids don't get bullied—so they don't feel bad, either. Do you have any ideas?"

Travis appeared to be considering the question, though, given his blank look, it wasn't easy to tell. Finally he spoke. "The other kids look up to me now. I don't want to lose the friends I have. I don't want kids to start bullying me again."

Mrs. Franco digested this information. "You're worried that if you stop giving kids a hard time then they wouldn't look up to you, and the kids who are your friends now won't be your friends anymore, and you might start getting treated badly again."

Travis nodded. Mrs. Franco waited for more. When Travis said nothing, Mrs. Franco wasn't sure what to do next. Then she remembered that solving the problem wasn't her job, it was *their* job. "I wonder what we could do about that."

Travis shrugged.

"This is a tough problem, Travis," said Mrs. Franco. "What do you think? How can we help you keep your friends and keep you from getting treated badly but make sure other kids don't get treated badly, either?"

Now Travis was rubbing his forehead. "I can't ease up unless I know kids are going to treat me OK, too."

"Yes, I understand. It's going to be hard for you to feel comfortable treating the other kids nicely without knowing if they'll return the favor."

"Yep."

"I'll be perfectly honest with you, Travis. I'm not sure how we'd do that. I think I need to think about it a little. Unless you have any ideas."

"Why don't you talk to the other kids about it, too? Not just me."

"I heard that in Mrs. Woods' class, they talk about this stuff all together, so everybody's working on it at the same time," said Mrs. Franco. "We could do that in our class. Do you think that would help?"

Travis shrugged. "Maybe. I don't know yet."

"Do you think the other kids would want to talk about it?"

"I don't know."

"I wonder if we should try it with the whole class and see how it goes. What do you think?"

"I guess."

"At the moment, I'm having trouble thinking of any other ideas. How about you?"

"No. OK, are we done?"

"I think we are. Thanks, Travis."

As Travis said, "Yep," and got up to leave, Mrs. Franco noticed the slightest smile on his face. I think I just did Plan B, she thought, allowing herself a fleeting moment of exhilaration. Then she started thinking about the hard work that lay ahead.

CHAPTER 8

School of Thought

We've come a long way. In the seven preceding chapters, we reviewed the lagging cognitive skills and unsolved problems that set the stage for kids' challenging behavior, covered how to identify and prioritize these lagging skills and problems, considered why traditional school discipline programs don't teach skills or resolve problems, covered the ins and outs of doing Plan B, and described how to go about using Plan B to teach skills, solve problems, and reduce challenging behavior with individual challenging kids and in an entire classroom. Now comes the really hard part: *changing the culture and practice of discipline in an entire school.* This is no small undertaking.

School systems and individual schools are so vastly different—in terms of personnel, leadership structures, organization, job responsibilities, schedules, populations served, existing disciplinary practices, unions, and so forth—that no fixed template can be applied to all schools mobilizing for and embarking on this challenge. But there are some key components that do cut across all schools:

- *Individuals* who create the impetus for change, who have a sense of a school's readiness for change, and who have the capacity to

respond to and help colleagues who are uneasy about or struggling with change

- *Structures* that foster the communication and teamwork needed to
  facilitate and sustain change, including those that would help parents
  and teachers "reach across the aisle" to work together more effectively. If these structures do not presently exist they must be created.
- *Leaders* who foster and encourage change and who cultivate a
  school climate that is geared toward continuous improvement

In this chapter, we'll consider each of these ingredients as they
relate to implementation of the CPS model, along with the manner by
which Plan B can help make the journey a bit smoother.

IMPETUS FOR CHANGE

Appreciation of how challenging students are being misunderstood,
treated in ways that are counterproductive, slipping through the
cracks, and losing their futures does not happen through osmosis.
Someone is going to have to get the ball rolling. I've heard it said that
the impetus for creating this awareness and mobilizing people for the
changes it brings must come from the leaders of a school or school system. There's no question that these tasks are easier if administrators
are on board, even if they're not leading the charge. But my experience is that the impetus for change can come from many different people. It could be a teacher who has lost faith in the existing system of
school discipline; a parent weary of seeing his or her child's lack of
behavioral progress at school; a school psychologist or social worker
with an unmanageable caseload; a guidance counselor wishing to
expose colleagues to some new ideas; a principal eager to turn things
around in an entire building; an assistant principal who has come to
appreciate the futility of the school's existing discipline problem; a special education director or school board member intent on reducing the
high cost of servicing kids who get lost along the way; or a superintendent trying to be responsive to teachers who have, for a long time,
been pleading for guidance and support in dealing with kids who are
disrupting the classroom process.

Some schools are more ready for change than others. In some schools, the staff and leaders have already come to recognize that their understanding of and approach to challenging kids need some serious adjustments, and are ready, perhaps even eager, to be introduced to the specifics of CPS. In other schools, staff and leaders aren't yet familiar with the research providing compelling evidence of lagging cognitive skills in challenging kids, haven't adjusted their views on the nature of these kids' difficulties, and therefore haven't begun to recognize the imperative to alter disciplinary practices. In these schools, raising awareness is often the first step, and it is often necessary to slowly get the ball rolling by quietly (or not so quietly, depending on your style) calling into question conventional wisdom and raising the consciousness of school staff about the tremendous harm caused when we fail to understand the difficulties of kids with behavioral challenges and fail to treat them in a way that is more enlightened and humane. This process can begin through conversations with colleagues ("I know Elena's a pain, but I can't help feeling that the way we're treating her is doing more harm than good"), in team meetings ("This is the nineteenth time Hector has been suspended this year. It's hard to imagine that more suspensions are going to fix what's really going on with that kid"), and in faculty meetings ("I've been reading some interesting material lately about why challenging kids are challenging; material that would have major ramifications for the way we do things around here"). The goal is not to be adversarial, but rather to raise awareness, get people talking, and help people take off their "sunglasses" and focus on the glaring reality that the needs of a meaningful subset of students are not being well addressed. Thinking big usually involves starting small.

You may find it easier at first to reach people at a purely practical level—since the current way they're approaching kids with behavioral challenges isn't going swimmingly—rather than hoping to tap into a wellspring of empathy for challenging kids. That said, Pam Charles, a principal at a public school for challenging kids in New York, has commented that fostering empathy for kids with behavioral challenges among her staff was the ingredient central to helping the kids at her school and reducing out-of-school suspensions from several hundred each year to zero. "The primary thing we focused on was empathy. . . . We knew the histories of the kids in our school, what they'd been through, one story worse than the next. We knew the brain research, why the kids were behaving the way they were. We wanted to be the place where empathy happens. We wanted to create something exceptional for kids who had no voice, to be the voice of the voiceless."

When people are ready for the specifics of CPS, you'll want to start by providing information about the lagging skills setting the stage for challenging behavior in kids, perhaps at a faculty meeting or an in-service. To help people sink their teeth into this material, it's often useful to provide copies of the ALSUP, to consider each lagging skill on the list, and, when possible, to practice completing it. Notice that providing information about Plan B does *not* come first. If people don't understand that lagging skills and predictable unsolved problems are setting the stage for challenging behavior, then Plan B won't make a great deal of sense and there will be a tendency to view Plan B as just another technique that can be dispensed with if it doesn't instantaneously reduce a kid's challenging behavior. Understanding the *why* of challenging behavior is what brings people back to Plan B even when the going gets rough.

If, after learning about CPS and discussing options, people are now eager to move toward implementation, there are some important considerations.

- Should implementation begin as a pilot program with individual students and/or teachers?
- Should initial implementation occur in selected classrooms, grades, learning communities, or teams?
- Should participation in training occur on a voluntary basis or as a school-wide initiative?
- What are the best mechanisms for ongoing training and teamwork so as to ensure the sustainability of the effort?

These questions must be answered in each individual school based on its needs. There's no right or wrong way to do this.

You'll want to plan ahead for the eventuality that some people are going to struggle with and passively or actively resist change. Modifications of standard practice aren't typically greeted with wild enthusiasm, and school discipline can be an especially thorny subject. Some people find the tenets of the CPS model to be incongruent with their own thinking or training. Some people feel they're already doing a good job with their challenging students and don't see the need to change course, or may be somewhat resentful of anyone's efforts to alter what they do in their classrooms. Others are "initiative weary," and have difficulty envisioning how they'll find the time to learn the skills or use the model. Still others believe that implementation of CPS will make the school less safe, or feel that helping kids with behavioral challenges falls outside the job description of educators. All are valid concerns, of course, and should be clarified and addressed.

How would one go about doing that? Well, clarifying concerns is something for which the Empathy step of Plan B is particularly well suited. The ingredients of Plan B are as important in adult-adult inter-actions as they are in adult-child interactions. Adults, just like kids, are more likely to participate in solving problems when they feel that their concerns aren't being disregarded.

Some concerns arise because of misconceptions about the CPS model, and some arise in response to change in general. If people have misconceptions, providing additional information to clarify relevant aspects of the CPS model will often be helpful. It's important, of course, for the additional information to be presented in a way that isn't dismissive. Most of the following examples have been covered elsewhere in this book, but not in this context:

> Concern: Look, maybe there's something to this CPS business, but I just can't see myself doing it.
> Response: *You can't see yourself doing it. Tell me more about that.*

> Concern: If I accept maladaptive behavior in my classroom, what sort of example does that set for the rest of my students?
> Response: *There is absolutely nothing about the CPS model that has you accepting challenging behavior in your classroom.*

> Concern: I'm not going to get jerked around by a kid or let him get away with disrupting my class.
> Response: *What is it about the model that makes you feel that you're going to get jerked around by a kid or let him get away with things?*

Concern: Anytime we capitulate to challenging kids, we let them know they have power over us.
Response: The CPS model doesn't involve capitulating. You're still the authority figure. But you're using your authority in a way that could be more productive.

Concern: We do our challenging students no favors by protecting them from the consequences of their actions.
Response: You're not protecting them from the consequences of their actions. They're still suffering all kinds of natural consequences for their actions. You're just not relying on artificial, imposed consequences to teach them the skills they lack or help them solve the problems that are setting the stage for their challenging behaviors.

Concern: Sounds like a new fad to me.
Response: That kids with behavioral challenges lack important skills is well documented. This is no fad. Thirty years ago, kids who had difficulty reading were often thought of as lazy or dumb. Now, no one thinks of them in that way, and many people have the know-how to teach them the skills they lack. This is no different.

Concern: I still think the kid is acting up for attention.
Response: I wonder why he's not seeking attention in a more adaptive way.

Concern: So we don't set limits on kids around here anymore?
Response: Now that would be a recipe for chaos! Don't forget, you're setting limits when you're using Plan B.

Concern: What if I try Plan B and it doesn't work?
Response: I guess we'd sit down and try to figure out why.

Concern: I don't have time for this.
Response: I hear you. It's true, learning new skills is going to take extra time, but I'm thinking it will save time (and kids) once we're good at it.

Concern: How much can I really do at school when the kid's going home to a mess?

Response: I guess we have two options. One is to continue making things as messy at school as we think they are at home so the kid has consistent messiness across settings. The other option, if we're convinced there's nothing we can do to make things better at home, is to make things better here at school, so at least the kid has one environment in which he's doing well. Better one than none.

Concern: Things were going a lot better around here before we started doing this CPS.

Response: It does feel that way sometimes, doesn't it? However, we weren't communicating very well before CPS, and we weren't helping very many challenging kids, either.

Concern: This is not how I was trained.

Response: Yeah, me neither. But it does make sense, doesn't it?

Overcoming the impediments to helping kids with behavioral challenges doesn't happen overnight. But in all the schools, inpatient psychiatric units, residential facilities, and juvenile detention centers in which the CPS model has been implemented thus far, many of those who were resistant early on are now among the most ardent advocates for challenging kids and the model.

STRUCTURES FOR SUPPORTING AND SUSTAINING CHANGE

These days, many schools are organized by teams or learning communities. That's because somewhere along the line we figured out that the challenges and problems faced by schools and teachers might be better resolved as a collaborative group rather than by individuals working in isolation. Some teachers who liked working in isolation haven't been so enthusiastic about the trend, but my experience is that most have been generally receptive. Good thing, too, because working toward a better understanding of kids with behavioral challenges and responding more effectively to their needs typically requires a collaborative group effort.

It is much easier to initiate change than to sustain it. Once people have begun implementing Plan B, they're going to need a structure that permits them to achieve a consensus on the lagging skills and unsolved problems of individual kids, to review their initial and ongoing attempts to implement Plan B, and to figure out why Plan B didn't go well, commiserate, express concerns, learn from others' experiences, support one another's efforts, and track progress. In many schools, team or learning community meetings are ideally suited to such activities. In the words of one junior high school principal, "My teachers have had enough one-day workshops. . . . I'm interested in providing them with help over the long haul."

Early on, some proportion of meeting time will be spent learning the CPS model. As familiarity and comfort with the model grows, meeting time will be spent considering individual kids, reviewing their progress, and revising high-priority skills and unsolved problems. If you need help keeping track of all the crucial elements—lagging skills, unsolved problems, priorities, who's doing Plan B on specific priorities, and what solutions they've arrived at—the CPS Plan and Plan B Flow Chart, available at lostatschool.org, should help. In addition to team meetings, many schools have found it necessary to carve out additional meeting time in which all relevant parties—administrators, clinicians, classroom teachers, and sometimes parents—meet (usually weekly) to discuss the "high priority" students about whom they have the greatest concerns.

If there's no structure in your school providing regular meeting time, then staff won't have an opportunity to commiserate, express concerns, figure out why Plan B didn't go well, learn from others' experiences, and support one another's efforts, in which case your school has a problem to solve. It is impossible to provide high-quality help to a challenging kid when adults don't have time to talk. That's true whether you're implementing CPS or any other effective model of care. It's only the ineffective models of care that don't require good communication.

The isolation of teachers is still ingrained in some school cultures, so collaboration must be systematically embedded in the daily life of the school. Fortunately, there are numerous existing models for structuring and organizing the efforts of a group to solve problems collaboratively. One that has been tailored to schools in particular, and that has been adopted (to varying degrees) by many schools, is the Professional Learning Communities (PLC) model. While the primary focus of PLCs is academics, the structure and organization provided by the model are equally applicable to challenging behavior. For the unfamiliar, PLCs are composed of teams whose members work interdependently to achieve common goals and engage in collective inquiry into the best practice. Team members focus on finding answers to a variety of questions related to the well-being of students, teachers, and the school in general, including the following (parentheses added, for obvious reasons):

- How can we clarify and communicate the mission, vision, and goals of our school (as they relate to challenging kids)?
- How can we initiate, implement, and sustain a change process (so as to better understand and address the needs of kids with behavioral challenges)?
- How can we shape organizational culture and provide structures that support the culture we seek (so that our new ways of responding to challenging kids endure over time)?
- How can we create collaborative processes that result in both individual and organizational learning (so that no one feels isolated in his or her efforts to respond more effectively to kids with behavioral challenges)?
- How can we foster an environment that is results-oriented yet encourages experimentation (as it relates to the ways in which we work with challenging kids)?

As is clear from these questions, PLCs provide more than just an organizational structure for working toward improvement. The model also promotes a *mentality* that encourages a relentless focus on continuous improvement. PLC team members are dedicated to examining and questioning the status quo, seeking new methods, testing those methods, and then reflecting on the results. This is good, because implementation of the CPS model requires the questioning of conventional wisdom and often draws attention to procedures, policies, and programs that are incongruent with a school's emerging mentality and practices relative to challenging kids.

PLCs are also *action-oriented*. This is also good, because one of the biggest obstacles to school-wide implementation of CPS is the existing school discipline program, which is usually the embodiment of Plan A, and is usually codified in a document that lists what kids can and can't do and what's going to happen to them if they do or don't do those things. CPS has prompted major revisions to the discipline code in many of the systems and facilities in which the model has been implemented. First, after seeing progress with Plan B, people usually begin to notice that the discipline code is both obsolete and no longer consistent with current beliefs and practices. Then a committee is usually formed to make proposed changes to the disciplinary code.

Members of a PLC are prepared to slosh around together in the mess, to endure temporary discomfort, to accept uncertainty, to celebrate their discoveries, and to move quickly beyond and learn from their mistakes. They realize that, even with the most careful planning, people will resort to old habits and things will go wrong. This is a good thing, too, because implementing Collaborative Problem Solving is, at least at first, messy and uncomfortable.

Reaching Across the Aisle

Another group of people—parents—needs to be included in the collaborative effort to improve things for challenging kids in a school. Parents often remark, "The folks at school don't listen to me. . . . They don't understand what we're going through at home . . . and they don't keep me informed about what they're doing. . . . They just blame me when it doesn't go well." Of course, teachers may say, "Those parents don't have the slightest idea what we're going through with that kid. We can't even get them to come in to meet with us . . . they just expect us to fix things when they send him to school."

Kids who exhibit challenges at school typically evidence challenges at home, too. On one hand, that's bad news, because it means that the kid is struggling in multiple environments. But on the other, it's good news, because it means that parents and teachers have something in common and it shouldn't be too difficult for each party to come to the realization that there are shared concerns and frustrations.

As Sarah Lawrence-Lightfoot notes in her insightful book, *The Essential Conversation: What Parents and Teachers Can Learn from Each Other,* great potential exists for productive collaboration between parents and teachers. Families and schools are overlapping spheres of socialization, and the successful learning and development of children depends on building bridges across them. Parents and teachers need each other and parent-teacher interactions can lead to new insights, deeper understanding, and mutual appreciation. When parents and teachers exchange highly specific information about the child—for our purposes, that initially means information about lagging skills and unsolved problems—the trust that is the bedrock of good communication between parents and teachers is fostered. Parents become convinced that they are being heard and that the teacher sees, knows, and cares about their child. Good communication also helps educators become convinced that parents are eager for information, eager to collaborate, and eager to help in any way possible. Both parties must do everything in their power to put children at the center of parent-teacher interactions.

Still, collaboration between the two parties is often loaded with emotion, especially when the topic is kids' social, emotional, and behavioral challenges. Dr. Lawrence-Lightfoot writes of the subtle barriers that make parents feel strangely unwelcome in their children's schools, almost as if they were trespassing on foreign ground, and of the natural tensions that exist in interactions between parents and teachers. Parents tend to be protective of their children, and entrusting their child to the care of a perfect stranger does not come easily to many. When things at school don't go as well as hoped, as is often the case with challenging kids, some parents may blame teachers, question their qualifications, and attempt to impose solutions, while others may feel so helpless and so unable to affect the goings-on at school that they avoid contact with it completely.

Not coincidentally, teachers often feel most uncertain, exposed, and defensive in interactions with parents, feeling that their competence and professionalism are challenged. Teachers often receive little if any preparation for working with parents in their educational training. Teacher education usually does not offer a conceptual framework for understanding the importance and complexities of building productive parent-teacher relationships, and many teachers feel ill-prepared to interact with parents collaboratively.

Why do parents and teachers have such trouble solving problems together? For the very same reasons kids and adults do: the blaming of one party or another; the attempt of one party to impose its will on another; the failure to achieve a consensus on the true nature of a kid's difficulties (lagging skills) and the true events (unsolved problems) precipitating his challenging behavior; the failure to identify the concerns of the different parties; dueling solutions. Some examples (not to be emulated) are:

Imposition of Will

SPECIAL EDUCATION COORDINATOR: *Mr. and Mrs. Nelson, we've decided that your son, Jeff, is no longer appropriate for the program he's in, so we're moving him to a different program in a different school. We need you to sign the revised IEP.*

Imposition of Will

PARENT: *My wife and I have come to the conclusion that this school is unable to meet the needs of our daughter, Leah, and we are pursuing placements outside of the school system and have been in contact with an attorney.*

Perfunctory Empathy

PRINCIPAL: *Ms. Donaldson, we understand that the past few months have been very difficult for you and Tony. We appreciate that. We know how hard that can be. But we have a school to run and the needs of many other students to consider.*

Perfunctory Empathy

PARENT: *Look, I know you all haven't had an easy time with Johnny. But I have to do what I think is best for my son.*

Failure to Achieve a Consensus

GUIDANCE COUNSELOR: *We really think Greg's difficulties trace back to the fact that he has no father figure in his life. We think he needs counseling so he can talk about that.*

PARENT: *Greg hasn't had a father figure in his life for a long time. I tried getting him a Big Brother, but it just never seemed to work out. Anyway, that's not why Greg is still having trouble. He's having trouble because he has no friends at school. I wish you all could find a way to help him make a friend.*

GUIDANCE COUNSELOR: *We just don't see it that way.*

PARENT: *I think I know my son.*

Dueling Solutions

SCHOOL PSYCHOLOGIST: *Jabbar needs to be in our self-contained classroom.*

ADVOCATE: *No way. What Jabbar needs are teachers who understand him and know how to work with him . . . and he needs to be around ordinary kids so he doesn't just emulate the bad behavior of other bad kids. I want him in an inclusion classroom.*

More Dueling Solutions

PARENT: *She needs an IEP.*

SPECIAL EDUCATION DIRECTOR: *She needs a 504 Plan.*

What's going wrong here? Dr. Lawrence-Lightfoot notes that the factors that lead to enmity and a breakdown in parent-teacher communication are fairly straightforward. They are defined by a *lack of empathy* and a *disregard for the other's role, perspective, and concerns,* factors that should sound familiar to you. Contrary points of view are commonplace, almost inevitable, as parents and teachers bring to the table unique and equally valuable perspectives about the child. It is far better for contrary points of view to be expressed openly than to be hidden behind a veil of civility and feigned deference. Dr. Lawrence-Lightfoot counsels, "Do not go to the table to say 'you must' or 'you need to.'" (She's referring here to Plan A, though she doesn't call it that.) In the parlance of CPS, this means that both parties need to concentrate their efforts on hearing each others' concerns rather than imposing solutions. In my experience, the vast majority of adversarial interactions between parents and school personnel can be traced back to the failure to achieve a consensus on a kid's lagging skills and unsolved problems. Both parties need to be part of the process of working toward a mutually satisfactory action plan—you're on the same team. *Let's see if we can get a handle on the skills that need some work and the problems that need to be solved . . . then we can work together to come up with a plan of action to teach those skills and help solve those problems.* Here's what that might look like:

TEACHER: *Mr. and Mrs. Knight, now that we're through talking about how Sally is doing academically—and I'm hoping you're getting the message that I think she's doing quite well and that I really enjoy having her in my class—there were a few other issues I wanted to discuss.*

MOTHER: *Uh-oh. We were waiting for this. She been giving you a hard time?*

TEACHER: *I take it I'm not the first.*

FATHER: *Nor the only. She's a handful at home, too.*

TEACHER: *How do you mean?*

FATHER: *Well, she doesn't take too well to being told what to do. We walk on eggshells. In the earlier grades, she didn't cause any trouble at school. But then they started seeing the same things at school that we were seeing at home. We've been to a lot of folks for help and I know she worked with a guidance counselor at school for a while.*

MOTHER: *Yes, she was in a social skills group at school for a while. We've also had her on some medicine to see if we could help her be a little less, you know, brittle. She's not on anything now, but she's still pretty much the same kid she's always been. Is that what you're seeing?*

TEACHER: *Well, yes, in a way. I've certainly noticed that she's not too keen on being corrected, especially when it's a behavioral issue, but also on academics. She seems to be quite the perfectionist. And I think the other kids think she's rather bossy. They say she always has to have her way.*

MOTHER: *That's our girl. Hope she's not giving you too hard of a time.*

TEACHER: *Well, we've definitely had our moments.*

MOTHER: *Do you think we should see about medicine again?*

FATHER: *Do you think she needs an IEP?*

TEACHER: *Oh, I'm not the one to be guiding you on medicine. And I guess we wouldn't know if she needed an IEP until we got a handle on the factors contributing to her difficulties. Around here these days we've actually come to view kids' challenging behavior as a sign that the kids are lacking some of the skills they need to behave appropriately. A learning disability of sorts.*

MOTHER: *A learning disability? I thought you said she was doing fine academically.*

TEACHER: *Yes, she is. I'm using the term "learning disability" to say that we don't really view behavioral challenges as being any different from some of the academic challenges a kid may exhibit at school.*

FATHER: *So if she has a learning disability, she needs an IEP, yes?*

TEACHER: *Well, even academic learning disabilities don't automatically lead to an IEP these days. But what I'm really saying is that Sally may need us to teach her some of the skills she's not quite up to speed on so she's not, to use your words, so much of a handful.*

FATHER: *So what kind of skills are we talking about here?*

TEACHER: *Glad you asked. I brought a form we use to try to identify the skills a child is lacking, and the problems that cause their challenging behavior. I wanted to get your input on the skills she's lacking, see if we could come to some sort of consensus. Then I thought we could talk about how we could help her.*

FATHER (examining the ALSUP): *This is a new take on things. Skills, eh? Never thought about it that way. I see a few items on here that would apply to Sally . . . in fact, more than a few.*

MOTHER: *I see a bunch here in the middle. Difficulty seeing the*

*"grays," concrete, literal, black-and-white thinking—geez,
that's her. Difficulty shifting from original idea or solution,
difficulty adapting to changes in plan . . .*

TEACHER: *Yes, I was thinking those might apply to Sally.*

FATHER: *So, does she need some kind of special school or
something?*

TEACHER: *I don't think so, but to tell you the truth, I hadn't
gotten that far yet. I do have some other parents coming in
just a few minutes for their conference, but I was thinking, if
we could schedule another meeting so we could put our
heads together and figure out what skills she's lacking and
what problems are causing her worst moments, then we
could come up with a plan for what to do.*

MOTHER: *She's already had her share of sticker charts and
missed recesses . . .*

TEACHER: *Oh, I wasn't thinking along those lines. I thought we
could talk about how we could work with Sally to address
her challenges together.*

FATHER: *I don't understand.*

TEACHER: *Well, I probably can't do this justice in the time we
have left, but I'm operating on the assumption that Sally is
already motivated to do well, but that there are some
problems she's having trouble solving on her own and needs
our help. We wouldn't help her learn how to solve those
problems if we solve them for her. She needs to be a
participant in solving them. I don't know if I'm making
sense with all of this . . .*

MOTHER: *I can't say that I understand completely, but we
don't want to hold you up. Can we take this form home
with us?*

TEACHER: *Yes, please. At the bottom there, where it says "Unsolved
Problems," that's where you list the problems that seem to set
the stage for her challenging behavior.*

FATHER: *That's easy. The word "no."*

TEACHER: *Well, we'd want to know what you were saying "no"
about if we wanted to be really precise about the specific
problem.*

FATHER: *Ah, got it. So, like "No, you can't tell your friend to go home just because she won't do things your way . . ." Right?*

TEACHER: *Exactly.*

FATHER: *So we fill this out and then meet with you again and come up with a plan?*

TEACHER: *That's what I was thinking.*

FATHER: *And the plan would involve us.*

TEACHER: *Well, you know her better than I do, so I'd certainly want you to be involved in the creation of the plan. We'd want to involve Sally in the plan, too. But I don't think we'll know what the plan looks like until we know what it is we're working on. Shall we try to find another time to meet?*

What happens when school personnel and parents start collaborating? My friend Pam Charles, the principal at a special education school for kids with behavioral challenges, puts it this way: "Once we started reaching out to parents, once we started helping their kids succeed at school, they stopped hanging up on us, they started returning our phone calls, they started showing up at school." And the father of a challenging kid I know offered his own perspective: "At some point, I stopped feeling like the people at school were judging me or blaming me. I started feeling like they weren't just paying lip service to my concerns. They wanted to work together. So did I."

LEADERSHIP

Leadership is a hot topic in schools these days, and for good reason: An effective school leader can make a world of difference for kids, teachers, and parents. Revamping school discipline is a daunting challenge, one that is unlikely to be met without *vision* (what we are trying to accomplish), *perseverance* (we won't accomplish it overnight), *resilience* (this isn't going very well yet, but I'm confident that it will), *collaboration* (let's put our heads together and figure out how to make it go better), *patience* (progress occurs at different paces for different individuals), *perspective* (let's not forget what we're trying to accomplish, but look at how far we've come already), and *a sense of purpose* (I know we have a lot of other things going on around here, but this is important).

As fate would have it, effective leadership involves many of the ingredients of Collaborative Problem Solving, except that the ingredients are now being applied to adult-adult interactions. When leaders use Plan A to solve problems, whether in adult-adult or adult-child interactions, they unwittingly promote a Plan A culture. As you already know, Plan A begets Plan A.

Fortunately, Plan B begets Plan B. As noted by Dr. Ron Heifetz, author of *Leadership Without Easy Answers,* effective leaders aren't "geniuses" and don't have all the answers. They recognize that their primary role is to *organize action,* to challenge and mobilize people to face and tackle tough problems for which there are no simple, painless solutions, and to facilitate exploration of new ways of doing things. When people look only to the leader to address problems, they become dependent on the leader's wisdom and the collective wisdom of the group is lost. In encouraging and energizing people to tackle tough problems, leaders elevate them from followers to problem-solvers.

Leaders also facilitate *invention.* They encourage debate, help people rethink, and help people recognize that simply redoubling their efforts to apply familiar strategies is rarely a productive approach. Often, solutions to persistent problems lie outside existing repertoires and therefore require outside-the-box thinking. Leaders encourage people to try new ideas on for size and explore novel solutions. They understand that the inclusion of different perspectives is essential to achieving durable, effective solutions.

Leaders help people *identify and stay focused on the difficult problems that need to be solved.* Who are the kids we aren't reaching? What do they need from us? Why are we still doing things in a way that isn't working for a lot of kids? What do we need to do differently to ensure they get what they need? What do *we* need—what training, what new structures—to accomplish the mission?

And if you're thinking that leadership can come only from those who occupy positions of leadership, think again. While we often look for leadership at the head of the table, leaders more often emerge from the foot.

Q & A

Question: Is CPS truly realistic in a middle, junior, or senior high school, where kids have multiple teachers who don't always have a chance to communicate with one another?

Answer: Many middle and high schools are organized in teams or learning communities these days, so that should make things a bit easier. Nothing takes the place of ensuring that staff has the time to talk about high-priority kids and meet periodically (preferably, at least weekly) to monitor the kids' progress and modify the CPS Plan and Plan B Flow Chart. Again, the only models of care that don't require good communication are the ineffective ones. CPS isn't the answer to all the communication and scheduling problems that plague some middle, junior, and senior high schools, but it can help address communication problems in two ways: first, by providing staff with a framework for organizing and communicating information about a challenging kid; and second, through Plan B, which provides staff with the key ingredients they'll need to tackle and solve their remaining communication problems. Perhaps even more daunting is the fact that secondary schools have to deal with a lot of kids whose challenges were misunderstood and poorly addressed in earlier grades. So it's not just the problems that have piled up over time; it's the kids, too. Where do you start? One kid and one problem at a time. Of course, the magnitude of this problem would be greatly reduced if the adults in the earlier grades started using CPS.

Question: If I'm working within a teaching team, how do we determine which of us should be doing Collaborative Problem Solving with a given student on a particular problem?

Answer: Early on, it will probably be whoever volunteers! But if you have several willing collaborators, you might want to give some thought to who has the best relationship with the student, who he's already talking to, and, if the problem is related to interactions with one member of the team, whether it would be better for that member to approach the kid or potentially more productive for him to talk about it with a different member.

Question: I'm a teacher, and I've been trying Plan B, but I don't think I'd give myself a very good grade yet. When will I feel like I've mastered it?

Answer: Maybe you're a tough grader. But, early on, I wouldn't be grading for proficiency; I'd be grading for bravery and effort. Like all new skills, the more you use Plan B, the more instinctive it becomes. And the mere fact that you recognize that you could do it even better—well, now, there's an unmistakable sign of progress.

Question: Yes, but how will I know I'm being successful?

Answer: An improved relationship with a given child, his increased receptivity to talk with you and provide information, his increasing willingness to work collaboratively to make things better—these are signs of success you may see before you start to see actual progress on the problems you're trying to solve and skills you're trying to teach. The time and effort you put into the process is never wasted, even though it can take a while to see all the fruits of your labors.

Question: I'm a school principal. I've been trying to help my teachers use Collaborative Problem Solving, and it's gone pretty well. But I have a few teachers who just aren't doing it. Advice?

Answer: Try to figure out why, starting with the Empathy step, as in "I've noticed that you haven't been participating much in our CPS work. What's up?" They may feel they don't have the skills to do Plan B yet. They may not be convinced about the rationale for Plan B. They may feel completely overwhelmed. They may be retiring soon and just don't see the point. We won't really know what their concerns are unless we ask. Then we can work toward ensuring that their concerns—and yours—are addressed.

Question: I understand the need for parents and teachers to collaborate with each other. But as a teacher, what if I really can't get the parents to work with me?

Answer: Sorry for the repetition, but try to figure out why, with particular emphasis on the Empathy step. Remember, the goal of the Empathy step is to gather information so as to understand a person's concerns or perspective. Maybe they've felt blamed for their kid's problems at school. Maybe they're embarrassed that they're not sure how to help their kid. Maybe they've been to so many mental health professionals, read so many books, and received so much advice—and still have nothing to show for it—that they've lost hope. Maybe they are so overwhelmed that trying to plug one more hole is simply beyond reach at the moment. If all else fails, never forget that you can still do a kid a lot of good in the six hours a day, five days a week, nine months a year that he's in school.

Question: Still, I can't help but feel that sometimes a kid's parents are undoing all that we're working on at school.
Answer: Feeling "undone" is usually a sign that people aren't yet communicating and working together as well as they could.

Question: Do you ever run into school personnel who refuse to participate in learning about CPS because they feel it goes outside of what they are paid to do?
Answer: Yes, but I find it's much more common for school personnel to be willing to go the extra mile, even without being paid for it, to learn new ways to help kids.

Question: How do you incorporate Collaborative Problem Solving into an IEP?
Answer: An IEP contains a great deal of information, but perhaps the most crucial components of an IEP are the problems or lagging skills being targeted for remediation and how these problems or lagging skills are to be addressed. If you've identified a kid's lagging skills and triggers (through use of the ALSUP) and established a set of priorities (through use of the CPS Plan), you're ready to incorporate those priorities into an IEP. You're also ready to document how Plan B will be used to address those lagging skills and problems. Quite frankly, since IEPs tend to be fairly static documents, you're likely to find the CPS Plan and Plan B Flow Chart to be far more effective at prioritizing and revising goals, tracking a kid's progress, deciding what skills have been satisfactorily trained and problems resolved, and helping adults and the kid appreciate the progress that's being made. IEPs become outdated rather quickly; the CPS Plan is a living, breathing plan of action.

Question: How do poverty and culture impact the effectiveness of the CPS model?

Answer: At the risk of seeming insensitive, I think poverty is overrated as an explanation for challenging behavior in kids (in his seminal book *Schools Without Failure,* Dr. William Glasser agreed). There are kids from impoverished circumstances who succeed. There are kids from wealthy backgrounds who don't. Those who come from wealth often have parents who will stop at nothing to access good care and have the resources and wherewithal to find and pay for it. Some receive very poor care anyway. Data[1] suggest that socioeconomic status is not a predictor of success with the CPS model.

People from similar backgrounds sometimes have an easier time connecting and communicating with each other. But I've yet to run into an ethnic group whose members don't value having their concerns heard and addressed. In fact, look at anyplace in the world where there's conflict right now and you'll see one people whose concerns are being disregarded and another imposing its will. It's very reliable.

Question: How will I know if our school has "turned the corner" in our treatment of challenging kids?

Answer: There's no single benchmark signifying that you've "arrived," given that improvement is an ongoing process. But there are some pretty clear indicators:

- The mentality toward challenging kids in your school is oriented toward lagging skills and unsolved problems, and people are actively using the ALSUP in their assessment of these kids and the CPS Plan and Plan B Flow Chart in monitoring their progress.
- People are skilled in and actively using Plan B.
- Structures supporting the use of CPS are in place, including mechanisms for (1) responding to behavior problems proactively rather than emergently; (2) communicating and collaborating across staff and with parents; (3) practicing, coaching, and monitoring Plan B skills; and (4) orienting new staff to the model.
- Mechanisms are in place for the continuous evaluation of school discipline, and discipline referrals, detentions, suspensions, and expulsions are on the decline.

- Adults understand that reducing challenging behavior is neither fleeting nor haphazard. Durable improvements occur when the kid's concerns are understood and addressed, problems are solved, and skills are taught.

Question: Does the CPS model apply to kids who shoot people in our schools?

Answer: Remember our mantra: *Behind every challenging behavior is either an unsolved problem or lagging skill.* Kids who act on the idea of shooting people at school are clearly having difficulty coming up with more adaptive solutions to problems they've been unable to solve. In many instances where kids have resorted to extreme violence, people were surprised that the kid went to such extremes. But we all have what might be called a "threshold of adversity," and we all have different levels of skill in dealing with adversity. When a person's threshold of adversity exceeds his skills, the likelihood of violence is heightened. That's why it's crucial to keep the lines of communication open with every kid so you're aware of his lagging skills and unsolved problems. Create a helping relationship. Work collaboratively toward solving the problems so the kid learns the skills.

The Story Continues . . .

Mrs. Westbrook buzzed into Mr. Middleton's office. "Crystal Caldwell is here."

Mr. Middleton had been mulling over Mr. Armstrong's latest discipline referral, and had asked Crystal to come talk with him before he decided what to do. "OK, send her back."

Mr. Middleton pointed Crystal to a chair as she entered his office. "Hi, Crystal."

"What'd I do now?"

"Well, I have some more discipline referrals from Mr. Armstrong here, but I also wanted to see how you're doing."

"Why?"

"I've noticed you've been absent a lot, and sometimes that's a sign that things aren't going so well."

"Look, whatever Armstrong is nailing me for, just give me the speech about my future and needing to respect authority and do what you gotta do."

"Well, I don't *gotta* do anything. I'd like to do something that helps."

Crystal smirked. "Helps?"

"I guess you're not too convinced."

"Look, I hate this place. If I was old enough, I'd drop out now."

"Yes, that's what I've heard. And from the looks of things, you've kind of started dropping out already. What do you do when you're not at school?"

Crystal smirked again. "I have fun. I have friends. They think school sucks, too."

"Does your grandma know who you're hanging out with?"

"My grandma has no clue about anything I do. Why, what's she gonna do about it?"

"These friends . . . they're skipping school, too?"

"Some of 'em . . . most of 'em have dropped out already."

"They're a lot older than you?"

"Some of 'em. Is there a point to this?"

"Just interested in knowing what you're up to when you're not here."

"Why, can you think of a good reason for me to be here?"

"Actually, no."

Mr. Middleton's honesty caught Crystal off guard. "What?"

"Well, when you're here you're in trouble a lot, and from what I can tell, you've always gotten in trouble a lot in school. I can't imagine that you think of school as a place where you're especially successful. Like you said, you hate this place, and when you're not here, you have fun and you have your friends. So, no, I can't think of why you'd want to be here."

"Then what am I doing here?"

"That's what I wanted to talk about." Mr. Middleton thought for a moment. "Crystal, can you remember a time when you ever felt good about school?"

Surprisingly, Crystal answered quickly. "Mrs. Morin . . . second grade. She was nice to me. I was living with my mom then. But my mom was drinking a lot, and Mrs. Morin . . ." Crystal's face had softened but then she caught herself. "Why are we talking about this?!"

"I'd like to help you feel good about school again."

Crystal crossed her arms. "Too late."

"I understand."

"You don't understand. You're not me."

"No, I'm not you."

"So you can't help me."

"I can't help you because I'm not you?"

"No one can help me. Help someone else. Look, what did Armstrong say I did?"

"He said he overheard you talking about drugs."

Crystal scowled. "Did anyone else get sent down here for that?"

"No. Just you."

"This is bullshit."

"What is?"

"A bunch of people in our class talk about drugs. How come I'm the only one getting crap for it?"

"I don't know."

"You wanna know why you haven't seen me at school much lately? Now you know."

"I don't understand."

"Why would I wanna come to a place where I get treated like crap?"

"Let's talk about that."

"Look, uh, Mr. Middleton, you're trying to be nice and everything, but I really don't want to do this."

"Crystal, are you still seeing that counselor from the mental health clinic?"

Crystal scowled. "No."

"How come?"

"'Cuz how often can you talk about how you feel about the father you never met and your mother's an alcoholic and she couldn't take care of you and dumped you on your grandma and she can't take care of you, either? It doesn't change anything! I'm done talking!" Crystal stood up. "Can I go?"

"Yes, you can go, in a second. I do have to give you three days of in-school suspension for the drug talk, Crystal, even though I know it's not going to help. But I also want to do something that will help."

"Like what?"

"I want to have a meeting between you, me, and Mr. Armstrong. To talk about how we can make things better for you here."

"No way!"

"Why not?"

"He doesn't want to make things better for me here!"

"I understand you feeling that way. And I know you won't believe this, but Mr. Armstrong is actually trying to do the right thing for you. But I know you don't think what he's trying to do is helping, so I think we should meet to talk about it."

"It's a waste of my time."

"Well, it might end up being a waste of my time, too. But I want to do it anyway. I'm afraid we're losing you, and I hate to see that happen."

"You lost me a long time ago."

"I want to find a way to get you back."

Early the next morning Mr. Middleton poked his head into Mrs. Galvin's office. "Got a minute?" he asked.

Mrs. Galvin looked up. "Of course."

"I've been thinking about something and I wanted to get your take on it."

"What's on your mind?"

"No big deal. Well, maybe it is a big deal. I don't mean to alarm you, but it's suddenly dawned on me that we have a double standard in our school."

Mrs. Galvin chuckled. "We probably have many double standards in our school. Probably a bunch we haven't even noticed yet."

Mr. Middleton pressed on. "I think this is one we haven't noticed yet. You know how we've been putting a lot of energy into our Response to Intervention and Professional Learning Community work? I've noticed that all that energy, all that time spent on developing a vision, thinking about our mission, establishing goals, gathering data, collaborating, it's all being devoted entirely to academics."

"What else would we be devoting ourselves to?"

"We're putting no energy whatsoever into applying the same principles to school discipline. If there was ever an aspect of our school that needed a new vision, and new goals, and better assessment and collaboration, it's how we deal with our challenging kids."

"Tell me more."

"We've put a lot of effort into examining whether our actions in this building are consistent with our stated vision for academics. We don't really even have a stated vision when it comes to how we handle our challenging students."

Mrs. Galvin pondered this observation. "Well, I suppose that's true. I guess we've been leaving it all up to you."

"That's exactly right! We've been leaving it all up to me!"

"So you don't think we should be leaving it all up to you?"

"No, the people the challenging kids are having trouble with are sending them to me to fix problems that have nothing to do with me. Take Crystal Caldwell. Mr. Armstrong is convinced she just needs him to be firm and consistent, and in the meantime, she's getting punished by me so often that she's spending more time out of school than in it. I mean, it's clearly not working."

Before Mrs. Galvin could respond, Mrs. Westbrook poked her head in the door. "Sorry to interrupt. Mr. Middleton, they're waiting for you down at Mrs. Woods' room."

"Oh, right, thank you," Mr. Middleton said. He looked back at Mrs. Galvin.

"Let's finish this conversation later," said Mrs. Galvin. "What's going on in Mrs. Woods' class?"

"A meeting with Joey's mom."

"Oh, no, did he—?"

"No, no, nothing like that," reassured Mr. Middleton. "Joey's doing great. His mother meets with Mrs. Woods every so often so she can learn more about what we're doing with him here at school. His mom's doing it at home now, too."

"You don't say."

Mr. Middleton got out of his chair. "Mrs. Woods has done an amazing job with that kid. She's a real trailblazer. I asked if I could sit in on the meeting today."

"I wonder . . ." Mrs. Galvin hesitated. "Do you think they'd mind if I sat in, too? You know, just for a few minutes. I don't want to intrude, but I'd like to hear about what they're doing."

"I don't see why not. Come on, I'm late already."

Mrs. Woods and Ms. Lowell were talking when Mr. Middleton and Mrs. Galvin entered the classroom.

"Oh, uh, hello, Mrs. Galvin," said Ms. Lowell, caught off guard. "Hello, Mr. Middleton."

"I hope it's OK if I sit in on part of your meeting," said Mrs. Galvin. "I've heard about how well things are going with Joey. I'd like to hear what you all are doing."

"Oh, sure," said Ms. Lowell, looking at Mrs. Woods.

"You're sure I'm not intruding?" asked Mrs. Galvin.

"If it's fine with Ms. Lowell, it's fine with me," said Mrs. Woods.

"Um, absolutely," said Ms. Lowell. "Mrs. Woods is doing some amazing things with Joey. She has me doing it at home, too."

"We're not meeting to talk about me," said Mrs. Woods. "Let's focus on Joey. He's working very hard. He's a great kid."

"Joey doesn't come to these meetings?" asked Mr. Middleton.

"No, he likes his mom to come alone," said Mrs. Woods. "Ms. Lowell was in the middle of telling me about some of the Plan B she's been doing with Joey."

"I'm not very good at it yet," said Ms. Lowell. "Although he and his brother are getting along a little better." The puzzled looks on the faces of Mr. Middleton and Mrs. Galvin suggested the need for further explanation. "See, Mrs. Woods found out that Joey was having some pretty negative thoughts about himself, and his older brother wasn't helping matters, so we've been doing double-barreled Plan B on that problem."

"So you've been doing Plan B at home and Mrs. Woods has been doing Plan B at school?" asked Mrs. Galvin.

"Yes, exactly," said Ms. Lowell. "Mrs. Woods had already made some headway on the problem before I started."

"That's wonderful," said Mrs. Galvin.

"And it's not just Joey," said Mr. Middleton. "Mrs. Woods is doing it with other kids, too."

"How do you find the time? How do you keep track of all this, I mean, with all the students you have?" asked Mrs. Galvin.

"Well, of course, I do have to find the time to do Plan B with individual kids," responded Mrs. Woods. "That's the hardest part—planning ahead for the discussions. But once a problem is solved, I don't really have to keep track of it or put time into it anymore. I just move on to the next problem. A lot of problems affect the entire class, so we've started trying to resolve those problems as a group."

"No one's ever reached Joey like Mrs. Woods has," said Ms. Lowell. "And believe me, many have tried. I can't tell you what we've been through."

Mrs. Galvin was genuinely moved by what she was hearing. "I'm very sorry for what you and Joey have been through. But it's wonderful to see you and Mrs. Woods working together on this. I'm so pleased that Joey is doing better. Everyone around here tries to do right by kids, but we don't always have all the tools we need." She looked at Mr. Middleton. "And sometimes we aren't even aware that we need new tools until we take a close look at what we're doing. I think Mr. Middleton and I will be talking some more about how some of the other kids in our school might benefit from what you've been doing with Joey."

Mrs. Galvin sat down in Mr. Middleton's office at the end of the school day. "Should we get back to our discussion?"

Mr. Middleton quickly picked up where he'd left off. "You know, our academic vision statement says we believe all students can learn and that every student has a right to access the learning opportunities we provide. But every day I still have an assembly line of challenging kids flowing in and out of my office and a mountain of discipline referrals. We're still sending kids home or to in-school suspension when they mess up around here. It's the same kids every week. Because of how we're dealing with them, we're actually making it *harder* for them to access learning. When it comes to school discipline, I think our vision and our actions are completely out of whack."

"That's probably because we don't have to report our disciplinary data the way we have to report our academic data with No Child Left Behind," said Mrs. Galvin. "No one knows how we're doing—or what we're doing—with discipline. Apparently no one cares. Imagine what would happen if we had to file annual yearly progress reports on discipline referrals!"

"These are the kids we're still losing," said Mr. Middleton. "I think we need to change how discipline is handled in our school. We need to think about what it would look like if we were really trying to do the right thing for challenging kids around here. Of course, if my ideas were ever realized, I might be out of a job. But my vision is that teachers will know how to handle discipline issues with a lot less assistance from me. Like what Mrs. Woods is doing. Do you know I haven't seen a discipline referral on a kid from her classroom in about ten weeks?"

Mrs. Galvin sighed. "Not everyone is Mrs. Woods."

"Well, maybe Mrs. Woods is special, but maybe she's special mostly because she was willing to try something new. I do know Mrs. Franco's trying Plan B, too. Mrs. Woods is coaching her."

"Interesting."

"The reality is that we don't know how everyone else would respond, but I think we need to find out."

"Maybe in our next faculty meeting we should start talking about this," suggested Mrs. Galvin. "Disruptive behavior is certainly one of the things people complain about the most. And maybe Mrs. Woods could tell everyone what she's doing with her kids, let other teachers hear about it. So now we need to figure out how to do this. I mean, how will we present this to our teachers?"

"Well, I don't want to tell you how to run a faculty meeting," said Mr. Middleton, "but it seems to me that, just like we've been doing with academics, we should stay focused on what we say we're going to do and what the data tell us we are actually doing. I'd be happy to present the data on referrals to my office—they really tell the tale. We have a lot of kids who are not getting full 'access to learning opportunities,' and I think we have many teachers who don't seem to think it's their job, or don't know how, to help kids make progress socially and behaviorally. Those areas are more important for some of these kids than academics."

"Should be an interesting discussion," said Mrs. Galvin. "I guess we should be ready for some fireworks."

Early one morning a few days later, Mr. Middleton stopped by Mr. Armstrong's classroom. This is not going to be fun, he thought. "Jerry, can we talk a minute?"

Mr. Armstrong looked up from some paperwork he was completing. "Sure, what about?"

"Crystal again."

Mr. Armstrong rolled his eyes. "If I put half the time I spend dealing with Crystal into the kids who actually want to learn, they'd all be going to Harvard."

Mr. Middleton walked into the classroom. "We've both been putting a lot of time into Crystal. Problem is, we don't have much to show for it."

"A kid's got to want to be helped. Some kids don't."

"I'm beginning to think that the help we've been giving Crystal isn't what she needs from us. In fact, I think it's pushing her further away from us. And I'm starting to think that's the case with a lot of the kids in this school who come my way."

"What does this have to do with me?"

"I want to start thinking about taking a different approach with Crystal. And I need your help."

"Look, if you're here to try to talk me into doing that Plan B nonsense, it's not going to happen. When Crystal learns that in the real world there are rules that need to be followed and certain ways you need to treat people, and that there's such a word as 'no,' she and the rest of us will be a lot better off."

"Jerry, how many times has someone told you 'no' in the last week?"

Mr. Armstrong looked puzzled and then considered the question. "None."

"How many times have you had to solve a problem in the last week?"

"A lot. I don't see how this applies to Crystal."

"Apparently, dealing well with the word 'no' isn't as crucial to life in the real world as it's made out to be. Plan B teaches kids how to solve problems, a skill you've just told me you used a lot in the last week. All the detentions and suspensions Crystal's had . . . they haven't helped her learn how to solve her swearing problem, or her fighting problem, or the fact that she hasn't felt good about school since the second grade, or the fact that the only place she feels good is when she's hanging out with a bunch of dropouts."

"Look, I agree the kid has problems. But I'm not going to let her interfere with the learning of the kids who are here to learn, and I'm not going to let her bring her swearing and drug talk into my classroom."

"So let's work with her on those things, Jerry! Because I'm not giving her detentions or suspensions for them anymore."

Mr. Armstrong looked stunned. "Our school discipline code says—"

"Our school discipline code says that discipline is administered at the discretion of the principal and assistant principal. And the assistant principal is not going to continue doing something that isn't working."

"Mrs. Galvin is on board with this?"

"Mrs. Galvin and I have been discussing how to work with all of our teachers to begin making the school discipline program more effective. We want to make sure this is a team effort, just like a lot of the other things we do around here. And I would like you to be part of the process."

Mr. Armstrong was speechless. Briefly. "You want me to be part of the process of turning the school discipline program into some namby-pamby, permissive—"

"Collaborative Problem Solving is not namby-pamby. And it's not permissive, either. It's very hard work. And I'd like you to learn more about it."

"It doesn't trouble you that if we don't give Crystal consequences for swearing and fighting and drug-talk, then she'll get the idea that she can get away with it?"

"There's nothing about Collaborative Problem Solving that will make Crystal think she can get away with swearing or fighting or talking about drugs."

"Crystal needs a show of strength. This is a show of weakness."

"It takes more strength to do Plan B than it does to continue proving to Crystal how strong we are. We have no credibility with Crystal. She doesn't think we know how to help her."

"We know what help she needs! You know her grandmother. You know about her mother. You know her brother. Come on, Bill!"

"Jerry, so long as we think she's swearing and talking about drugs because of her mother and her brother and her grandmother, we'll never fix the problem. There are a lot of kids in this school who don't have Ward and June Cleaver for parents. Most of them don't swear or fight at school. Until we figure out and address whatever is getting in her way, we'll continue spinning our wheels."

"Well, I don't have the slightest idea how to do it."

At last, something to work with, thought Mr. Middleton. "Now *that* we can do something about. I'd like to have a meeting—me, you, and Crystal. I want to talk about the difficulties she's having and how much she hates this place and how we can help her. She and I have already talked about it a little. Now we need you to join us."

"You've talked about it already?"

"This is a very unhappy kid, Jerry. She's already written us off. She thinks we've written her off. If we don't switch gears with her—"

"So what's one meeting going to accomplish?"

"It won't be just one meeting. One meeting's a start. She needs to know she can rely on us to help make school good for her again."

Mr. Armstrong shook his head. "It's all about us, as usual. When things aren't working in a kid's life, blame the teacher."

"No, it's about her, too. That's why we need to talk about it together. We need to hear about and address her concerns, she needs to hear about and address ours. Tell you what, you don't need to say anything. Just sit there. Listen. Get to know her."

Mr. Armstrong considered this arrangement. "Look, Bill, we go way back. You know I've always been all about the kids. No one wants Crystal to do well more than I do. And it's not like we never talk to kids around here."

"I know that. This is a different kind of talking."

Mr. Armstrong looked at his watch. "The kids'll be here any minute. I have to think about this."

"OK, think about it. There's no down side, Jerry. Just remember that. There's no down side."

"We should probably get started," Mrs. Galvin called the faculty meeting to order one week later. She set forth her agenda for the meeting. "I would like to focus on something a little different today. For a long time some of you have been asking for help with some of the kids who are frequent flyers in our discipline program. I was thinking maybe it would be a good idea for us to take a look at our vision and mission, and examine whether our school discipline practices are really living up to what we say we want to accomplish.

"We have a lot of kids who are missing class time because of discipline referrals, and a lot of kids who are still being disruptive in classrooms, on the bus, in the cafeteria, but it's always the same kids and all we're doing is sending them to Mr. Middleton. We thought that it might be a good thing for us to look at as a school."

None of the teachers said anything. Mrs. Woods and Mrs. Franco looked anxiously at each other. Mr. Armstrong looked down at his hands.

"Mr. Middleton has prepared some data for us to consider," said Mrs. Galvin, nodding to the assistant principal.

Mr. Middleton held up a sheet of paper. "Here are some data I've pulled together. I've given you each a copy. Take a look at the number of students who have visited my office, the amount of time they've been out of class, and the number of 'repeat offenders.' These kids are clearly not fully accessing our 'learning opportunities,' and we are clearly not addressing their difficulties."

Mrs. Galvin chimed in. "I think a lot of you are spending more time on discipline than you'd like, sometimes to the detriment of the teaching you want to be doing. I thought we could try to come up with a better plan . . . together."

Mr. Armstrong looked up from the sheet. "What kind of a plan?"

"Well, a plan that would have your input and that would work better for everyone than the current plan," said Mrs. Galvin.

"I'd like to jump in again here," said Mr. Middleton. "To be blunt, I think the role I've been playing as primary disciplinarian in the school has become obsolete. Kids act up in classrooms, they get sent to me. I have some vague idea of what happened, but I also know it's more complicated than what I'm being told. But I talk to them anyway and apply punishments as dictated by our discipline code, and the next day or the next week, sometimes even the next *hour*, they're back in front of me and I'm doing the same thing all over again. It's always the same kids and the same problems. I'm not in a great position to solve problems that occur in your classrooms. The problems are between you and the kids. I think my job is to help you solve those problems. But I can't do it effectively with the existing setup and I can't do it without your involvement."

Ms. Estrada, the new seventh-grade teacher, hesitantly raised her hand. "I think I'm one of the people who've been sending kids to the office a lot. And I'm very sorry to report that I'm one of those people who've been spending huge amounts of time handling behaviors in my classroom. Maybe it's because I'm a new teacher, so maybe some of you have some experience that I don't have, but I would love the chance to talk about how to change things for the better. I'd even chair the committee!"

Ms. Estrada's earnestness brought smiles to some faces.

"Thank you, Ms. Estrada," said Mrs. Galvin. "I appreciate your candor. Any other thoughts?"

"Mr. Middleton, I agree that the role you've been playing doesn't make a whole lot of sense anymore," said Mrs. Franco. "And I agree that the whole discipline program doesn't make much sense anymore, either.

I've felt that way for a long time. But beyond that, I don't understand what you want from us."

"I guess we're looking for your ideas about the best way for us to change something that many people feel isn't working, and that is completely inconsistent with our stated vision and mission," said Mr. Middleton.

"This just goes back to inclusion," said Mr. Armstrong. "Someone comes up with the great idea that we should have lots of kids in our classrooms who used to be in special ed, kids with all kinds of issues, and then we get these kids dumped on us, and no one gives any thought to what we're supposed to do with them. Now we're getting Response to Intervention dumped on us, too. So it's no wonder a lot of us rely on the office for help on the problem kids. We're not getting help from anywhere else."

There were scattered nods of approval.

"I agree that we have a lot of kids in our classrooms who wouldn't have been there ten years ago," said Mrs. Franco. "And I probably run a tighter ship than I used to because of it. I mean, I do need to get some teaching done every day. But these difficult kids—the ones we wouldn't have given any thought to fifteen years ago because they would've been somewhere else—they aren't going anywhere. I mean, maybe some of us wish they'd disappear—and I'm not saying I do—but they aren't going anywhere. They're ours for keeps. So we'd better figure it out."

"Unless our vision and mission are just empty words, we need to start talking more about how we help them," said Mr. Middleton. "When we say 'all students,' I think we'd better mean it."

"So what would that look like?" asked Mrs. Galvin. "Mr. Middleton's data tells us the way we're handling our challenging kids isn't working very well and we want those kids to stay in our classrooms without impacting the learning of other students. How can we work together on a plan that will help us accomplish those apparently competing goals?"

"Well, you said you had some ideas," said Mr. Armstrong. "I'd like to hear them. Although I think I already know where this is heading."

Mr. Middleton smiled. "Yes, you probably do. We have some teachers doing something called Collaborative Problem Solving with some of their challenging kids. It's something Dr. Bridgman brought into our school. It's very hard work, and it is a major departure from the way we've been doing things. But some of our teachers are having success with it. We were thinking it might be useful to have Mrs. Woods tell us about it, maybe at our next faculty meeting. That way everyone can hear about it and we can talk about it together. That's what we were thinking. But we wanted to discuss this as a general topic with you before we did anything."

"I don't want to be a stick-in-the-mud," said Mr. Duncan, an eighth-grade teacher. "But I don't know anything about this problem-solving program you're talking about, so I don't know if I believe in it. I need to hear more about it. And I need to know how we're going to balance that program with all the other initiatives we have going around here."

"Well, I think that's what we're talking about here," said Mr. Middleton. "I think we're asking if you all want to spend some time in faculty meetings learning more about it and talking about other ways in which we might not be 'walking the talk.'"

"I'd like to talk about how we get parents more involved around here," said Mrs. Franco. "There are some kids, well, we just can't do it all by ourselves."

"There are some parents you don't want to have involved around here," said Mr. Armstrong, prompting scattered nods of agreement.

"I wonder if we can really make headway with our challenging kids without getting input from parents," said Mrs. Franco. "I mean, these are *their* kids . . . why are we doing this all by ourselves? I don't think we do a very good job of communicating with parents or involving them."

"We've never tried to address this problem together before," said Mr. Middleton. "Not just together meaning us, but together meaning them. Maybe we need to get a group of parents together to help us out with this."

"I know a few who'd love to help out," said Mrs. Franco. "By the way, I don't think we do a very good job of communicating about our challenging kids among ourselves, either."

"Sounds like we have some things to work on," said Mrs. Galvin. "And sounds like there is a general consensus that we are willing to examine our discipline practices, yes?"

"You're assuming that all of us are unhappy with the present setup," said Mr. Armstrong. "And that we're all in agreement with what you're calling our stated mission and vision when it comes to behavior problems."

"What do you mean?" said Mr. Middleton.

"You're using your data to argue that what we're doing now isn't working," continued Mr. Armstrong. "How do you know that these kids are going to do any better using some other system? At least with the current setup we may not be helping the kids with problems, but at least they're not disrupting the learning of the kids who come to school to learn. I think there's something to be said for that. So I'm not all gung-ho about doing something that's going to take more time, detract from the learning of the other kids, and has no guarantee of being successful. It's hard enough teaching what we need to teach without having to put time into the kids who don't want to be here in the first place and probably never will."

Several others nodded vigorously.

Mrs. Woods reluctantly raised her hand. "I understand your concerns, Jerry. I can't speak for everyone, but I'm betting lots of people in here are concerned about the same things. And you know I'm no rabble-rouser. But I just want to let you know that what I've been doing in my classroom isn't taking more time, it's taking less. I'm finally understanding and solving problems that have been getting in the way for these kids—and taking up a lot of time—for a long time. So it's not detracting from the learning of anybody. And you're right, there's no guarantee of success. These are our toughest kids. But I've come to agree with the perspective that they need something from us that our school discipline program doesn't give them. I don't see the down side to thinking about how to change things. That's all I had to say."

"I mentioned to Mrs. Woods that we might want her to do a little overview on Collaborative Problem Solving in our next meeting, but we wanted to clear the idea with you all first," said Mr. Middleton. "Then we can decide as a group how we might want to take things further."

"Why don't we have Mrs. Woods say a little about Collaborative Problem Solving now?" proposed Mrs. Franco. "I mean, it's hard to talk about something that very few people in here know anything about. We have some time left." She looked at Mrs. Galvin. "Unless you have something else you want us to cover."

"No, no, that would be terrific, if Mrs. Woods is willing and others are interested," said Mrs. Galvin. "Does anyone object?"

No one said anything. "Mrs. Woods, what do you think?" asked Mrs. Galvin.

"Well, I didn't really prepare anything," Mrs. Woods said, a little flustered. "But I suppose I could do a little introduction." Mrs. Woods stood up. "Here's the deal on Collaborative Problem Solving. In some ways it's pretty simple, in others, it's a little more complicated. I'll just talk about the simple parts right now. The challenging kids in our school are lacking important thinking skills. If I'd known I was going to be doing this, I would have brought the list of skills. But we can go over them next time. It's like they have a learning disability, but not in the areas we're used to—you know, reading, writing, arithmetic—but in other areas, like handling frustration, or social skills, or being flexible, or problem-solving. Just like any other learning disability, our job is to teach them the skills they're lacking. And one of the ways to teach those skills and help them solve the problems they're having is Collaborative Problem Solving, which is called Plan B. The important point, and this is what Mr. Middleton was talking about earlier, is that what we usually do, telling them what to do, rewarding and punishing—that's called Plan A—doesn't teach the kids the skills they lack or solve their problems. That's why they keep showing up in Mr. Middleton's office. Now there are some specific steps to Plan B, and I've been doing it with some of my kids, and it's really been helpful. It's changed my understanding of difficult kids and how I interact with them. I don't want to go overboard, but it's been kind of reinvigorating."

"Can you tell us more about what this Plan B looks like?" asked Mr. Armstrong.

Mrs. Woods explained the three Plans and the three steps for doing Plan B. She explained the distinction between Proactive Plan B and Emergency Plan B and why the former was far preferable. Then she provided examples of Proactive Plan B that she'd done with several of her students.

"Can we practice?" asked Ms. Estrada.

"I want to be mindful of the time," said Mrs. Galvin. "Should we save the practice for the next time?"

"I wouldn't mind seeing it now," said Mr. Armstrong.

"Should we take, say, ten more minutes?" asked Mrs. Galvin. "Then come back to it in our next meeting?"

The group nodded. Ms. Estrada agreed to be the guinea pig.

"So, Ms. Estrada, is there a student in your class who you're thinking of doing Plan B with?" asked Mrs. Woods.

"Oh, I need to do Plan B with pretty much every one of them," said Ms. Estrada. The group laughed.

"All in good time," said Mrs. Woods. "But pick a kid who needs Plan B badly. Someone you've been sending down to Mr. Middleton a lot."

"OK, I have someone in mind. She and Mr. Middleton have become well acquainted this year."

"And what have you been sending her down to the office for?" asked Mrs. Woods, thinking it would be easiest to demonstrate Plan B by focusing on a specific problem.

"She's obnoxious," said Mrs. Estrada. The grouped laughed again. "Guess that's not specific enough."

"No, we'd need something a little more precise," said Mrs. Woods.

Mr. Middleton chimed in. "If it's who I'm thinking you're talking about, one of the big things is sexual talk."

"Yes, that's her," said Ms. Estrada. "But I can't talk to her about that! I don't even know what she's talking about half the time!" More laughter.

"Yes, but that's why *I've* been talking to her about it!" said Mr. Middleton.

"So, Ms. Estrada," said Mrs. Woods, "if you wanted to talk to her about that using Plan B, how would you begin? Remember, the Empathy step is first."

"Um, how about, 'I think that you need to tone down the sexual talk so you don't get into trouble.'"

"Ah, yes," said Mrs. Woods. "That's *your* concern. But with Plan B, you're starting with *her* concern."

"But I don't know what her concern is," said Ms. Estrada.

"That's what the Empathy step is for," said Mrs. Woods. "You need to find out."

"I don't get this. What do I say?"

"If you're doing Proactive B—and on this topic, I don't think you want to use Emergency B—you'd make an observation, like 'I've noticed that you talk about sex a lot.'" Mrs. Woods thought better of saying "What's up?" on this particular topic, so she replaced it with "What's going on?"

"So what's she going to say?" asked Ms. Estrada.

"We don't know," said Mrs. Woods. "But I suppose there are a lot of things she could say. Maybe she'll say it makes her feel popular. Maybe she'll say she feels a lot of pressure to do whatever she's talking about. Maybe she'll say it's normal. Maybe she'll say she likes it. Maybe she'll say she doesn't know what else to talk about. Whatever she says, that's probably what you two are working on. But you aren't done with the Empathy step until you feel as if you have a clear understanding of her concern. Then the next step is the Define the Problem step. That's where you're getting your concern on the table."

Ms. Estrada was ready. "So that's where I say that I hate to see her getting into trouble for it."

"If that's really your biggest concern," said Mrs. Woods. "Anything you're concerned about more than that?"

"Well, given the possibilities you mentioned, I'm concerned that she's talking about sex because she thinks it makes her popular or if she's feels like she's under pressure to do the stuff she's talking about."

"So it's not just her getting into trouble that concerns you, it's things even more important than that, yes?"

"Yes."

Now Mr. Armstrong had some concerns of his own. "We're allowed to talk to kids about this stuff? Isn't this the kind of conversation that could get us into trouble? I mean, if this ever came up with a girl in my class, I'm not comfortable talking with her about it."

Mrs. Galvin weighed in. "I think that we probably do need to think about the line for when we need professional assistance on certain topics. But I'm also hearing that Mr. Middleton has been trying to talk about this with this student anyway. And it's possible that Ms. Estrada might be a better option on this particular topic."

Mr. Armstrong wasn't convinced. "But aren't there just some things that need to be talked about at home? That is, if there's anyone at home to do it? What if she's been abused or something?"

Mr. Middleton cleared his throat. "If she's been abused, we want to know, don't we? And in this particular case, I'm not sure we can bank on someone talking about it at home. But, I must say, we've never actually tried to find that out."

"All important issues," said Mrs. Galvin, looking at her watch. "But, just for the sake of what we're trying to accomplish right now, let's just see what the three steps of Plan B look like."

Mrs. Woods continued. "OK, so let's say the girl's concern is that she isn't sure what else she can talk about to be popular with the other kids . . . and, Ms. Estrada, let's say your concern is that you're not sure that sex-talk is the best or most reliable way to be popular. We now have two concerns on the table. Time for the Invitation. That's where you're inviting her to solve the problem together."

"I have no idea what I'd say next," admitted Ms. Estrada.

"Well, the Invitation is a summary of the two concerns that are now on the table. It might be something like, 'I wonder if there's a way for us to help you be popular with the other kids without you talking about sex to do it.' Then you give her the first stab at the solution, something like, 'Do you have any ideas?'"

"This *is* hard!" said Ms. Estrada.

"It does take some getting used to," said Mrs. Woods.

"So what's the solution?" asked Mr. Armstrong.

"We don't know yet," said Mrs. Woods. "Because they haven't talked about it yet. But good solutions are solutions that address both concerns."

"Maybe you could talk a little about when you find the time to do this?" asked Mr. Middleton.

"First thing in the morning, during P.E., lunch, after school," said Mrs. Woods. "Finding the time isn't my biggest problem. Like I said, in the end, doing Plan B saves me time because I'm not dealing with the same problem over and over again. But the hardest part is doing Plan B well. Some kids are so accustomed to Plan A that they don't realize you're trying a different approach. You have to stick with it until they trust what you're doing."

"So this is what we're supposed to be doing in place of consequences?" asked Mr. Armstrong.

"It's what some of our teachers are doing in place of consequences," said Mr. Middleton.

"So we don't do consequences around here anymore?" asked Mr. Armstrong.

"Well, all we've done so far is have you learn a little bit about Collaborative Problem Solving," said Mr. Middleton. "Nothing's been decided. We really do want this to be a group effort. In fact, we were thinking it might be a good idea to form a working group at some point to talk about this in more detail and then make some suggestions for the entire group. I'd want to be on the committee, since this topic is of particular concern to me. Any other volunteers?"

Ms. Estrada, Mrs. Franco, and Mrs. Woods all raised their hands. "Mr.

Armstrong, I think your point of view should be represented as well," said Mr. Middleton.

"I had a feeling you might nominate me," said Mr. Armstrong. "Naturally, I'm delighted to serve."

Mrs. Franco raised her hand. "Shouldn't we have some parents on our committee, too? I mean, maybe not right in the beginning, but we're always complaining about lack of parental involvement. I've already heard from one mom about why she found it so difficult to work with us. Isn't that something we need to know more about?"

Mr. Middleton agreed.

The meeting ended. Afterward, Mr. Armstrong approached Mr. Middleton. "Well, if I'm going to be on the committee, I should probably know more about Plan B. And I've been giving some thought to what you proposed with Crystal."

"I knew you would," said Mr. Middleton. "And?"

"And I think it would be good for me to see what Plan B would look like."

"Ah, good. Should I set up a meeting?"

"That would be fine. I don't have to say anything, right?"

"Right."

"This should be interesting."

"I certainly hope so."

Mr. Armstrong and Crystal assembled in Mr. Middleton's office a few days later. "Crystal, as you know, I was hoping the three of us could talk about some of the problems you're having here at school so we could work on them together," began Mr. Middleton.

Crystal feigned a yawn.

"Now, come on, Crystal," Mr. Middleton prodded. "We've never had Mr. Armstrong in here to help us out. Let's try."

Crystal rolled her eyes. "Help out? All he does is tell me what I'm doing wrong! And send me to the office so I can get detentions! I don't want his help. He's the problem!"

"I hear you," said Mr. Middleton.

"What does that mean, 'You hear me'?" demanded Crystal.

"You said all we do is tell you what you're doing wrong and give you detentions and that you don't want our help," said Mr. Middleton. "What I mean is that I can understand how you might feel that way."

"You agree with me?" said a puzzled Crystal. Mr. Armstrong found himself wondering the same thing.

"I'm not agreeing or disagreeing," said Mr. Middleton. "I'm just trying to listen and make sure I understand what you're saying."

This seemed to satisfy Crystal. Briefly. "It doesn't matter anyway. I'm dropping out as soon as I'm old enough."

"Yes, you said that the last time we talked," said Mr. Middleton. "And I suppose that's one solution. But here's what I'm thinking. You feel like we don't listen to you and just tell you what you're doing wrong and give you detentions and you don't want our help if that's the only kind of help we can offer. I'm hearing you loud and clear. But, see, my concern is that you're swearing a lot and talking about things that are pretty inappropriate, and that if everyone in the building was running around swearing and calling one another names then it wouldn't be the kind of place any of us would really want to hang out in. I'm wondering if there is any other kind of help we can offer—you know, other ways for us to help you with the swearing and the fighting—besides us giving you detentions and you dropping out?"

Crystal tipped her head against the back of her chair and looked at the ceiling. "I don't know! I just swear when I get mad. It just comes out. And when people piss me off."

"So you don't swear just for the fun of it?" asked Mr. Middleton, partially for the benefit of Mr. Armstrong. "It's only when you get mad?"

"What's fun about getting into trouble?" asked Crystal. "Not that I care."

"I've always assumed there was nothing fun about getting into trouble," said Mr. Middleton, "unless I'm missing something. When did you stop caring about getting into trouble?"

Crystal scowled. "When? I don't know. Eventually, you just get into trouble so much, year after year, teacher after teacher, and nothing anybody says to you or does to you helps. You just kinda figure you're always gonna be in trouble."

"I think I understand," said Mr. Middleton, adding the qualifier, "even though I'm not you. I'm asking you to think about taking a big chance. You've written us off. At this point, it's easier for you to just give up on us. But I'm asking you to give us one last chance. There are some problems that have piled up for you over the years, and it's going to take awhile for us to sort through them. But that means you'd have to start trying again. And I think that's going to be hard, too."

Mr. Armstrong found himself caught up in what Mr. Middleton was saying. He suddenly leaned toward Crystal. "I'd like to find a way to help you with the swearing and the fighting."

Crystal looked at Mr. Armstrong quizzically. "Huh?"

"I don't want to be your enemy. I want to help."

"Well, you sure fooled me."

"But I don't know how to do it."

"Well, me either."

"Crystal, you and Mr. Armstrong have never actually tried to solve this problem together, have you?" asked Mr. Middleton.

Crystal looked at Mr. Armstrong. "Me and him have never tried to solve *anything* together."

"Maybe it would be better for the three of us to try to solve this one," said Mr. Middleton. "You know, until you two get better at it. That sound OK to both of you?"

Crystal and Mr. Armstrong eyed each other and nodded tentatively.

"I think this problem could take awhile to talk about, and we don't really have much more time today," said Mr. Middleton. "Why don't we find a time to talk tomorrow? That'll give us all some time to think of possible solutions."

"I'm not getting detentions anymore for swearing and fighting?" asked Crystal.

"You're willing to work with me and Mr. Armstrong on those problems?" asked Mr. Middleton.

Crystal nodded.

"Then we're going to try this for a while without the detentions for the swearing. I don't know that I can go quite that far on the fighting."

"I haven't been in a fight for a while," said Crystal.

Mr. Middleton looked surprised. "What about that episode between you and Ashlee?"

"Never laid a hand on her," said Crystal with some satisfaction.

"Crystal, I'm going to try very hard not to suspend you or give you detentions while we're working on these things. I need you to try very hard to keep it under control until we come up with a plan."

Crystal smiled.

"Are you both available to meet before school tomorrow morning?" asked Mr. Middleton.

"I am," said Mr. Armstrong.

"My grandma works the night shift, so she gets home early in the morning," said Crystal. "She can drive me to school when she gets home."

"I'd like to meet with your grandma again one of these days," said Mr. Middleton. He saw Crystal stiffen. "Not to tell her you're in trouble," he reassured. "Just to see if maybe she can help us out, too."

Crystal looked skeptical. "She can't help with anything. She's, um," Crystal hesitated, "she's pretty stressed out, you know, what with working all night . . . and no one knowing where my brother is. I don't know if she could handle— If it's OK, can we leave her out of this for now?"

"I think that's fine," said Mr. Middleton. "I'll see you both bright and early."

The next morning, Mr. Armstrong and Mr. Middleton found themselves looking at the clock in Mr. Middleton's office. Crystal was fifteen minutes late for their meeting, and their small talk about professional football and boys' hockey had run its course.

"I know what you're thinking, Jerry, but don't say it," said Mr. Middleton, craning his neck toward the door to see if there was any sign of Crystal.

"What I'm thinking is that I have things to do in my classroom if she's not going to show up," said Mr. Armstrong.

Suddenly, Crystal and her grandmother, who was still wearing her work uniform, appeared in the outer office. Mr. Middleton rose to greet them.

"Lord have mercy, they're both here," murmured Mr. Armstrong to himself.

Mr. Middleton knew Crystal's grandmother from their prior dealings about Crystal's older brother. "It's nice to see you, Ms. Eldredge."

"Crystal told me you wanted her here early, but she wouldn't tell me why," said Ms. Eldredge. "I'm here to find out for myself."

Mr. Middleton looked anxiously at Crystal to gauge her reaction. Crystal looked down at her feet.

"Crystal, I know this isn't what we talked about," said Mr. Middleton softly. "But I should probably meet with your grandma for a few minutes. That OK with you?"

"Whatever," muttered Crystal.

"Do you want to come in with us?" Mr. Middleton asked Crystal.

"OK."

"Ms. Eldredge, this is Mr. Armstrong, Crystal's team leader," said Mr. Middleton.

"Nice to meet you," said Ms. Eldredge, taking her seat. "So what's this meeting about?" Crystal sat in the chair next to her grandmother, her head down.

"We're just talking with Crystal about different ways we can help her here at school," said Mr. Middleton.

"Her brother got in trouble at school a lot, too," said Mrs. Eldredge. "Mr. Middleton, I'm sure you remember Bobby."

"Yes, Bobby was quite a spitfire," said Mr. Middleton.

Ms. Eldredge sighed. "Well, now he's disappeared." Crystal closed her eyes, knowing what was coming.

"You don't know where he is?" asked Mr. Middleton.

"No, I don't," said Ms. Eldredge, her voice catching. "I mean, I've done my best with both of 'em, but if I don't work nights, I won't have a job, and I need my sleep during the day. I can't watch 'em as close as I'd like, and now I see Crystal heading down the same path." She pulled a tissue out of her purse. "I sure hope you all can get her turned around."

"We're going to do our best," said Mr. Middleton. "We think she's a good kid."

"Well, it's nice to hear you say that," said Ms. Eldredge, dabbing at her eyes. "When she was little, she was an angel. I don't know what happened to her. It's not easy, a girl growing up without her mother." Crystal, sitting with her knees against her chest and her head down, looked as if she wanted to disappear.

"I understand," said Mr. Middleton, glancing over at Mr. Armstrong, who was looking at Ms. Eldredge with what appeared to be genuine compassion.

"What's she in trouble for now?" asked the grandmother.

"Oh, we're just trying to help her with how she handles disagreements with people," said Mr. Middleton, looking at Crystal. "And her choice of words is sometimes more colorful than we can allow around here."

"She gets that from her brother. 'Course, I slip up myself sometimes. But I've told her a million times she can't talk that way at school."

"We appreciate that," said Mr. Middleton. "We seem to be learning that all the detentions and suspensions we've been giving her haven't helped with that problem. We're trying to think of other ways that we can help."

"Let me know if you come up with anything. Lord knows I'll do whatever I can to help her."

"That's good to hear," said Mr. Middleton.

Ms. Eldredge began to get out of her chair. "I guess I'll let you all get on with your conversation. I really appreciate you trying to help her out."

"Well, that's what we're here for," said Mr. Middleton. "If you don't mind bringing her early like this sometimes, we can catch you up on what we're doing when we see you again."

"That's fine. Sorry to hold you up. I was just a little late leaving the hospital this morning."

Mr. Middleton ushered Ms. Eldredge out of his office. "Not a problem. We'll see you soon."

Mr. Middleton sat back down at his desk and looked at Crystal, whose head was still buried in her knees. "Crystal?"

"I told you she couldn't help with anything," came her voice from between her knees. "She can't even deal with her own life."

Mr. Middleton chose his words carefully. "I understand that you feel that way. I can see that she worries about you."

"I don't want to do this."

"You don't want to do what?"

"I don't want your help."

"I'm sorry to hear you say that," said Mr. Middleton. "I thought you wanted to give us a chance."

"You're wasting your time."

"Maybe so."

"You can't help me."

"That could be true."

Crystal lifted her head. "Don't you get it?"

"I don't understand what you mean."

Crystal stared hard at Mr. Middleton. "I don't belong here. The other kids, they're going somewhere. I'm going nowhere. Just like my mother. Just like my brother."

"OK."

"You agree?"

"No, actually I don't agree. But I'm trying to understand."

"How can you understand? Did you know your father? Was your mother an alcoholic? Did she disappear? Did she dump you on some old lady?" Crystal caught herself and returned to the original question. "How can you understand?"

Mr. Middleton wondered if he'd bitten off more than he could chew, but pressed on. "Crystal, I did know my father. And my mother was not an alcoholic. And she did not disappear."

"Well, there you go."

"And I'm not giving up on you even though those things happened to you."

Crystal stared at Mr. Middleton. "Well, I have."

"I know." Mr. Middleton paused. "So we have a problem, don't we?"

"Huh?"

"You've given up on you and we haven't."

Crystal was still staring at Mr. Middleton. "Why are you doing this?"

Mr. Middleton paused to consider the question. "Crystal, this is going to sound a little corny, but a long time ago—this was before I became an assistant principal—I went into teaching because I really liked working with kids. But somewhere along the way I got so caught up in all the other stuff that goes on in a school that—like I said, this is going to sound a little corny—I lost track of why I got into this business in the first place. I like helping kids, Crystal. And I haven't been helping you. That's why I'm doing this."

Crystal suddenly turned her attention to Mr. Armstrong. "What about him?"

Mr. Armstrong cleared his throat. "Me, too."

Crystal looked a little confused. "This is freaky."

"I can imagine," said Mr. Middleton.

"So now I'm just supposed to, like, be an angel 'cuz you guys have decided to help me?"

"I don't think it's going to be that easy," said Mr. Middleton. "I think we have a lot of hard work ahead of us."

"I don't know if I can stop swearing when I get mad."

"I think that, at the moment, I'm more concerned about helping you start caring than about helping you stop swearing. Then we'll try to figure out when you're swearing the most and see if we can come up with a plan to help you. And we'll figure out what your disagreements with people are about and we'll see if we can get some of those disagreements settled without the fighting."

"I fight when people say crap—I mean stuff—about my mother, or about my brother. That just pisses me— I mean, makes me mad."

"So, when you're ready, we'll start there," said Mr. Middleton. "We'll see if we can figure out when that happens and see if we can come up with a plan so it doesn't get to that point. It sounds like we'll need a plan for what you can do, instead of fighting, if it does get to that point."

"I'm not making any promises."

Mr. Middleton nodded. "I know, Crystal, I'm not looking for any promises. I'm just looking for you to let yourself start caring again so you can work on it with us." Mr. Middleton suddenly looked at the clock. "Oh, geez, it's late. I guess we're going to have to save that for the next time. We need to get you off to homeroom. Shall we continue this discussion tomorrow morning?"

"OK," said Crystal.

Mr. Armstrong nodded. "Crystal, I'm going to have a quick word with Mr. Middleton. I'll meet you at the room."

The two men watched as Crystal left.

"That was interesting," said Mr. Armstrong.

"Gotta feel for her," said Mr. Middleton.

"I'm not sure what we just accomplished," said Mr. Armstrong. "What's our plan?"

"For what?"

"For the swearing. And the fighting."

"We don't have a plan yet. I don't think she trusts us yet. She doesn't think we're reliable yet. She's not convinced that we can help her, either. Plus, we need her help coming up with the plans."

"And we're doing that tomorrow?"

"We'll try, but I'm not sure that thinking we'll be reliable and having faith that we can help her are going to happen overnight."

"So what am I supposed to do if she swears today or gets into a fight?"

"If she swears, remind her that's something you're going to help her with. If she gets into a fight, send her down to me."

"And what are the other kids going to think if she doesn't get punished?" asked Mr. Armstrong.

Mr. Middleton looked at all the discipline referrals on his desk. "I'm more worried about what they think when we do punish her and still have nothing to show for it."

CHAPTER 9

Lives in the Balance

You've made it to the last chapter. While there are a few more strands left to weave together before the book ends, some threads have intentionally been left hanging. By now you've probably realized that this book doesn't contain a solution for every social, emotional, and behavioral challenge a kid might exhibit at school. But you've also probably come to recognize that it wasn't the goal of this book to provide a solution for every challenge. There is no single solution for any challenge, only what the kid and his adult caregivers come up with to address their respective concerns. And there's sticking with it when the first solution doesn't quite accomplish the mission and when the helping relationship bumps along through the inevitable ups and downs.

You've also probably come to recognize that Collaborative Problem Solving looks different in every classroom and every school and every school system where it's implemented. There's no fixed template. What it looks like in each school is determined by that school's administrators, teachers, students, and parents working together toward common goals. The goal of this book is to get the ball rolling. The rest is up to you.

You do have some vital, unshakable basic elements to rely on. A philosophy: *Kids (and adults) do well if they can.* A mantra: *Behind*

*every challenging behavior is an unsolved problem or a lagging skill,
or both.* Knowledge: *Traditional school discipline does not teach
skills or help kids solve problems.* Some goals: *Significantly improve
your understanding of the challenging kids in your classroom and
school. Create mechanisms for responding to their needs proactively
rather than emergently.* A mission: *If we were going to start doing
right by the challenging kids in our school, what would that look like?*
A new methodology: *Plan B.* Three ingredients: *Empathy, Define the
Problem, and the Invitation.* And, of course, the paperwork: the
Analysis of Lagging Skills and Unsolved Problems and the *CPS Plan*
and *Plan B Flow Chart.* The rest is practice, tenacity, patience, perseverance, team work, and a desire for continuous improvement. And
hope. Your last mantra (paraphrasing a colleague, Dr. Robert Kin-
scherff):

*Remain calmly optimistic and
relentlessly persistent in the face of all odds.*

Transforming school discipline won't be easy or fast. We humans
tend to resist change. Collaborative Problem Solving requires change.
We like to be comfortable. New ways of doing things make people
uncomfortable. We're very busy and have competing priorities. Helping challenging kids has to become a priority in each classroom, each
school, each school system. Millions of kids are still getting lost. But
it doesn't have to be that way.

The potential wasted, the price paid by so many kids, teachers,
parents—all of us—is too massive and tragic to comprehend. The
misery, though it can sometimes be hard to recognize, is unmistakable. There are lives in the balance.

The kids are waiting for you. Now it's your turn.

The Story Continues . . .

Fast-forward to the end of the school year. It's been eight months since
Dr. Bridgman first met Joey and his mother. Seven months since Mrs.

Franco made her first attempt at Plan B with Travis. Six months since Mr. Middleton started rethinking school discipline and changing his approach with Crystal.

Joey entered Mrs. Woods' class for his last early-morning meeting with his teacher.

"Hi Joey," said Mrs. Woods.

"Hi," said Joey glumly.

"I bet you're excited that there are only four days left of school," said Mrs. Woods.

Joey was unenthusiastic. "Um, I guess."

Mrs. Woods looked carefully at Joey. "What are you doing this summer?"

"Not much," said Joey.

More silence. "Cat got your tongue?" asked Mrs. Woods, forgetting briefly about how black-and-white Joey could be.

"I don't own a cat," said Joey, looking slightly confused.

Mrs. Woods suppressed a smile. "I'm sorry. It's just an expression. You just seem a little quiet today."

"Oh," said Joey.

"So is everything OK?"

"Yeah, I guess."

"I'm a little sad today myself."

"You are?" asked Joey, looking concerned.

"Well, it's our last meeting together," said Mrs. Woods, "and I've kind of gotten used to seeing you in the morning."

"Yeah, me too," said Joey.

"It's been quite a year," said Mrs. Woods. "We've really made some good strides this year, haven't we?"

Joey nodded.

"I've learned a lot this year," said Mrs. Woods.

"You have?" Joey seemed surprised to hear that teachers were in need of any additional learning.

"Yes, I have," said Mrs. Woods. "I'm really glad you were in my class."

"Me too," said Joey.

"That's why I'm a little sad. You'll be in someone else's class next year."

Joey reached into his pocket, pulled out a small pewter object, and handed it to Mrs. Woods. "I got this for you."

"What's this?" asked Mrs. Woods.

"A wizard."

Mrs. Woods examined the object. "Yes, so it is. This is for me?"

"Yes, I got it for you. So you can remember how you helped me."

"Joey, this is so sweet of you. I'm going to put it right here on my desk." She fought back tears. "And when I have kids next year who need my help, I'm going to look at that wizard and remember all the hard work we did together."

Joey seemed pleased.

"Speaking of next year," said Mrs. Woods, "I was wondering if maybe you could come to my class for a visit every once in a while. Maybe even help me with some of next year's students. I've already asked Mrs. Galvin about it, and she said it would be fine, if you want to, and if it's OK with your teachers."

Joey's face brightened. "That would be good."

On the afternoon of the last day of school, Mr. Middleton dropped by Mr. Armstrong's classroom. "Have a good summer, Jerry."

Mr. Armstrong looked up from his desk. "Yes, you too, Bill."

"Interesting year, eh?"

Mr. Armstrong smiled. "Very interesting. I take it you're talking about our discipline working group. And Crystal."

Mr. Middleton walked into the classroom. "Yes, of course."

"I think we made some headway."

"I agree."

"I mean, it's not like she never swears anymore. And she did have that fight a few months ago. But I haven't heard her mention dropping out in a while."

Mr. Middleton nodded. "We're not out of the woods with her yet. But I'm glad you were able to hook her up with that summer program. That was a great idea. And she thought it was a good idea, too. Better than having her spend all her time with that crowd she runs with."

"Maybe it's wishful thinking, but I got the feeling maybe she was starting to trust us a little," said Mr. Armstrong.

"She didn't know what to make of us. She's so sure people are going to abandon ship on her."

"She's a tough kid."

"I don't think she had much choice."

"You know, you were right, Bill."

"Right about what?"

"At one point you told me it didn't matter what plan we came up with until she started caring again, and until she believed we could give her the kind of help she needed. Well, it's true. Not that I think we should totally get rid of suspensions and detentions. I still think there's a place for that stuff for some kids."

"I know you do. And that's what we'll keep sorting out in our working group. I'm glad you decided to help out with that."

"Me too," said Mr. Armstrong.

After everyone had left the building, Mrs. Galvin walked through the quiet hallways of the school, simultaneously enjoying the solitude and missing the sounds of kids. The stillness was broken as she passed Dr. Bridgman's office. Through the crack in the door, she heard him talking loudly on the phone. Then the conversation ended abruptly. She knocked.

"Yeah," he said curtly.

"I'm sorry, I think I'm intruding," said Mrs. Galvin, pushing the door open. "I just wanted to say I hope you have a nice summer."

Dr. Bridgman turned toward the door, a little embarrassed. "Oh, Mrs. Galvin, I'm sorry, I didn't know it was you. Please, sit down." He hastily removed a stack of files from a chair.

"Everything OK?" asked Mrs. Galvin.

"Not exactly."

"What's wrong?"

Dr. Bridgman made no effort to hide his annoyance. "It was your fellow principal over at East School."

"Ah, Dr. Sanders. She's giving you a hard time?"

"Suffice to say that she hasn't been quite as receptive to my ideas as you have. And it's really hurting a lot of kids at that school. I was hoping to get some Collaborative Problem Solving training going at East School next year—nothing mandatory, just for people who are interested—and she nixed the idea. Says her teachers have enough on their plates as it is. They don't have *time* for Collaborative Problem Solving. She just doesn't get it."

"You know, I didn't get it so fast myself," said Mrs. Galvin.

"Yeah, but at least you had an open mind. She just won't do what she needs to do."

Mrs. Galvin looked carefully at her school psychologist. Then she chuckled, saying, "Well, I'll be."

"What's so funny?"

"It's just that I never thought I'd see the day."

"What day?"

"The day *I* helped *you* do Plan B," said Mrs. Galvin.

"I don't get it," said Dr. Bridgman.

"From the sounds of it, you need my help doing Plan B with Dr. Sanders."

"She doesn't do Plan B. She's a closed-minded, shortsighted—"

Mrs. Galvin's laughter interrupted Dr. Bridgman's rant before it gathered momentum. "Dr. Bridgman, is it safe for me to assume that you have legitimate concerns about what's being done with challenging students over at the East School?"

"Yes, there are so many kids they could be helping . . ."

"And have you put those concerns on the table?"

Dr. Bridgman considered the question. "Well, yes, I mean, I think so."

"Because it sounds to me like you have a *solution* on the table right now, not a *concern*," observed Mrs. Galvin. "And tell me, is it also safe to assume that Dr. Sanders has legitimate concerns of her own?"

"I wouldn't know," groused Dr. Bridgman.

"Well, of course she does. You know the kind of time pressures we operate under and how many new initiatives are always coming down the pike. We all have more on our plates than we can handle."

"Yeah, but Collaborative Problem Solving would save them time!"

"Yes, I understand that she doesn't quite appreciate that yet. But what we have here is a classic case of dueling solutions. Classic."

Dr. Bridgman said nothing. Then a sheepish smile slowly spread across his face. "So the Plan B guy got caught doing Plan A."

"The Plan B guy is human," said Mrs. Galvin. "And has very good intentions. But, and I've learned this the hard way, it seems we all head for Plan A when we're under duress."

"And you think it's possible to do Plan B with that . . . that . . ."

"Dr. Sanders," supplied Mrs. Galvin. "Yes, I do. She's not easy to deal with. But I've known her for a long time. She has a heart. If you want, I can call her tomorrow. I've already told her a little about what we've been doing with our challenging kids. Maybe she needs some of the details. Maybe she has some concerns I don't know about. Then we'll set up a meeting. Me, you, and her. And we'll do some Collaborative Problem Solving."

Dr. Bridgman couldn't quite hide his amazement. "You really know how to do it now."

"You've had quite an impact on us, Dr. Bridgman. But we're not over the hump yet. We still have a lot of teachers in this school who aren't very good at Plan B. And I've been trying to set up a meeting with the superintendent to talk about integrating Collaborative Problem Solving into the disciplinary policies for the entire district. You game?"

Dr. Bridgman's eyes widened. "I'm game."

Mrs. Galvin began getting out of her chair. "So are you staying here all night?"

"A few minutes ago, I wasn't sure what I was doing," admitted Dr. Bridgman.

"Come on," said Mrs. Galvin. "I hear next year's incoming class is completely out of control. We've got a lot of hard work ahead. And I'm not doing it all by myself."

Child's Name_____ Date _____

LAGGING SKILLS

____Difficulty handling transitions, shifting from one mind-set or task to another

____Difficulty doing things in a logical sequence or prescribed order

____Difficulty persisting on challenging or tedious tasks

____Poor sense of time

____Difficulty reflecting on multiple thoughts or ideas simultaneously

____Difficulty maintaining focus

____Difficulty considering the likely outcomes or consequences of actions (impulsive)

____Difficulty considering a range of solutions to a problem

____Difficulty expressing concerns, needs, or thoughts in words

____Difficulty understanding what is being said

____Difficulty managing emotional response to frustration so as to think rationally

____Chronic irritability and/or anxiety significantly impede capacity for problem-solving or heighten frustration

____Difficulty seeing the "grays"/concrete, literal, black-and-white thinking

____Difficulty deviating from rules, routine

____Difficulty handling unpredictability, ambiguity, uncertainty, novelty

____Difficulty shifting from original idea, plan, or solution

____Difficulty taking into account situational factors that would suggest the need to adjust a plan of action

____Inflexible, inaccurate interpretations/cognitive distortions or biases (e.g., "Everyone's out to get me," "Nobody likes me," "You always blame me," "It's not fair," "I'm stupid")

____Difficulty attending to and/or accurately interpreting social cues/poor perception of social nuances

____Difficulty starting conversations, entering groups, connecting with people/lacks other basic social skills

____Difficulty seeking attention in appropriate ways

____Difficulty appreciating how his/her behavior is affecting other people

____Difficulty empathizing with others, appreciating another person's perspective or point of view

____Difficulty appreciating how s/he is coming across or being perceived by others

UNSOLVED PROBLEMS

HOME

____Waking up/getting out of bed in the morning

____Completing morning routine/getting ready for school

____Sensory hypersensitivities

____Starting or completing homework or a particular academic task

____Food quantities/choices/preferences/timing

____Time spent in front of a screen (TV, video games, computer)
____Going to/getting ready for bed at night
____Boredom
____Sibling interactions
____Cleaning room/completing household chores
____Taking medicine
____Riding in car/wearing seat belt

SCHOOL
____Shifting from one specific task to another (specify)
____Getting started on/completing class assignment (specify)
____Interactions with a particular classmate/teacher (specify)
____Behavior in hallway/at recess/in cafeteria/on school bus/waiting in line
(specify)
____Talking at appropriate times
____Specific academic tasks/demands, e.g., writing assignments (specify)
____Handling disappointment/losing at a game/not coming in first/not being first
in line (specify)

OTHERS (list)

Sources

Introduction

1. Teaching interrupted: Do discipline policies in today's public schools foster the common good? (2004). *Public Agenda.*

   Skiba, R. J., and R. L. Peterson (1999). The dark side of zero tolerance: Can punishment lead to safe schools? *Phi Delta Kappan, 80,* 372–382.

   Skiba, R. J., and R. L. Peterson (2000). School discipline at a crossroads: From zero tolerance to early response. *Exceptional Children, 66,* 335–347.

2. American Psychological Association Zero Tolerance Task Force (2006). *Are Zero Tolerance Policies Effective in the Schools? An Evidentiary Review and Recommendations.* Washington, D.C.: American Psychological Association.

3. U.S. Department of Education, Office for Civil Rights, OCR Elementary and Secondary School Survey, 2002.

Chapter 1

1. Wald, J., and D. J. Losen (2003). *New Directions for Youth Development: Deconstructing the School-to-Prison Pipeline.* San Francisco: Jossey-Bass.

   Atkins, M., M. McKay, S. Frazier, L. Jakobsons, P. Arvanitis, T. Cunningham, C. Brown, and L. Lambrecht (2002). Suspensions and detentions in an urban, low-income school: Punishment or reward? *Journal of Abnormal Child Psychology, 30,* 361–372.

Chapter 2

1. McClellan, J. (2005). Commentary: Treatment guidelines for child and adolescent bipolar disorder. *Journal of the American Academy of Child & Adolescent Psychiatry, 44,* 236–239.

2. Abikoff, H., and R. G. Klein (1992). Attention-deficit hyperactivity disorder and conduct disorder: Comorbidity and implications for treatment. *Journal of Consulting and Clinical Psychology, 60,* 881–892.

    Greene, R. W., J. Biederman, S. Zerwas, M. Monuteaux, J. Goring, and S. V. Faraone (2002). Psychiatric comorbidity, family dysfunction, and social impairment in referred youth with oppositional defiant disorder. *American Journal of Psychiatry, 159,* 1214–1224.

    Hinshaw, S. P., B. B. Lahey, and E. L. Hart (1993). Issues of taxonomy and comorbidity in the development of conduct disorder. *Development and Psychopathology, 5,* 31–49.

    Lahey, B. B., and R. Loeber (1994). Framework for a developmental model of oppositional defiant disorder and conduct disorder. In D. K. Routh (ed.), *Disruptive Behavior Disorders in Childhood.* New York: Plenum.

    Moffitt, T. E. (1993). The neuropsychology of conduct disorder. *Development and Psychopathology, 5,* 135–151.

3. Angold, A., and E. J. Costello (1993). Depressive comorbidity in children and adolescents: Empirical, theoretical, and methodological issues. *American Journal of Psychiatry, 150,* 1779–1791.

    Belden, A. C., N. R. Thomson, and J. Luby (2008). Temper tantrums in healthy versus depressed and disruptive preschoolers: Defining tantrum behaviors associated with clinical problems. *Journal of Pediatrics, 152,* 117–122.

    Garland, E. J., and M. Weiss (1996). Case study: Obsessive difficult temperament and its response to serotonergic medication. *Journal of the American Academy of Child and Adolescent Psychiatry, 35* (7), 916–920.

    Greene et al., Psychiatric comorbidity. *American Journal of Psychiatry, 159,* 1214–1224.

    Loeber, R., and K. Keenan (1994). Interaction between conduct disorder and its comorbid conditions: Effects of age and gender. *Clinical Psychology Review, 14* (6), 497–523.

    Stifter, C. A., T. L. Spinrad, and J. M. Braungart-Rieker (1999). Toward a developmental model of child compliance: The role of emotion regulation in infancy. *Child Development, 70* (1), 21–32.

Zoccolillo, M. (1992). Co-occurrence of conduct disorder and its adult outcomes with depressive and anxiety disorders: A review. *Journal of the American Academy of Child and Adolescent Psychiatry, 31,* 547–556.

4. Bloomquist, M. L., G. J. August, C. Cohen, A. Doyle, and K. Everhart (1997). Social problem solving in hyperactive-aggressive children: How and what they think in conditions of controlled processing. *Journal of Clinical Child Psychology, 26,* 172–180.

Dodge, K. A. (1993). The future of research on the treatment of conduct disorder. *Development and Psychopathology, 5,* 311–319.

Dodge, K. A., and J. D. Coie (1987). Social information processing factors in reactive and proactive aggression in children's peer groups. *Journal of Personality and Social Psychology, 53,* 1146–1158.

Greene, R. W., J. Biederman, S. V. Faraone, J. Sienna, and J. Garcia-Jetton (1997). Adolescent outcome of boys with attention-deficit/hyperactivity disorder and social disability: Results from a 4-year longitudinal follow-up study. *Journal of Consulting and Clinical Psychology, 65* (5), 758–767.

Vitiello, B., and D. M. Stoff (1997). Subtypes of aggression and their relevance to child psychiatry. *Journal of the American Academy of Child and Adolescent Psychiatry, 36* (3), 307–315.

5. Baker, L., and D. P. Cantwell (1987). A prospective psychiatric follow-up of children with speech/language disorders. *Journal of the American Academy of Child and Adolescent Psychiatry, 26,* 546–553.

Beitchman, J. H., J. Hood, and A. Inglis (1990). Psychiatric risk in children with speech and language disorders. *Journal of Abnormal Child Psychology, 18,* 283–296.

Beitchman, J. H., J. Hood, J. Rochon, and M. Peterson (1989). Empirical classification of speech/language impairment in children. II. Behavioral characteristics. *Journal of the American Academy of Child and Adolescent Psychiatry, 28,* 118–123.

Snowling, M. J., D. V. M. Bishop, S. E. Stothard, B. Chipchase, and C. Kaplan (2006). Psychosocial outcomes at 15 years of children with a preschool history of speech-language impairment. *Journal of Child Psychology and Psychiatry, 47,* 759–765.

6. Little, S. S. (1993). Nonverbal learning disabilities and socioemotional functioning: A review of recent literature. *Journal of Learning Disabilities, 10,* 653–665.

Rourke, B. P., and D. R. Fuerst (1995). Cognitive processing, academic achievement, and psychosocial functioning: A neurodevelopmental perspective. In D. Cicchetti and D. J. Cohen (eds.), *Developmental*

Psychopathology (Vol. 1): *Theory and Methods,* 391–423. New York: John Wiley & Sons.

   Semrud-Clikeman, M., and G. W. Hynd (1990). Right hemispheric dysfunction in nonverbal learning disabilities: Social, academic, and adaptive functioning in adults and children. *Psychological Bulletin, 107,* 196–209.

Chapter 3

1. Greene, R. W., J. S. Ablon, M. Monuteaux, J. Goring, A. Henin, L. Raezer, G. Edwards, J. Markey, and S. Rabbitt (2004). Effectiveness of Collaborative Problem Solving in affectively dysregulated youth with oppositional defiant disorder: Initial findings. *Journal of Consulting and Clinical Psychology, 72,* 1157–1164.

   Greene, R. W., S. A. Ablon, and A. Martin (2006). Innovations: Child psychiatry: Use of Collaborative Problem Solving to reduce seclusion and restraint in child and adolescent inpatient units. *Psychiatric Services, 57* (5), 610–616.

Chapter 7

1. Comer, J. P. (2005). Child and adolescent development: The critical missing focus in school reform. *Phi Delta Kappan, 86,* 757–763.
2. Sugai, G., and R. H. Horner (2002). The evolution of discipline practices: School-wide positive behavior supports. *Child and Family Behavior Therapy, 24,* 23–50.

   Sugai, G., R. H. Horner, G. Dunlap, M. Hieneman, T. Lewis, C. Nelson, E. Scott, C. Liaupsin, W. Sailor, A. P. Turnbull, H. R. Turnbull, D. Wickham, M. Reuf, and B. L. Wilcox (2000). Applying positive behavioral support and functional assessment in schools. *Journal of Positive Behavior Interventions, 2,* 131–142.

Chapter 8

1. Greene et al. (2004). Effectiveness of Collaborative Problem Solving. *Journal of Consulting and Clinical Psychology, 72,* 1157–1164.

Books Cited and Other Recommended Reading

Ayers, William, Bernadine Dohrn, and Rick Ayers (eds.). *Zero Tolerance: Resisting the Drive for Punishment in Our Schools.* New York: The New Press, 2001.

Brown-Chidsey, Rachel. *Assessment for Intervention: A Problem-Solving Approach.* New York: Guilford Press, 2005.

Brown-Chidsey, Rachel, and Mark Steege. *Response to Intervention: Strategies for Effective Practice.* New York: Guilford Press, 2005.

Charney, Ruth. *Teaching Children to Care: Classroom Management for Ethical and Academic Growth.* Greenfield, Mass.: Northeast Foundation for Children, 2002.

Danforth, Scot, and Terry Jo Smith. *Engaging Troubling Students: A Constructivist Approach.* Thousand Oaks, Cal.: Corwin Press, 2005.

DuFour, Richard, and Robert Eaker. *Professional Learning Communities at Work: Best Practices for Enhancing Student Achievement.* Bloomington, Ind.: Solution Tree, 1998.

Egan, Gerard. *The Skilled Helper: A Problem-Management and Opportunity-Development Approach to Helping.* Belmont, Cal.: Wadsworth Publishing, 2006.

Gibbs, Jeanne. *Tribes: A New Way of Learning and Being Together.* Windsor, Cal.: Centersource Systems, 2001.

Glasser, William. *Schools Without Failure.* New York: Harper & Row, 1969.

Gordon, Thomas. *Teacher Effectiveness Training: The Program Proven to Help Teachers Bring Out the Best in Students of All Ages.* New York: Three Rivers Press, 2003.

Heifetz, Ronald. *Leadership Without Easy Answers.* Cambridge, Mass.: Belknap Press, 1998.

Kohn, Alfie. *Beyond Discipline: From Compliance to Community.* Alexandria, Va.: Association for Supervision and Curriculum Development, 1996.

———. *What to Look for in a Classroom.* New York: John Wiley & Sons, 1998.

———. *The Schools Our Children Deserve: Moving Beyond Traditional Classrooms and "Tougher Standards."* New York: Houghton Mifflin, 1999.

Lawrence-Lightfoot, Sarah. *The Essential Conversation: What Parents and Teachers Can Learn from Each Other.* New York: Random House, 2003.

Stutzman Amstutz, Lorraine, and Judy Mellett. *Restorative Discipline for Schools: Teaching Responsibility; Creating Caring Climates.* Intercourse, Pa.: Good Books, 2005.

Tomlinson, Carol Ann. *The Differentiated Classroom: Responding to the Needs of All Learners.* Alexandria, Va.: Association for Supervision and Curriculum Development, 1999.

Watson, Marilyn. *Learning to Trust: Transforming Difficult Elementary Classrooms Through Developmental Discipline.* San Francisco: Jossey-Bass, 2003.

Acknowledgments

Completing this book would not have been possible without the assistance of many dedicated and talented people. I received stellar editing and guidance from my editor at Scribner, Samantha Martin. My thanks to the dozens of educators and parents who provided input on various drafts of the book, and to two in particular: Julie Benay, principal at Swanton (Vermont) Elementary School; and Laura Baker, head of school at Greenfield (Massachusetts) Center School. Many parts of this book are a reflection of their wisdom. Lynn Heitman provided very helpful feedback on the running story section in the book.

Also deserving of recognition are the many educators throughout North America and beyond who are already implementing Collaborative Problem Solving in their schools and classrooms, and who tirelessly devote themselves to helping colleagues understand and treat challenging kids in more humane, compassionate ways. They have my heartfelt gratitude and admiration.

As always, my thanks to my friend and agent, Wendy Lipkind, who saw this book through thick and thin.

And to Talia, Jacob, and Melissa for all the love and for keeping it real.

Index

academic vision statements, 258
actions:
  accountability for, 57–58
  failure to gauge impact of, 14, 17, 18, 24–25, 31, 32, 39
  impulsive, 14, 17–18, 31, 32, 33, 38–39, 167
  inhibition and modification of, 17–18, 25
  manipulative, 6, 8, 12, 17
  organizing of, 247
  repeating vs. changing course of, 24
  setting limits on, 57
  surprise by response to, 15, 24
aggressiveness, 2–5, 7, 12, 19, 29, 38–39, 167, 188
alienation, 11
  feelings of, 14, 23, 29, 30, 32, 47, 68–69, 72, 178–79, 184
American Psychological Association, ix
Amstutz, Lorraine Stutzman, 200
anxiety, 7, 14, 19, 20, 21, 46, 167
approval, 34, 36, 76, 198
Asperger's disorder, 15, 22
Assessment of Lagging Skills and Unsolved Problems (ALSUP), 27, 29, 31, 32, 35–36, 49, 67–69, 71–73, 95, 113, 167, 197, 207, 210, 244–46, 250, 251, 281, 287–88

attention deficit hyperactivity disorder (ADHD), 7, 15, 18, 38
attention seeking, 6, 8, 12, 15, 32, 36, 39, 61, 198
attention span, 167
autism spectrum disorders, 39, 169

Beyond Discipline: From Compliance to Community (Kohn), 186, 196
biases, 14, 22
  cognitive, 23, 68–69, 72
  intentionality attributional, 37, 68, 77–78
bipolar disorder, 15, 21
brain, 39, 100, 152, 185
  injury of, 15
Brown-Chidsey, Rachel, 58
bullying, 21, 33, 38, 188, 218, 222–24, 228–29

cafeteria, 22, 26
  problems in, 38, 128, 262
challenging behavior:
  connection of lagging skills to, 11–12, 16, 17, 19, 27, 31, 35, 38–39, 49, 97, 148, 155, 252, 280–81
  connection of unsolved problems to, 25–27, 49, 113, 148, 166, 252, 280–81